T0375116

DUMBARTON OAKS
MEDIEVAL LIBRARY

Jan M. Ziolkowski, General Editor

OLD TESTAMENT NARRATIVES

DOML 7

Old Testament Narratives

Edited and Translated by

DANIEL ANLEZARK

*D*UMBARTON OAKS
*M*EDIEVAL *L*IBRARY

HARVARD UNIVERSITY PRESS
CAMBRIDGE, MASSACHUSETTS
LONDON, ENGLAND
2011

Library of Congress Cataloging-in-Publication Data
Old Testament narratives / edited and translated by Daniel Anlezark.
    p. cm.—(Dumbarton Oaks medieval library; DOML 7)
    Includes bibliographical references and index.
    Parallel Old English text with English translation.
    ISBN 978-0-674-05319-9 (alk. paper)
    1. English poetry—Old English, ca. 450–1100—Translations into
English. 2. Bible. O.T.—History of Biblical events—Poetry. 3. Christian
poetry, English (Old) I. Anlezark, Daniel.
PR1508.O57 2011
829'.108—dc22   2010049065

Contents

Introduction

The five Old English poems edited and translated in this volume survive in two separate manuscripts. The first four— *Genesis A, Genesis B, Exodus,* and *Daniel*—are found in Junius XI in the Bodleian Library, Oxford; *Azarias* is found in the Exeter Book.[1] Another poem in Junius XI, *Christ and Satan,* was added to the manuscript in the decades after the Old Testament narratives were copied.[2] Both Junius XI and the Exeter Book date from the latter part of the tenth century and were copied at a time when the Anglo-Saxons took a great interest in their culture's poetic tradition. The authors of these poems are not known, nor are the original dates of composition. In the centuries between the renewed interest in Anglo-Saxon literature during the Reformation and the development of modern philology in the nineteenth century, it was believed that the Anglo-Saxon cowherd Cædmon, whose story is told in Bede's *Ecclesiastical History,*[3] had composed these works. Cædmon was in the employ of the great Anglo-Saxon monastery at Whitby in the late seventh century, where, as a result of his reluctance to join in singing with others at a late-night party, he received both an angelic vision and a divine poetic inspiration. When he was presented to the Abbess Hild, she recognized the gift, accepted him as a monk, and had him instructed in the scriptures and doctrine. The resulting corpus of biblical poems—

apparently still familiar two generations later—were, according to Bede, the first to incorporate Christian subject matter into Old English alliterative verse.

While the Exeter Book has been kept at Exeter Cathedral since it was donated by Bishop Leofric in 1072, we do not know the exact whereabouts of Junius XI before 1651, when it was given by James Ussher, archbishop of Armagh, to the Dutch scholar Franciscus Junius. Junius published the first edition of all the poems in the manuscript in Amsterdam in 1655, with the traditional attribution to Cædmon; the "Cædmon manuscript" became Junius XI when it was bequeathed by him to the Bodleian Library.[4] The attribution to Cædmon was current until Benjamin Thorpe's edition of 1832, after which scholars established, on a variety of linguistic and stylistic grounds, that the poems could not have been written by one author, although critical opinion continues to favor an early date, probably before 800.[5] The one exception is *Genesis B,* which probably dates from the tenth century.

The Old Testament portion of Junius XI was designed to be illustrated and presents the poems as a continuous narrative in numbered sections. However, the cycle of illustrations is incomplete, and not all the poems' sections (or fitts) have their numbers. In various places pages are missing from the manuscript, disrupting the text. The first of the poems, logically enough, is *Genesis A*. The author's treatment is generally faithful to the course of the biblical narrative, with a tendency to eliminate repetitive passages. The poet also augments the story with material drawn from apocryphal sources, most notably concerning Lucifer's rebellion and the fall of the angels, which are not found in the book of

Genesis. Other additions to the narrative derive from the
biblical commentary tradition and commonplace medieval
interpretations of certain episodes. At times the poet's handling of emotionally charged moments—such as Cain's murder of Abel and Abraham's expulsion of Hagar and Ishmael
—suggests an interest in the characters' psychology beyond
their theological import. Both in these additions and in the
rendering of the Latin text, the poet fully incorporates the
Old English heroic idiom, which serves to emphasize and
draw out the martial aspect of the biblical source. The opening section of the poem (1–14) lauds the creator and closely
echoes the preface to the Canon of the Mass, a reminder for
the modern reader that the medieval reader was most likely
to encounter the Bible as a collection of texts used in the
liturgy; the idea of the Bible as a single book was unknown.[6]
In fact, it seems most likely that the structure of the Old
Testament narrative and the selection of texts in Junius XI
were guided by the series of readings set down for the Easter Vigil.[7] Junius XI is itself the earliest example in the English language of a continuous narrative drawn from books
spread widely across the Old Testament, and as such has an
important place in the historical development both of the
idea of the Bible as a book and of the Bible in English.

The narrative proper begins with an account of the fall of
the angels—Lucifer's envy and arrogance are answered by
God's anger and fury. The reason for the creation of the human race emerges in this context, as the thrones of heaven
vacated by the fallen angels must be filled; this idea draws
on a medieval theological commonplace. The poem often
explains motivation where this is not found in the biblical
original. The six days of creation are described (103–205), al-

though the passage is curtailed by the loss of Old English text. The creation is followed by a description of the four rivers flowing from Eden (206–34), after which the text is disrupted, probably by the loss of manuscript leaves. When it resumes, it does so abruptly midsentence, and in the interpolated *Genesis B,* which is discussed below. The transition back to *Genesis A* is so smooth at the narrative level that it reveals the work of an editor splicing the two texts together. The action resumes with God's visit to paradise after the sin of Adam and Eve, now aware of their nakedness (852–71). In a substantial addition to the biblical narrative (939–66), the poet explains to his audience (the poet's gender is assumed rather than known) that this sin and the consequent banishment are the source of current misery in the world and, in an equation of paradise with heaven (which is implicit throughout), explains that no guilty man may journey there. This homiletic commentary also balances the account of God's wrath with the observation that God did not abandon the human race but gave it a rich and beautiful world to live in, even if it includes suffering and death. Such commentary is more characteristic of the earlier parts of the poem than of the later account of the wanderings of Abraham. Another homiletic expansion follows soon after, in the description of the malignant tree that grows from Abel's innocent blood and the poet's recollection that all this misery is ultimately to be blamed on Eve (982–1001). The tree of sin is undoubtedly included to recall the Fall, but it also reveals the poet's knowledge of the motif from Aldhelm's *Carmen de Virginitate,* written in the early eighth century for the nuns of Barking Abbey.[8] The emotion of the "downhearted" Cain's banishment is more intense in the

Old English, and his exile matches a familiar experience in the Anglo-Saxon warrior life and its poetry. Anglo-Saxon taste is also evident in the poetic expansion of the genealogy of Genesis 4:17–26 (1055–1247), which considers not just the passing of generations but also the transmission of hereditary nobility and ancestral wealth.

With the arrival of Noah the pace of the narrative in both the biblical source and the poem changes, and the propagation of the human race gives way to its threatened extinction, along with all other earthly life. In the development of the poem's ideas a threat becomes apparent to the royal line of Adam through Seth, a theme enhanced by the martial language in which the story of the Flood is cast. The rising waters are depicted as a menacing army (1375–86), but Noah and his family are protected in the towering fortress that is the ark. Noah is a holy man obedient to God, but also a prince and a father of princes. One recurrent element of the biblical narrative that the poet emphasizes is sacrifice: Noah's sacrifice (1497–1510) recalls Abel's, and the poet observes that Noah's virtues date from his youth and merit the grace God has given him, though he removes the direct reference to the sacrifice of animals (Gen 8:20). That this is no accident is indicated by the fact that the poet does the same thing by omitting animal sacrifice from his description of Abraham's sacrifice at Gen 16:9–17. His primary interest appears to lie in providing an English version of the historical narrative of Genesis, and such omissions suggest a lay audience for whom the example set by the patriarchs might have been confusing.

The poet's fondness for genealogy does not equate with a fondness for lists, and almost all the names found in Gen-

esis 10 are omitted. However, this is balanced by a continued interest in the royal line that will lead to Abraham and
the passing on of family wealth (1598–1648). The account
of Abraham's wandering life takes up about one third of
the poem as it survives. From the outset, the poet includes
new thematic emphases while developing motifs running
through the biblical story: Abraham's nobility and his place
within a family order; Abraham's desire for a son and heir;
the favor shown by God to faithful Abraham; Abraham's
need of a homeland; the formation of a lasting covenant between God and Abraham. The result, when augmented by a
focus on Abraham's emotional response to his various ad-
ventures, is a fuller human character than is found in the
biblical text. The same is true of Sarah, and to an extent of
Hagar as well. The handling of the three-way relationship of
these characters is complex and subtle, and reveals a poet
mindful of the implications of the example of patriarchal
sexual conduct for his Anglo-Saxon audience and aware of a
Christian theological tradition which had long since developed strategies for explaining the difficult moral detail of
much of Genesis.[9] Abraham, as might be expected, is never
condemned directly for his concubinage, and the poet removes any implication of polygamy, or of Abraham's willing
participation in Sarah's plan to gain him a son by the servant woman. The overall result, enhancing the same themes
found in the book of Genesis, is the presentation of Abraham and Sarah as a heterosexual married couple producing
legitimate offspring alongside the sexual irregularity prac-
ticed by the Sodomites and by Lot and his daughters, and
the sexual incontinence of Pharaoh and Abimelech.[10]

The sacrifice of Isaac, the final episode of the poem,

echoes the account of Cain and Abel in its emphasis on Abraham's intention of killing his "kinsman." More significant is the poet's choice to end his epic at this point, revealing an interest in the mystical significance of the Old Testament text, informed by the commentary tradition. Isaac is a typological representation of Christ par excellence and illustrates the dominant Christian method of interpreting the events of the Old Testament as prefiguring Christ or the Church. The sacrifice of Isaac thus foreshadows Christ's true sacrifice on Calvary.[11] The final passage, emphasizing Abraham's thanksgiving (2930–36), is not found in Genesis but shows a poet returning to where he began, recalling for his audience their link to these ancient events, through the life of Christ, by their participation in the Eucharistic sacrifice of thanksgiving. The skillful inclusion of such learned theological perspectives in a poem which is most obviously interested in a historical narrative revealing God's providence at work in human affairs, along with the lesson that those who call themselves God's people should obey his commandments, tells us something about the poet and his intended audience. The poet-translator enjoyed a Latinity that extended well beyond knowledge of the biblical text; in addition to revealing his awareness of biblical typology, he often develops bilingual onomastic puns.[12] However, this learning is carried lightly, and informs rather than dominates a poem probably intended for a lay audience that valued ancestry, power, land, and wealth as well as the God who ruled over them all.

It is not known why *Genesis B* was interpolated into *Genesis A*—whether it was part of the original design of the larger poem, or was necessitated by the accidental loss of text from

Genesis A, or was the result of deliberate substitution at an earlier stage of transmission by a copyist who preferred the alternative account of Adam and Eve's sin.[13] While text is missing at the transition to *Genesis B,* the transition back to *Genesis A* is seamless at the narrative level, which suggests an expert hand in placing the interpolation. Unlike *Genesis A,* which follows the Latin Vulgate, *Genesis B* is a close translation from an Old Saxon original, as Eduard Sievers deduced on philological grounds in 1875. His theory was confirmed by the discovery of a fragment of an Old Saxon *Genesis* in the Vatican Library, which corresponds precisely to lines from the Old English.[14] One striking difference between the two parts of the combined Old English *Genesis* (immediately apparent by the lineation in a modern edition) is found in the meter. *Genesis A* employs the normal two-stress alliterative line; it does not include a single hypermetric line.[15] By contrast, *Genesis B* carries over an abundance of long verse lines from the Old Saxon original, some of which may be normal verses with extra syllables, while others are well-formed hypermetric half-lines. The Old English also reflects the influence of the Old Saxon in its lexicon (for example, the unusual *hearra* for "lord") and orthography.[16] Another consequence of the interpolation is a reiteration of the fall of the angels, beside a thematically linked account of the fall of Adam and Eve. Among the most striking literary aspects of *Genesis B* beside *Genesis A* are its relative freedom with the biblical narrative and the originality of its treatment of both character and episode. The character of Lucifer/Satan is more fully developed than in *Genesis A,* as the poem explores his arrogance and insolence, both of which remain intact after his banishment to hell with his supporters. His attitudes, motivations, and emotions are explored in a series of long, lively speeches which reveal his bitterness and hatred toward God and Adam. The poem's great invention is the character of Satan's demonic envoy, who flies from hell and enters paradise disguised as a serpent. This devil's prickly character, sharp intellect, and clever lies overwhelm first Eve and then Adam. In their interactions we find a poet interested in questions of gender and having a complex attitude toward women, expressed in the character of Eve.[17] The careful exploration of human psychology is accompanied by a subtle exploration of the process of sin; neither Adam nor Eve intends to do wrong, but in the end they are convinced that direct disobedience of God's command is a reasonable course of action. The reader is drawn into this process and so shares the poet's bewilderment that such trickery has been allowed to happen.

Exodus carries the greater narrative of Junius XI forward to the escape of the Hebrews from Egypt, from the tenth plague to the crossing of the Red Sea (Exodus 12:29–15:21). One effect of the compiler's choice to follow *Genesis A* with *Exodus* (a selection that may have been limited by the poems available to him) is an emphasis on the theme of exile and a desire to return to the land promised to Abraham. That this is more than coincidental is suggested by the recurrence of the theme in *Daniel:* in the poems of Junius XI the Promised Land is the focus of exiled desire rather than joyful habitation. *Exodus* begins by explicitly mentioning these themes, but in language which from the outset establishes a mystical relationship between the geographic journey of the Israelites and the spiritual journey of the Anglo-Saxon Christian, moving toward "heavenly life." The land promised to Abraham, the destination of the nation fleeing from Egyptian captivity, is allegorically also the promised land of heaven. However, the poet maintains a careful focus on historical events throughout, and especially on the figure of Moses, who is both lawgiver and war leader, a great general whose fine speeches rally his troops and whose special relationship with God assures his people of victory.

The author of *Exodus* delights in both the poetry of history and the play of poetic language and metaphor, all of which combine to produce a poem of stunning complexity and originality. This originality is found as much in the poet's vocabulary as in its narrative mode, as *Exodus* is the Old English poem with the highest frequency of poetic compound nouns, many clearly the poet's invention. The poet's highly successful attempt to recast what essentially was a slave escape as an epic victory for the Hebrew army rests not only on his depiction of the Hebrews' willingness to undertake the hopeless battle before the miracle at the Red Sea, but also on his treatment of the miraculous phenomena found in the biblical source. The pillar of fire is transformed from a guide by night into a cosmic warrior guardian, while the returning Red Sea—with strong echoes of the treatment of the waters of the Flood in *Genesis A*—becomes alternately an invincible and merciless army and a weapon in God's vengeful hand. The allegorical shift is never far away from the literal story, though, and is clearly manifest in the poet's unusual representations, which parallel his inventive diction. The pillar of cloud becomes a magnificent sail, the Hebrew people mariners crossing the desert, the pursuing Egyptians landsmen. The metaphor makes sense only in terms of the Christian figural understanding of the Church as a ship, along with the belief that the Chosen People of the Old Testament prefigure the followers of Christ in the New. This typological way of reading also accounts for the major narrative digression that occurs as the Israelites enter the Red Sea, where the poet begins a genealogical recollection of Israel, then leaps back to Noah and the Flood before recalling Abraham and the sacrifice of Isaac. All represent allegorical high points relating to the mystery of Christ, the Christian redemption, and the Church, with a particular focus on the typology of baptism.

The poem's language and style converge to engage the reader. The juxtaposition of familiar words in new and often unusual compound nouns invites new meanings of mysterious events. For example, *flod-weard* ("flood-guardian," line 494), a word found only in *Exodus,* invites the reader to reflect on God's power over nature, but also evokes a complex set of interpretive associations extending back to Genesis 1:2, when God moved over the waters. The narrative technique adopts a similar approach, best exemplified in the account of the crossing of the Red Sea, where the juxtaposition of the Flood story with the sea crossing evokes not only the historical link between the two events as acts of God's deliverance, but also their association as lections in the Easter Vigil and their shared baptismal typology.

Daniel opens with the recollection of the exodus and the happy occupation of the Promised Land. It is impossible to know whether the poem's opening originally and serendipitously coincided with the conclusion of *Exodus* or an anthologizing scribe recrafted the inherited verse to match *Daniel*'s new context. However, the two poems' approaches to the biblical narrative are quite different, as the *Daniel* poet is almost exclusively interested in the historical (and with it the moral) aspect of the biblical narrative. Daniel is in fact a prophetic book with a historical opening that creates the setting for a series of apocalyptic visions. The poet is clearly interested in the history, and it is unlikely that the poem in Junius XI ever continued much beyond its present ending at Belshazzar's feast, if at all. Daniel remains an important character and a great interpreter of dreams, but the poet omits much of the material regarding his character.

By basing his narrative on the first five chapters of Daniel, the poet has created a poem that is mostly about the Chaldean king Nebuchadnezzar and his place in the passing of power between earth's great empires under the ultimate sovereignty of God.[18] It is the king who sends his armies to sack Jerusalem, though in the poet's telling the sin of the Hebrews comes first, so that the Chaldean destruction of the city is an expression of God's wrath with those who have broken his covenant. In the Hebrews' Babylonian exile, the king selects three noble Hebrew youths—Hananiah, Azariah, and Mishael—for instruction. Daniel first emerges in the story as an interpreter of the king's dream of a statue with a golden head and feet of clay, though only the dream's meaning and none of its biblical content is briefly accounted for in the poem. Beside Daniel's streamlined role as interpreter and adviser in the poem, the three holy youths are more carefully cast as devout keepers of God's covenant who defy the king. Their refusal of idolatry and Nebuchadnezzar's futile attempt to incinerate them for it becomes the first step on the king's path to conversion; this is inseparable in the poem from the national repentance they articulate among the flames. The king's own repentance comes during his exile for seven years in the wilderness. Again the poet pares down the tale, leaving out the biblical description of the king's physical transformation and so emphasizing psychological and spiritual change. Nebuchadnezzar's role continues even after his death, as the final destruction of the Babylonian empire under Belshazzar is expressed by the poet in terms of Belshazzar's failure to honor God as his predecessor had done.

The text of *Azarias* reveals an obvious and very close relationship to *Daniel,* corresponding to the section of the longer poem recounting the attempted destruction of the holy youths in the Chaldean furnace and the two canticles they sing there.[19] Very little Old English poetry survives in more than one version or copy, and the separate survival of the canticles in *Azarias* owes something to their use in the monastic Office (they were also included in the Vulgate text of the book of Daniel). The exact nature of the relationship between the two poems is more difficult to define, and their textual divergence is best explained by the formulaic character of Old English verse.[20] Within this tradition poets (and scribes) felt a degree of freedom in their roles as transmitters of received verse and could happily substitute words, or metrically acceptable half-lines, or even greater portions of a poem. The excerption of *Azarias* from a longer poem (if this is what happened), however, has changed more than a few lines. The second canticle, which praises God in creation, diverges more and more both from the version in *Daniel* and from the biblical text, producing a poem with a greater emphasis on nature in its vitality and beauty. Another consequence of divorcing the martyrdom of the youths (as it was understood by medieval authors) from its

wider narrative context is that Nebuchadnezzar appears to
be more violent and capricious, perhaps a necessary corol-
lary in a poem where emphasis has been put on the faith
in God shown by Hananiah, Azariah, and Mishael. However, as in all the poems collected in this volume, this God
is firmly Christian. The thorough appropriation of the Old
Testament by Christian authors is perfectly exemplified by
the conclusion of the second canticle in both *Daniel* and
Azarias, where in a final doxology God is praised as Father,
Son, and Holy Spirit. This is almost certainly a reflex of the
use of the canticle in the monastic cycle of daily prayer, but
it nevertheless provides an insight into the medieval understanding of Old Testament saints such as Noah, Abraham,
and Moses, all of whom were regarded as prophets of the
Christian covenant.

Notes

1 Published facsimiles are Gollancz, *The Cædmon Manuscript of Anglo-
Saxon Biblical Poetry;* Muir, *A Digital Facsimile of Oxford, Bodleian Library,
MS. Junius XI;* Chambers, Förster, and Flowers, *The Exeter Book of Old En-
glish Poetry;* Muir, *The Exeter Anthology of Old English Poetry*.

2 *Christ and Satan* is made up of three separate poems based on the gos-
pels and apocryphal narratives that accrued to the Old and New Testa-
ments; it is edited in a separate volume in this series. Other Exeter Book
poems appear in separate volumes in this series; one other surviving Old
English narrative poem based on the Old Testament, *Judith*, appears in
the third volume of the Dumbarton Oaks Medieval Library, *The* Beowulf
Manuscript, ed. R. D. Fulk (Cambridge, Mass., 2010).

3 *Bede's Ecclesiastical History of the English People,* 4.24.

4 *Caedmonis monachi paraphrasis poetica*.

5 Thorpe, *Cædmon's Metrical Paraphrase of Parts of the Holy Scriptures in
Anglo-Saxon.* The most recent thorough attempt at a relative dating of
much Anglo-Saxon verse is by R. D. Fulk, *A History of Old English Meter,*

390–92, who dates *Genesis A* to before *Exodus*, which is no later than ca. 825, and *Daniel*, which is no later than ca. 725 (if Mercian, or a century later if Northumbrian, contemporary with *Beowulf*). Doane, *The Saxon Genesis,* 54, dates *Genesis B* to ca. 900.

6 On the shape and text of the medieval Bible, see Marsden, "Wrestling with the Bible."

7 See Remley, *Old English Biblical Verse,* 94–167.

8 Wright, "The Blood of Abel and the Branches of Sin.".

9 See Anlezark, "Old English Biblical and Devotional Poetry."

10 See Godden, "The Trouble with Sodom."

11 See Hauer, "The Patriarchal Digression in the Old English *Exodus.*" For medieval Christian typology in general, see Auerbach, "*Figura.*"

12 See Robinson, "The Significance of Names in Old English Literature."

13 Doane, *The Saxon Genesis,* 30–34.

14 Ibid., 7.

15 See Fulk, *Old English Meter*, 390–92.

16 See Doane, *Saxon Genesis*, 47–53, and Fulk, *Old English Meter*, 298, 333–34.

17 Renoir, "Eve's I.Q. Rating."

18 Anderson. "Style and Theme in the Old English *Daniel*."

19 See Remley, "*Daniel*, the *Three Youths* Fragment," for a detailed discussion of their textual relationship.

20 See Jones, "*Daniel* and *Azarias* as Evidence."

GENESIS

Genesis A

1
Us is riht micel   ðæt we rodera weard,
wereda wuldor-cining,   wordum herigen,
modum lufien.   He is mægna sped,
heafod ealra   heah-gesceafta,
5   Frea ælmihtig.   Næs him fruma æfre
or geworden,   ne nu ende cymþ
ecean Drihtnes,   ac he bið a rice
ofer heofen-stolas.   Heagum þrymmum
soðfæst and swið-feorm   swegl-bosmas heold,
10   þa wæron gesette   wide and side
þurh geweald Godes   wuldres bearnum,
gasta weardum.   Hæfdon gleam and dream,
and heora ord-fruman,   engla þreatas,
beorhte blisse.   Wæs heora blæd micel!
15   Þegnas þrymfæste   þeoden heredon,
sægdon lustum lof,   heora Lif-Frean
demdon, Drihtenes   dugeþum wæron
swiðe gesælige.   Synna ne cuþon,
firena fremman,   ac hie on friðe lifdon,
20   ece mid heora aldor.   Elles ne ongunnon
ræran on roderum   nymþe riht and soþ,
ærðon engla weard   for ofer-hygde

Genesis A

It is very right for us that we should praise with words the ¹ guardian of the heavens, the glorious king of hosts, should love him in our minds. He is abundant in powers, head of all lofty creatures, the Lord almighty. There never was a beginning for him, nor an origin brought about, nor presently will come an end of the eternal Lord, but forever he will be sovereign over the thrones of heaven. Righteous and potent in supernal powers, he has held the expanses of heaven, which were established broad and wide through God's rule for the sons of glory, for the guardians of spirits. The hosts of angels had rejoicing and happiness, bright bliss and their source of being. Their glory was great!

Triumphant attendants glorified the prince, eagerly spoke   15 praise, honored their Lord of life, were very happy in blessings of the Lord. They did not know of sins, the doing of evil deeds, but rather they lived in peace, eternally with their leader. They strove to exalt nothing else but right and truth, until by arrogance the guardian of the angels strayed into er-

dwæl on gedwilde.   Noldan dreogan leng
heora selfra ræd,   ac hie of sib-lufan
25 Godes ahwurfon.   Hæfdon gielp micel
þæt hie wið Drihtne   dælan meahton
wuldorfæstan wic   werodes þrymme,
sid and swegl-torht.

Him þær sar gelamp,
æfst and ofer-hygd   and þæs engles mod
30 þe þone unræd ongan   ærest fremman,
wefan and weccean   —þa he worde cwæð,
niþes ofþyrsted—   þæt he on norð-dæle
ham and heah-setl   heofena rices
agan wolde.   Þa wearð yrre God
35 and þam werode wrað   þe he ær wurðode
wlite and wuldre.   Sceop þam wer-logan
wræclicne ham   weorce to leane,
helle-heafas,   hearde niðas.

Heht þæt wite-hus   wræcna bidan,
40 deop, dreama leas,   Drihten ure,
gasta weardas,   þa he hit geare wiste,
syn-nihte beseald,   susle geinnod,
geondfolen fyre   and fær-cyle,
rece and reade lege.   Heht þa geond þæt rædlease hof
45 weaxan wite-brogan.   Hæfdon hie wroht-geteme
grimme wið God gesomnod;   him þæs grim lean becom!
Cwædon þæt heo rice,   reðe-mode,
agan woldan   and swa eaðe meahtan.
Him seo wen geleah   siððan waldend his,
50 heofona heah-cining,   honda arærde,
hehste wið þam herge.   Ne mihton hygelease,
mæne wið metode,   mægyn bryttigan,

ror. They no longer wished to act for their own advantage, but they turned away from God's intimacy. They had the great boast that they could partition with the Lord the glorious dwelling, the splendor of the host, ample and sublimely radiant.

A sorrow befell them there, the envy and the arrogance 28 and the mind of the angel who first began to fabricate, weave and awaken the deceit—when he spoke in a word, thirsted for hatred—that he would possess a home and a throne in the northern part of the kingdom of heaven. Then God became angry and furious with the troop that he had honored with beauty and splendor. He formed a home in banishment for that traitor as a reward for his work, the howls of hell, hard tortures.

Our Lord commanded the guardians of spirits to endure 39 that torture chamber of exiles, deep, deprived of joy, when he knew it was ready, bound in unending night, filled with torment, pervaded with fire and intense cold, fumes and red flame. Then he commanded monstrous tortures to intensify throughout that abode for the perverse-minded. They had grimly gathered a group of conspirators against God; a grim reward befell them for that! The violent ones said that they would have the kingdom and could do so easily. This expectation deceived them, when the ruler, high King of the heavens raised his most high hands against that army. Those thoughtless ones could not share power with the creator,

ac him se mæra   mod getwæfde,
bælc forbigde.

           Þa he gebolgen wearð
55   besloh syn-sceaþan   sigore and gewealde,
dome and dugeðe,   and dreame benam
his feond, friðo   and gefean ealle,
torhte tire,   and his torn gewræc
on gesacum swiðe   selfes mihtum
60   strengum stiepe.   Hæfde styrne mod,
gegremed grymme   grap on wraðe
faum folmum   and him on fæðm gebræc
yrre on mode;   æðele bescyrede
his wiðer-brecan   wuldor-gestealdum.
65   Sceof þa and scyrede   scyppend ure
ofer-hidig cyn   engla of heofnum,
wærleas werod.   Waldend sende
laðwendne here   on langne sið,
geomre gastas;   wæs him gylp forod,
70   beot forborsten,   and forbiged þrym,
wlite gewemmed.   Heo on wrace syððan
seomodon swearte,   siðe ne þorfton
hlude hlihhan,   ac heo hell-tregum
werige wunodon   and wean cuðon,
75   sar and sorge,   susl þrowedon,
þystrum beþeahte,   þearl æfter-lean
þæs þe heo ongunnon   wið Gode winnan.

but the mighty one ended their pride, humbled their bab-
bling.

When he became enraged he thrust down the evildoers 54
from victory and authority, from glory and prosperity, and
deprived his enemy of joy, security and all delight, radiant
glory, and for his injury vehemently took vengeance upon
his enemies by his own powers with a forceful toppling. He
had a stern mind, grimly aggrieved he angrily gripped them
with hostile hands and crushed them in his grasp, wrathful
in mind; he completely cut off his adversaries from the native land, from the glorious dwellings.

Then our creator shoved out and cut off that insolent 65
race of angels from the heavens, the faithless troop. The
ruler sent the hostile army on a long journey, the sad spirits;
their vaunting was exhausted, the boast utterly broken, their
triumph humbled, beauty defiled. Afterward they hung
about darkly in exile, they had no cause to laugh loudly, but
they accursedly dwelled in hell's tortures and knew about
woe, sore and sorrowful, endured torment, suffocated in
darkness, and cruel recompense because they undertook to
fight against God. Then as before there was true friendship

GENESIS

Þa wæs soð swa ær   sibb on heofnum,
fægre freoþo-þeawas,   Frea eallum leof,
80 þeoden his þegnum;   þrymmas weoxon
duguða mid Drihtne   dream-hæbbendra.

II

Wæron þa gesome   þa þe swegl buað,
wuldres eðel.   Wroht wæs asprungen,
oht mid englum   and orleg-nið,
85 siððan here-wosan   heofon ofgæfon,
leohte belorene.   Him on laste setl,
wuldor-spedum welig,   wide stodan
gifum growende   on Godes rice,
beorht and geblædfæst,   buendra leas,
90 siððan wræc-stowe   werige gastas
under hearm-locan   heane geforan.

Þa þeahtode   þeoden ure
mod-geþonce   hu he þa mæran gesceaft,
eðel-staðolas   eft gesette,
95 swegl-torhtan seld,   selran werode,
þa hie gielp-sceaþan   ofgifen hæfdon,
heah on heofenum.   Forþam halig God
under roderas feng,   ricum mihtum,
wolde þæt him eorðe   and uproder
100 and sid wæter   geseted wurde
woruld-gesceafte   on wraðra gield,
þara þe forhealdene   of hleo sende.

Ne wæs her þa giet   nymþe heolster-sceado
wiht geworden,   ac þes wida grund
105 stod deop and dim,   Drihtne fremde,
idel and unnyt.   On þone eagum wlat
stið-frihþ cining,   and þa stowe beheold,

8

in the heavens, the beautiful customs of peace, the Lord
dear to all, the Prince among his attendants; the glories of
the blissful hosts grew with the Lord.

Those who inhabit the sky, the homeland of glory, were   II 82
then united. Enmity, hostility, and rancor among the angels
were shattered after the warmongers abandoned heaven,
deprived of light. In their wake stood thrones, bountifully
prosperous, abroad in God's kingdom, gracefully flourishing, bright and thriving without occupants after the accursed spirits traveled abjectly to the place of exile in their
prison.

Then our prince considered in his thought how he might   92
settle with a better troop the great creations and the native-
seats after that, the bright radiant thrones, those which the
boastful destroyers had given up, high in the heavens. Therefore holy God took control under the skies, with royal powers, intended that the earth and sky above and the broad
water be established as a created world in compensation for
the hateful, rebellious ones, whom he banished from his
protection.

Then was nothing yet here except darkness, but this vast   103
abyss stood deep and dark, alien to the Lord, idle and use-
less. The resolute king looked upon it with his eyes, and beheld the place, without joys, saw the dark mist hanging in

dreama lease, geseah deorc gesweorc
semian sin-nihte sweart under roderum,
110   wonn and weste, oðþæt þeos woruld-gesceaft
þurh word gewearð wuldor-cyninges.
Her ærest gesceop ece Drihten,
helm eall-wihta, heofon and eorðan,
rodor arærde, and þis rume land
115   gestaþelode strangum mihtum,
Frea ælmihtig. Folde wæs þa gyta
græs ungrene; gar-secg þeahte
sweart syn-nihte, side and wide,
wonne węgas.
               Þa wæs wuldor-torht
120   heofon-weardes gast ofer holm boren
miclum spedum. Metod engla heht,
lifes brytta, leoht forð cuman
ofer rumne grund. Raþe wæs gefylled
heah-cininges hæs; him wæs halig leoht
125   ofer westenne, swa se wyrhta bebead.
Þa gesundrode sigora waldend
ofer lagu-flode leoht wið þeostrum,
sceade wið sciman. Sceop þa bam naman,
lifes brytta. Leoht wæs ærest
130   þurh Drihtnes word dæg genemned,
wlite-beorhte gesceaft. Wel licode
Frean æt frymðe forþ-bæro tid,
dæg æresta; geseah deorc sceado
sweart swiðrian geond sidne grund.

III
135   Þa seo tid gewat ofer timber sceacan
middan-geardes; metod æfter sceaf

perpetual night, black under the skies, gloomy and void, until this created world came into existence by the word of the king of glory. The eternal Lord, protector of all things, first created here heaven and earth, raised up the sky, and the Lord almighty established this spacious land by his strong powers. The surface was not yet green with grass; dark perpetual night oppressed the ocean far and wide, the gloomy waves.

Then the gloriously splendid spirit of heaven's keeper 119 hovered over the sea with great success. The creator of angels, the giver of life, commanded light to come forth over the spacious abyss. The high king's order was quickly fulfilled; for them there was a holy light over the void, as the maker commanded. Then the ruler of victories separated light from darkness across the flowing sea, shadow from radiance. Then the giver of life shaped names for both: first, light was called "day" by the Lord's word, the splendidly bright creature. In the beginning the Lord was well pleased, in that fruitful moment, the first day; he saw the dark shadow disappear across the broad abyss.

III
Then the moment went hurrying over the material of 135
middle-earth; afterward the creator, our maker, drew up the

scirum sciman,   scippend ure,
æfen ærest.   Him arn on last
þrang þystre genip,   þam þe se þeoden self
140   sceop nihte naman.   Nergend ure
hie gesundrode;   siððan æfre
drugon and dydon   Drihtnes willan,
ece ofer eorðan.   Ða com oðer dæg,
leoht æfter þeostrum.   Heht þa lifes weard
145   on mere-flode   middum weorðan
hyhtlic heofon-timber.   Holmas dælde
waldend ure   and geworhte þa
roderas, fæsten,   þæt se rica ahof
up from eorðan   þurh his agen word,
150   Frea ælmihtig.

                    Flod wæs adæled
under heah-rodore   halgum mihtum,
wæter of wætrum,   þam þe wuniað gyt
under fæstenne   folca hrofes.
Ða com ofer foldan   fus siðian
155   mære mergen þridda.   Næron metode ða gyta
wid-lond ne wegas nytte,   ac stod bewrigen fæste
folde mid flode.   Frea engla heht
þurh his word wesan   wæter gemæne,
þa nu under roderum   heora ryne healdað,
160   stowe gestefnde.   Ða stod hraðe
holm under heofonum   swa se halga bebead,
sid ætsomne,   ða gesundrod wæs
lago wið lande.   Geseah þa lifes weard
drige stowe,   dugoða hyrde,

first evening to glow with splendor. In its track the shade of darkness came running, hastening, for which the prince himself created the name "night." Our savior separated them; ever after they have carried out and done the Lord's will, eternally across the earth. Then came the second day, light after the darkness. Life's guardian then commanded the exultant heavenly material to arise in the midst of the sea-stream. Our ruler divided the seas and then made the heavens, the firmament, which the powerful one, the Lord almighty, lifted up from the earth by his own word.

The flood was divided under the high sky by holy powers, 150 water from waters, for those who still dwell under the firmament of the people's roof. Then the glorious third morning quickly came traveling over the earth. As yet neither the wide land nor the waves were useful to the creator, but earth stood firmly covered with the flood. By his word the Lord of angels commanded the waters to be gathered, which now hold their course under the heavens, fixed in their place. Then the ocean quickly stood, wide and united under the heavens as the holy one commanded, when the sea was divided from the land. Then life's guardian, the shepherd of

165   wide æteowde,   þa se wuldor-cyning
eorðan nemde.   Gesette yðum heora
onrihtne ryne,   rumum flode,
and gefetero

* * *

IV

    Ne þuhte þa gerysne   rodora wearde,
170   þæt Adam leng   ana wære
neorxna-wonges,   niwre gesceafte,
hyrde and healdend.   Forþon him heah-cyning,
Frea ælmihtig   fultum tiode;
wif aweahte   and þa wraðe sealde,
175   lifes leoht-fruma,   leofum rince.
He þæt andweorc   of Adames
lice aleoðode,   and him listum ateah
rib of sidan.   He wæs reste fæst,
and softe swæf,   sar ne wiste,
180   earfoða dæl,   ne þær ænig com
blod of benne,   ac him brego engla
of lice ateah   liodende ban,
wer unwundod,   of þam worhte God
freolice fæmnan.
                   Feorh in gedyde,
185   ece saula.   Heo wæron englum gelice
þa wæs Eue,   Adames bryd,
gaste gegearwod.   Hie on geogoðe bu
wlite-beorht wæron   on woruld cenned
meotodes mihtum.   Man ne cuðon
190   don ne dreogan,   ac him Drihtnes wæs
bam on breostum   byrnende lufu.
Þa gebletsode   blið-heort cyning,

hosts, saw the dry place, widely revealed, which the glorious king named "earth." He set for the waves their correct course, for the spacious flood, and restricted

* * *

It did not then seem fitting to the guardian of the skies that Adam should be alone any longer, the keeper and custodian in paradise, the new creation. Therefore the high king, the Lord almighty, furnished support; the origin of life's light created a woman and then gave her as a help to the dear man. He drew that substance from Adam's body, and carefully pulled a rib from his side. He was fast asleep and softly slumbered, felt no soreness, no share of pain, nor did any blood come from the wound, but the prince of angels drew out from his body a living bone, the man unwounded, from which God made a noble woman.

He put life into her, an eternal soul. They were like the 184 angels when Eve, Adam's bride, was adorned with a spirit. Beautiful in youth, they both were born into the world by the creator's powers. They did not know how to do or commit sin, but the burning love of the Lord was in the breast of both. Then the happy-hearted king, creator of all things,

metod alwihta,   monna cynnes
ða forman twa,   fæder and moder,
195   wif and wæpned.   He þa worde cwæð:
"Temað nu and wexað,   tudre fyllað
eorðan ælgrene,   incre cynne,
sunum and dohtrum.   Inc sceal sealt wæter
wunian on gewealde   and eall worulde gesceaft.
200   Brucað blæd-daga   and brim-hlæste
and heofon-fugla.   Inc is halig feoh
and wilde deor   on geweald geseald,
and lifigende,   ða ðe land tredað,
feorh-eaceno cynn   ða ðe flod wecceð
205   geond hron-rade.   Inc hyrað eall."
    Þa sceawode   scyppend ure
his weorca wlite   and his wæstma blæd,
niwra gesceafta.   Neorxna-wong stod
god and gastlic,   gifena gefylled
210   fremum forðweardum.   Fægere leohte
þæt liðe land   lago yrnende,
wylle-burne.   Nalles wolcnu ða giet
ofer rumne grund   regnas bæron,
wann mid winde,   hwæðre wæstmum stod
215   folde gefrætwod.   Heoldon forð-ryne
ea-streamas heora   æðele feower
of þam niwan   neorxna-wonge.
Þa wæron adælede   Drihtnes mihtum
ealle of anum,   þa he þas eorðan gesceop,
220   wætre wlite-beorhtum,   and on woruld sende.
    Þæra anne hatað ylde,   eorð-buende,
Fison folc-weras;   se foldan dæl
brade bebugeð   beorhtum streamum

16

blessed the first two of the human race, father and mother, woman and man. Then he made this speech:

"Now be fruitful and multiply, fill the all-green earth with 196 offspring, the progeny of you two, with sons and daughters. The salt water and all the worldly creation shall remain under your rule. Enjoy fruitful days and the sea's bounty and the birds of heaven. Blessed cattle and wild beasts are given into the power of you two, and those living things that tread the land, and that fecund race that stirs up the current across the whale-road. All will obey you two."

Then our maker looked on the beauty of his work and the 206 glory of his fruits, and new creations. Paradise stood good and sanctified, filled with the lasting benefits of his graces. A running pool, a wellspring, fairly irrigated that pleasant land. Not at all did clouds then bring rains across the wide ground, gloomy with the wind, but nonetheless the earth stood adorned with fruits. Four noble river streams had their common source from the fresh paradise. By the Lord's powers they were all divided from the one beautifully bright pool, when he created this earth, and sent them into the world.

Men inhabiting the earth, the nations, call one of them 221 Phison; it broadly meanders in bright streams around

Hebeleac utan. On þære eðyl-tyrf
225 niððas findað nean and feorran
gold and gym-cynn, gum-þeoda bearn,
ða selestan, þæs þe us secgað bec.
Þonne seo æftre Ethiopia
land and liod-geard beligeð uton,
230 ginne rice —þære is Geon noma.
Þridda is Tigris, seo wið þeodscipe,
ea inflede, Assirię belið;
swilce is seo feorðe, þa nu geond folc monig
weras Eufraten wide nemnað.

* * *

GENESIS B

v
235 "... ac niotað inc þæs oðres ealles, forlætað þone ænne
beam,
wariað inc wið þone wæstm. Ne wyrð inc wilna gæd."
Hnigon þa mid heafdum heofon-cyninge
georne togenes and sædon ealles þanc,
lista and þara lara. He let heo þæt land buan;
240 hwærf him þa to heofenum halig Drihten,
stið-ferhð cyning. Stod his hand-geweorc
somod on sande; nyston sorga wiht
to begrornianne, butan heo Godes willan
lengest læsten. Heo wæron leof Gode
245 ðenden heo his halige word healdan woldon.
vi
Hæfde se alwalda engel-cynna
þurh hand-mægen, halig Drihten,
tene getrimede, þæm he getruwode wel

Havilah, that region of the earth. In that homeland the people, the sons of nations, find the best gold and gemstones
near and far, as books tell us. Then the second encompasses
the land and realm of Ethiopia, the vast kingdom—its name
is Gihon. Tigris is the third, the coursing river that encircles
the nation of Assyria; as does the fourth, which men widely
across many a nation now call Euphrates.

* * *

GENESIS B

"... but enjoy all the others for yourselves, renounce that one   V
tree, guard yourselves against the fruit. For you two there   235
will be no unsatisfied desire." Then they eagerly bowed their
heads toward heaven's king and said thanks for all things, for
his creative skill and his teachings. He allowed them to occupy that land; then the holy Lord, the resolute king, turned
toward the heavens. His handiwork stood together on the
sand; they knew nothing at all about lamenting sorrows, but
rather they should fulfill God's desire for the longest time.
They were beloved of God while they intended to keep his
holy word.

The ruler of all, the holy Lord, had arrayed ten orders of   VI
angels by the power of his hand, whom he well trusted would   246

þæt hie his giongorscipe   fyligan wolden,
250   wyrcean his willan   —forþon he him gewit forgeaf.
And mid his handum gesceop   halig Drihten,
gesett hæfde he hie swa gesæliglice;   ænne hæfde he swa
    swiðne geworhtne,
swa mihtigne on his mod-geþohte,   he let hine swa micles
    wealdan
hehstne to him on heofona rice,   hæfde he hine swa
    hwitne geworhtne,
255   swa wynlic wæs his wæstm on heofonum   þæt him com
    from weroda Drihtne,
gelic wæs he þam leohtum steorrum.
256   Lof sceolde he Drihtnes wyrcean,
dyran sceolde he his dreamas on heofonum,   and sceolde
    his Drihtne þancian
þæs leanes þe he him on þam leohte gescerede   —þonne
    læte he his hine lange wealdan.
Ac he awende hit him to wyrsan þinge,   ongan him winn
    up ahebban
260   wið þone hehstan heofnes waldend,   þe siteð on þam
    halgan stole.
Deore wæs he Drihtne urum;   ne mihte him bedyrned
    weorðan
þæt his engyl ongan   ofer-mod wesan,
ahof hine wið his hearran,   sohte hete-spræce,
gylp-word ongean,   nolde Gode þeowian,
265   cwæð þæt his lic wære   leoht and scene,
hwit and hiow-beorht.
266   Ne meahte he æt his hige findan
þæt he Gode wolde   geongerdome,
þeodne þeowian.   Þuhte him sylfum

follow in his obedience, work his will—because he granted
them intelligence. And the holy Lord created them with his
hands, he had established them so blessedly; one he had
made so potent, so mighty in his intellect, so much he let
him rule, highest after him in the kingdom of the heavens,
so radiant had he made him, so delightful in the heavens was
his stature that came to him from the Lord of hosts, that he
was like the dazzling stars.

He should have performed the Lord's praise, should have   256
cherished his joys in the heavens, and should have thanked
his Lord for the reward that he bestowed on him in that
light—then he would have allowed him to rule for a long
time. But he exchanged it for a worse outcome for himself,
began to raise up strife against the most high ruler of heaven,
who sits on the holy throne. He was dear to our Lord; it
could not be kept hidden from him that his angel began to
be insolent, exalted himself against his master, sought cal-
umny and defiant words against him, would not serve God,
said that his body was radiant and shining, luminous and
brightly colored.

He could not find it in his mind that he would serve God,   266
the prince, in obedience. It seemed to him alone that he had

þæt he mægyn and cræft   maran hæfde
270   þonne se halga God   habban mihte
folc-gestælna.   Feala worda gespæc
se engel ofer-modes.   Þohte þurh his anes cræft
hu he him strenglicran   stol geworhte,
heahran on heofonum;   cwæð þæt hine his hige speone
275   þæt he west and norð   wyrcean ongunne,
trymede getimbro;   cwæð him tweo þuhte
þæt he Gode wolde   geongra weorðan.
    "Hwæt sceal ic winnan?" cwæð he.   "Nis me wihtæ
þearf
hearran to habbanne.   Ic mæg mid handum swa fela
280   wundra gewyrcean.   Ic hæbbe geweald micel
to gyrwanne   godlecran stol,
hearran on heofne.   Hwy sceal ic æfter his hyldo ðeowian,
bugan him swilces geongordomes?   Ic mæg wesan god swa
he.
Bigstandað me strange geneatas,   þa ne willað me æt þam
striðe geswican,
285   hæleþas heard-mode.   Hie habbað me to hearran
gecorene,
rofe rincas;   mid swilcum mæg man ræd geþencean,
fon mid swilcum folc-gesteallan.   Frynd synd hie mine
georne,
holde on hyra hyge-sceaftum.   Ic mæg hyra hearra wesan,
rædan on þis rice.   Swa me þæt riht ne þinceð,
290   þæt ic oleccan   awiht þurfe
Gode æfter gode ænegum.   Ne wille ic leng his geongra
wurþan."
    Þa hit se allwalda   eall gehyrde,
þæt his engyl ongan   ofer-mede micel
ahebban wið his hearran   and spræc healic word

22

greater power and skill, more comrades than the holy God could have. The angel of insolence spoke many words. He planned how he would create a stronger throne for himself through his unique power, higher in the heavens; he said that his mind urged him that he should begin to create, west and north, an edifice; he said that it seemed doubtful that he would continue to be an underling for God.

"Why must I toil?" he said. "It is not at all necessary for me to have a master. I can create as many wonders with my hands. I have great authority to adorn a better throne, higher in heaven. Why must I grovel for his favor, and bow to him with such obedience? I can be a god as he is. Strong companions stand beside me, tough-minded warriors who will not fail me in the strife. They have chosen me as their master, the brave soldiers; with such supporters one can consider plans, undertake them with such as these. They are my zealous friends, loyal in their hearts. I can be their master, govern in this kingdom. So it does not seem right to me that I need flatter God to get anything good. I will no longer be his underling." 278

When the ruler of everything heard it all, that his angel began to raise a great insolence against his master and foolishly spoke lofty words against his Lord, then he had to pay 292

295 dollice wið Drihten sinne,   sceolde he þa dæd ongyldan,
worc þæs gewinnes gedælan,   and sceolde his wite habban,
ealra morðra mæst.   Swa deð monna gehwilc
þe wið his waldend   winnan ongynneð
mid mane wið þone mæran Drihten.   Þa wearð se mihtiga
                                                                          gebolgen,
300 hehsta heofones waldend,   wearp hine of þan hean stole.
Hete hæfde he æt his hearran gewunnen,   hyldo hæfde
                                                                          his ferlorene,
gram wearð him se goda on his mode.   Forþon he sceolde
                                                                          grund gesecean
heardes helle-wites,   þæs þe he wann wið heofnes
                                                                          waldend.
Acwæð hine þa fram his hyldo   and hine on helle wearp,
305 on þa deopan dala,   þær he to deofle wearð,
se feond mid his geferum eallum.   Feollon þa ufon of
                                                                          heofnum
þurhlonge swa   þreo niht and dagas,
þa englas of heofnum on helle,   and heo ealle forsceop
Drihten to deoflum.   Forþon heo his dæd and word
310 noldon weorðian,   forþon he heo on wyrse leoht
under eorðan neoðan,   ællmihtig God,
sette sigelease   on þa sweartan helle.
Þær hæbbað heo on æfyn   ungemet lange,
ealra feonda gehwilc,   fyr edneowe,
315 þonne cymð on uhtan   easterne wind,
forst fyrnum cald.   Symble fyr oððe gar,
sum heard geswinc   habban sceoldon.
Worhte man hit him to wite   —hyra woruld wæs
                                                                          gehwyrfed—

for the deed, share the suffering of the struggle, and had to have his punishment, the greatest of all miseries. So does each person who begins to struggle with sin against this ruler, against the famous Lord. Then the mighty one, the highest ruler of the heavens, was enraged, threw him off the high throne.

He had won hate from his master, had lost his favor, the   301 good one had become hostile toward him in his mind. Therefore he had to seek the abyss of hard hell-punishments, because he contended with heaven's ruler. He banished him from his favor and threw him into hell, into the deep cleft, where he became a devil, the enemy with all his companions. They fell then from the heavens above continuously for three nights and days, the angels from heaven into hell, and the Lord misshaped them all into devils. Because they did not desire to respect his word and deed, therefore he, almighty God, set them in a worse light underneath the earth, defeated in dark hell.

There each and every enemy has an eternally kindled   313 flame in an evening boundlessly long; then in the dawn the east wind comes, a frost tormentingly cold. Fire or cold, they must always have some hard affliction. It was made for their torture from the beginning—their world was over-

　　　forman siðe,　　fylde helle
320　　mid þam andsacum.　　Heoldon englas forð
　　heofon-rices hehðe,　　þe ær Godes hyldo gelæston.
　　Lagon þa oðre fynd on þam fyre,　　þe ær swa feala hæfdon
　　gewinnes wið heora waldend.　　Wite þoliað,
　　　hatne heaðo-welm　　helle tomiddes,

VII

325　　brand and brade ligas,　　swilce eac þa biteran recas,
　　　þrosm and þystro,　　forþon hie þegnscipe
　　　Godes forgymdon.　　Hie hyra gal beswac,
　　　engles ofer-hygd,　　noldon alwaldan
　　　word weorþian,　　hæfdon wite micel,
330　　wæron þa befeallene　　fyre to botme
　　　on þa hatan hell　　þurh hygeleaste
　　　and þurh ofer-metto,　　sohton oþer land,
　　　þæt wæs leohtes leas　　and wæs liges full,
　　　fyres fær micel.　　Fynd ongeaton
335　　þæt hie hæfdon gewrixled　　wita unrim
　　　þurh heora miclan mod　　and þurh miht Godes
　　　and þurh ofer-metto　　ealra swiðost.
　　Þa spræc se ofer-moda cyning,　　þe ær wæs engla scynost,
　　　hwitost on heofne　　and his hearran leof,
340　　Drihtne dyre,　　oð hie to dole wurdon,
　　　þæt him for galscipe　　God sylfa wearð
　　mihtig on mode yrre.　　Wearp hine on þæt morðer innan,
　　　niðer on þæt nio-bedd,　　and sceop him naman siððan,
　　　cwæð se hehsta　　hatan sceolde
345　Satan siððan,　　het hine þære sweartan helle
　　　grundes gyman,　　nalles wið God winnan.
　　　Satan maðelode,　　sorgiende spræc,
　　　se ðe helle forð　　healdan sceolde,

26

turned—hell was filled with those apostates. Henceforth, the angels who had maintained God's favor held the heights of the kingdom of heaven. The others, enemies, lay in the fire, who earlier had such great strife with their ruler. They suffer torture, the hot hostile surge in the midst of hell,

VII
325
conflagration and broad flames, so also the bitter fumes, smoke and darkness, because they rejected God's service. Their passion deceived them, the angel's insolence, they did not wish to respect the word of the ruler of all, they had great punishment, when they all plummeted to the fire's depth in the hot hell through thoughtlessness and through insolence, they sought out another land, that was without light and was full of flame, a great barrage of fire. The fiends realized that in the exchange they gained endless tortures through their great pride and by God's power and most of all through their insolence.

Then the haughty king spoke, who earlier had been the 338 brightest of angels, most brilliant in heaven and beloved of his master, dear to the Lord, until they became foolish, so that for their passion mighty God himself became angry in mind. He threw him right into that death, below into that tomb, and afterward created him a name, the most high said that from then on he should be called Satan, and commanded him to govern hell's dark abyss, in no way to struggle against God. Satan made a speech, spoke sorrowing, he who had to keep hell henceforth, govern the abyss.

gieman þæs grundes.   Wæs ær Godes engel,
350   hwit on heofne,   oð hine his hyge forspeon
and his ofer-metto   ealra swiðost,
þæt he ne wolde   wereda Drihtnes
word wurðian.   Weoll him on innan
hyge ymb his heortan,   hat wæs him utan
355   wraðlic wite.   He þa worde cwæð:
       "Is þæs ænga styde   ungelic swiðe
þam oðrum ham   þe we ær cuðon,
hean on heofon-rice,   þe me min hearra onlag,
þeah we hine for þam alwaldan   agan ne moston,
360   romigan ures rices.   Næfð he þeah riht gedon
þæt he us hæfð befælled   fyre to botme,
helle þære hatan,   heofon-rice benumen;
hafað hit gemearcod   mid mon-cynne
to gesettanne.   Þæt me is sorga mæst,
365   þæt Adam sceal,   þe wæs of eorðan geworht,
minne stronglican   stol behealdan,
   wesan him on wynne,   and we þis wite þolien,
hearm on þisse helle.   Wa la, ahte ic minra handa
                                                                    geweald
and moste ane tid   ute weorðan,
370   wesan ane winter-stunde,   þonne ic mid þys werode!—
ac licgað me ymbe   iren-benda,
rideð racentan sal.   Ic eom rices leas;
habbað me swa hearde   helle-clommas
fæste befangen.
                          "Her is fyr micel,
375   ufan and neoðone.   Ic a ne geseah
laðran landscipe.   Lig ne aswamað,
hat ofer helle.   Me habbað hringa gespong,

Earlier he had been God's angel, brilliant in heaven, until his thought deceived him, and his insolence most of all, so that he had not wished to respect the word of the Lord of hosts. His thought surged inside him about his heart, outside him heat was a cruel torture. He spoke these words:

"This constricted space is very unlike the other home 356 that we knew before, high in the kingdom of heaven, which my master granted me, though because of the ruler of all we could not keep it, expand our realm. However, he did not do right when he cast us into the depth of fire, the hot hell, deprived us of the kingdom of heaven; he has planned to settle it with the human race. It is the greatest sorrow to me, that Adam, who was made of earth, shall occupy my mighty throne, be in joy, and we should suffer this torture, pain in this hell. Alas! If I had power over my hands and could be out of here for one moment, one winter's hour, then with this troop!—but iron shackles surround me, a halter of chains sits on me. I am powerless; hell's hard fetters have so firmly imprisoned me.

"A great fire is here, above and below. I never saw a more 374 loathsome landscape. The flame does not fail, hot across hell. Linked chains, a bitterly cruel halter has marred my

slið-hearda sal   siðes amyrred,
afyrred me min feðe;   fet synt gebundene,
380   handa gehæfte.   Synt þissa hel-dora
wegas forworhte,   swa ic mid wihte ne mæg
of þissum lioðo-bendum.   Licgað me ymbe
heardes irenes   hate geslægene
grindlas greate.   Mid þy me God hafað
385   gehæfted be þam healse,   swa ic wat he minne hige
cuðe;
and þæt wiste eac   weroda Drihten,
þæt sceolde unc Adame   yfele gewurðan
ymb þæt heofon-rice,   þær ic ahte minra handa geweald.

VIII
"Ac ðoliaþ we nu þrea on helle   —þæt syndon þystro and
hæto—
390   grimme, grundlease.   Hafað us God sylfa
forswapen on þas sweartan mistas;   swa he us ne mæg
ænige synne gestælan,
þæt we him on þam lande lað gefremedon,   he hæfð us
þeah þæs leohtes bescyrede,
beworpen on ealra wita mæste.   Ne magon we þæs wrace
gefremman,
geleanian him mid laðes wihte   þæt he us hafað þæs
leohtes bescyrede.
395   He hæfð nu gemearcod anne middan-geard,   þær he hæfð
mon geworhtne
æfter his onlicnesse,   mid þam he wile eft gesettan
heofona rice mid hluttrum saulum.   We þæs sculon hycgan
georne,
þæt we on Adame,   gif we æfre mægen,

movement, cut off my passage; my feet are bound, hands tied. The roads through these hell-gates are blocked, so that there is no way I can escape from these bonds. Great grids of hard iron forged in heat surround me. With these God has tethered me by the neck, so I know he reads my mind; and he also knows this, the Lord of hosts, that between me and Adam things would turn evil concerning the kingdom of heaven, if I had power over my hands.

"But now we suffer afflictions in hell—they are darkness and heat—cruel, abysmal. God himself has swept us into these dark mists; though he could not accuse us of any sin, that we carried out any harm in that land, he has nevertheless cut us off from the light, cast us into the greatest of all tortures. We cannot carry out revenge for this, repay him with any harm at all, because he has cut us off from the light. Now he has surveyed a middle world, where he has created a man after his likeness, with whom afterward he desires to settle the kingdom of the heavens with pure souls. We must eagerly consider how we can make amends through Adam

VIII
389

and on his eafrum swa some,   andan gebetan,
400   onwendan him þær willan sines,   gif we hit mægen wihte
aþencan.
"Ne gelyfe ic me nu þæs leohtes furðor   þæs þe he him
þenceð lange niotan,
þæs eades mid his engla cræfte.   Ne magon we þæt on
aldre gewinnan,
þæt we mihtiges Godes mod onwæcen.   Uton oðwendan
hit nu monna bearnum,
þæt heofon-rice, nu we hit habban ne moton,   gedon þæt
hie his hyldo forlæten,
405   þæt hie þæt onwendon þæt he mid his worde bebead.
Þonne weorð he him wrað on mode,
ahwet hie from his hyldo.   Þonne sculon hie þas helle
secan
and þas grimman grundas.   Þonne moton we hie us to
giongrum habban,
fira bearn on þissum fæstum clomme.   Onginnað nu ymb
þa fyrde þencean!
"Gif ic ænegum þægne   þeoden-madmas
410   geara forgeafe,   þenden we on þan godan rice
gesælige sæton   and hæfdon ure setla geweald,
þonne he me na on leofran tid   leanum ne meahte
mine gife gyldan,   gif his gien wolde
minra þegna hwilc   geþafa wurðan,
415   þæt he up heonon   ute mihte
cuman þurh þas clustro,   and hæfde cræft mid him
þæt he mid feðer-homan   fleogan meahte,
windan on wolcne,   þær geworht stondað
Adam and Eue   on eorð-rice

for our anger, if we ever can, and through his heirs as well, to pervert his desire there, if we can devise it in any way.

"I do not hope for that light for me any more, which he   401
intends to enjoy with them forever, a blessedness with the power of his angels. Across the ages we cannot achieve it, that we might weaken the purpose of the mighty God. Let us now turn it away from the children of men, the kingdom of heaven, now that we cannot have it, bring it about that they abandon his favor, that they turn their back on what he commanded by his word. Then he will become angry with them in his mind, cast them away from his favor. Then they will have to seek out this hell and these awful abysses. Then we can have them as our underlings, the children of men in these stiff chains. Let us begin now to plan this expedition!

"If I once gave princely treasures to any follower, while   409
we sat happily in the good kingdom and had the rule of our thrones, then he could never repay me for my grace with requital at a more cherished moment, if still one of my followers would become my helper, so that upwards and onwards he out might pass through these gates, and had the skill in him that he might fly with a feather-cloak, wind through the sky to where Adam and Eve stand created in the earthly

420   mid welan bewunden,   and we synd aworpene hider
on þas deopan dalo.

"Nu hie Drihtne synt
wurðran micle,   and moton him þone welan agan
þe we on heofon-rice   habban sceoldon,
rice mid rihte;   is se ræd gescyred
425   monna cynne.   Þæt me is on minum mode swa sar,
on minum hyge hreoweð,   þæt hie heofon-rice
agan to aldre.   Gif hit eower ænig mæge
gewendan mid wihte   þæt hie word Godes
lare forlæten,   sona hie him þe laðran beoð.
430 Gif hie brecað his gebodscipe,   þonne he him abolgen
wurðeþ;
siððan bið him se wela onwended   and wyrð him wite
gegarwod,
sum heard hearm-scearu.   Hycgað his ealle,
hu ge hi beswicen!   Siððan ic me sefte mæg
restan on þyssum racentum,   gif him þæt rice losað.
435   "Se þe þæt gelæsteð,   him bið lean gearo
æfter to aldre,   þæs we her inne magon
on þyssum fyre forð   fremena gewinnan.
Sittan læte ic hine wið me sylfne,   swa hwa swa þæt secgan
cymeð
on þas hatan helle,   þæt hie heofon-cyninges
440 unwurðlice   wordum and dædum
lare . . ."

* * *

XI
Angan hine þa gyrwan   Godes andsaca,
fus on frætwum,   —hæfde fæcne hyge—,

kingdom, surrounded by good things, and we are thrown here into this deep cleft.

"Now they are much more honored by the Lord, and can have for themselves the prosperity that we should have in the kingdom of heaven, the kingdom by right; the benefit is allotted to mankind. That is so painful to me in my mind, grates in my heart, that they will hold the kingdom of heaven forever. If any of you can in any way make it turn out that they abandon God's word and teaching, immediately they will be more hateful to him. If they break his commandment, then he will become enraged with them; after that the goodness will be taken away from them and torment will be made ready for them, some harsh punishment. All of you, consider how you might trick them in this! Afterward, if they lose that kingdom themselves I can more easily rest in these chains. 421

"Whoever achieves that, a reward will be ready for him forever afterward, of whatever goods we can obtain here within these fires from now on. I will let him be seated beside me, whoever returns to this hot hell to say that they dishonorably [have abandoned] with words and deeds the instruction of heaven's king . . ." 435

*   *   *

Then God's enemy began to prepare himself, eager in his armor—he had evil intentions—he put a disguising helmet XI 442

hæleð-helm on heafod asette   and þone full hearde

geband,

445   spenn mid spangum;   wiste him spræca fela,

wora worda.   Wand him up þanon,

hwearf him þurh þa hell-dora,   —hæfde hyge strangne—

leolc on lyfte   laþwende-mod,

swang þæt fyr on twa   feondes cræfte:

450   wolde dearnunga   Drihtnes geongran,

mid man-dædum   men beswican,

forlædan and forlæran,   þæt hie wurdon lað Gode.

He þa geferde   þurh feondes cræft

oððæt he Adam   on eorð-rice,

455   Godes hand-gesceaft,   gearone funde,

wislice geworht,   and his wif somed,

freo fægroste,   swa hie fela cuðon

godes gegearwigean,   þa him to gingran self

metod man-cynnes   mearcode selfa.

460   And him bi twegin   beamas stodon

þa wæron utan   ofætes gehlædene,

gewered mid wæstme,   swa hie waldend God,

heah heofon-cyning   handum gesette,

þæt þær yldo bearn   moste on ceosan

465   godes and yfeles,   gumena æghwilc,

welan and wawan.   Næs se wæstm gelic!

Oðer wæs swa wynlic,   wlitig and scene,

liðe and lofsum,   þæt wæs lifes beam;

moste on ecnisse   æfter lybban,

470   wesan on worulde,   se þæs wæstmes onbat,

swa him æfter þy   yldo ne derede,

ne suht sware,   ac moste symle wesan

lungre on lustum   and his lif agan,

on his head and fastened it very firmly, fixed it with clasps; he knew many a fine speech of twisted words. From there he wound his way upward, turned through the gates of hell— he had a firm intention—swooped in the air with a mind turned to evil, whipped the fire aside with a fiend's skill: he wished to deceive the Lord's underlings by stealth, with sinful deeds, to mislead and to misguide, so that they would become hateful to God.

Then he traveled with a fiend's skill until he found Adam,   453 God's creation wisely wrought, ready in the earthly kingdom, together with his woman, the fairest lady, as they knew how to bring about much good, whom the creator of mankind himself designated as his underlings. And they stood between two trees that were laden all over with fruit, covered with produce, just as the ruler God, high king of heaven had planted with his hands, so that the children of men could choose good or evil there, each person, prosperity or woe. The fruit was not alike!

One was so joyous, beautiful and bright, gracious and   467 praiseworthy—that was the tree of life; he who bit into that fruit could live ever after, remaining in the world into eternity, so that afterward he would not be harmed by old age, nor severe sickness, but straight away he could be among joys and possess his life forever, the favor of the king of

37

hyldo heofon-cyninges   her on worulde,
475   habban him to wæron   witode geþingþo
on þone hean heofon,   þonne he heonon wende.
    Þonne wæs se oðer   eallenga sweart,
dim and þystre;   þæt wæs deaðes beam,
se bær bitres fela.   Sceolde bu witan
480   ylda æghwilc   yfles and godes
gewand on þisse worulde,   sceolde on wite a
mid swate and mid sorgum   siððan libban,
swa hwa swa gebyrgde   þæs on þam beame geweox.
    Sceolde hine yldo beniman   ellen-dæda,
485   dreamas and drihtscipes,   and him beon deað scyred.
    Lytle hwile   sceolde he his lifes niotan,
secan þonne landa   sweartost on fyre,
sceolde feondum þeowian,   þær is ealra frecna mæste
leodum to langre hwile.   Þæt wiste se laða georne,
490   dyrne deofles boda   þe wið Drihten wann.
    Wearp hine þa on wyrmes lic   and wand him þa
ymbutan
þone deaðes beam   þurh deofles cræft,
genam þær þæs ofætes   and wende hine eft þanon
þær he wiste hand-geweorc   heofon-cyninges.
495   Ongon hine þa frinan   forman worde
se laða mid ligenum: "Langað þe awuht,
Adam, up to Gode?   Ic eom on his ærende hider
feorran gefered,   ne þæt nu fyrn ne wæs
þæt ic wið hine sylfne sæt.   Þa het he me on þysne sið
faran,
500   het þæt þu þisses ofætes æte,   cwæð þæt þin abal and
cræft
and þin mod-sefa   mara wurde,

heaven here in the world, could have as his pledge guaranteed honors in the high heaven when he turned hence.

But the other was completely black, dim and dark; that 477
was the tree of death, which bore much that was bitter.
Whatever person tasted of what grew on that tree, must
know how good and evil turn in this world, must ever after
live in torment with sweat and with sorrow. Old age must
deprive him of valiant deeds, pleasures and nobility, and
death be allotted to him.

For a brief while should he enjoy his life, then seek out 486
the darkest of lands in the fire, must serve the fiends, where
there is the greatest of all horrors for people, for a longer
time. The hateful one readily knew that, the devil's secret
messenger who strove against God. He cast himself then in
the likeness of a serpent and wound himself about the tree
of death through his devil's skill, took some fruit there and
turned back to where he knew the king of heaven's handiwork to be.

Then the hateful one deceptively asked him with his first 495
word: "Is there anything at all, Adam, which you long for
from God above? I have come traveling here from afar on
his errand, it is not long now since I was seated beside him.
Then he commanded me to go on this journey, commanded
that you should eat of this fruit, said that your ability and
skill and your mental capacity would grow greater, and your

and þin lic-homa   leohtra micle,
þin gesceapu scenran,   cwæð þæt þe æniges sceates
ðearf
ne wurde on worulde.   Nu þu willan hæfst,
505   hyldo geworhte   heofon-cyninges,
to þance geþenod   þinum hearran,
hæfst þe wið Drihten dyrne geworhtne.   Ic gehyrde hine
þine dæd and word
lofian on his leohte   and ymb þin lif sprecan.
"Swa þu læstan scealt   þæt on þis land hider
510   his bodan bringað.   Brade synd on worulde
grene geardas,   and God siteð
on þam hehstan   heofna rice,
ufan alwalda.   Nele þa earfeðu
sylfa habban   þæt he on þysne sið fare,
515   gumena Drihten,   ac he his gingran sent
to þinre spræce.   Nu he þe mid spellum het
listas læran.   Læste þu georne
his ambyhto,   nim þe þis ofæt on hand,
bit his and byrige.   Þe weorð on þinum breostum rum,
520   wæstm þy wlitegra.   Þe sende waldend God,
þin hearra þas helpe   of heofon-rice."
Adam maðelode   þær he on eorðan stod,
self-sceafte guma: "Þonne ic Sige-Drihten,
mihtigne God,   mæðlan gehyrde
525   strangre stemne,   and me her stondan het,
his bebodu healdan,   and me þas bryd forgeaf,
wlite-sciene wif,   and me warnian het
þæt ic on þone deaðes beam   bedroren ne wurde,
beswicen to swiðe,   he cwæð þæt þa sweartan helle
530   healdan sceolde   se ðe bi his heortan wuht

body much more radiant, your shape more beautiful, he said that you would not need any treasure in the world. You have now obtained the favor of heaven's king, have gratefully served your master, you have made yourself precious to the Lord. In his light I heard him praise your word and deed and speak about your life.

"So you must fulfill in this land here what his messengers 509 deliver. The green regions are wide in the world, and God the ruler of all sits above in the highest kingdom of heaven. He does not wish to have the trouble himself that he, the Lord of men, would travel on this journey, but he sent his underling to speak with you. Now he has commanded me with words to impart skills to you. Carry out his command eagerly, take this fruit in hand, bite it and taste! You will become more capacious in mind, and your form the more beautiful. The ruler God, your master, has sent you this help from the kingdom of heaven."

Adam made a speech where he stood on the earth, the 522 independent man: "When I heard the Lord of victory, the mighty God, dictate with a strong voice, and he ordered me to remain here, to keep his commandments, and gave me this bride, the radiantly beautiful woman, and commanded me to beware that I not be brought to destruction, too greatly deceived, by this tree of death, he said that the dark hell would hold anyone who produced any evil from his

laðes gelæde.   Nat þeah þu mid ligenum fare
þurh dyrne geþanc   þe þu Drihtnes eart
boda of heofnum.   Hwæt, ic þinra bysna ne mæg,
worda ne wisna   wuht oncnawan,
535 siðes ne sagona.

      "Ic wat hwæt he me self bebead,
nergend user,   þa ic hine nehst geseah;
he het me his word weorðian   and wel healdan,
læstan his lare.   Þu gelic ne bist
ænegum his engla   þe ic ær geseah,
540 ne þu me oðiewdest   ænig tacen
þe he me þurh treowe   to onsende,
min hearra þurh hyldo.   Þy ic þe hyran ne cann:
ac þu meaht þe forðfaran.   Ic hæbbe me fæstne geleafan
up to þam ælmihtegan Gode   þe me mid his earmum
              worhte,
545 her mid handum sinum.   He mæg me of his hean rice
geofian mid goda gehwilcum   —þeah he his gingran ne
              sende."

XII

  Wende hine wrað-mod   þær he þæt wif geseah
on eorð-rice   Euan stondan,
sceone gesceapene,   cwæð þæt sceaðena mæst
550 eallum heora eaforum   æfter siððan
wurde on worulde: "Ic wat, inc waldend God
abolgen wyrð,   swa ic him þisne bodscipe
selfa secge,   þonne ic of þys siðe cume
ofer langne weg,   þæt git ne læstan wel
555 hwilc ærende swa   he easten hider
on þysne sið sendeð.   Nu sceal he sylf faran
to incre andsware   —ne mæg his ærende

42

heart. I do not know, however, if you have come deceitfully with hidden intentions or if you are a messenger of the Lord from heaven. Indeed, I cannot penetrate any of your logic, your words or reasoning, your mission or utterances.

"I know what he himself commanded me, our savior, 535 when I saw him last; he told me to honor his words and hold them well, to fulfill his teaching. You are not like any of his angels who I saw before, nor have you revealed to me any sign that my master might send to me as a pledge of his favor. For these reasons I cannot obey you: but you can get out of here. I have a firm belief above in almighty God, who created me with his own arms and hands. He can bestow every good thing from his high empire on me—without sending his underling."

XII

Angry-minded he turned to where he saw the woman Eve 547 standing in the earthly kingdom, beautifully formed, and said that afterward the greatest injuries in the world would arise for all their heirs: "I know, the ruler God will become enraged with you two, when I personally make this report to him, when I come from this mission across the long road, say that you two did not well fulfill this message that he sends here on this mission from the east. Now he himself shall journey to you two with an answer—his messenger

his boda beodan— þy ic wat þæt he inc abolgen wyrð,
mihtig on mode.   Gif þu þeah minum wilt,
560   wif willende,   wordum hyran,
þu meaht his þonne rume   ræd geþencan.
   "Gehyge on þinum breostum   þæt þu inc bam twam
meaht
wite bewarigan,   swa ic þe wisie.
Æt þisses ofetes!   Þonne wurðað þin eagan swa leoht
565   þæt þu meaht swa wide   ofer woruld ealle
geseon siððan,   and selfes stol
herran þines,   and habban his hyldo forð.
Meaht þu Adame   eft gestyran,
gif þu his willan hæfst   and he þinum wordum getrywð.
570   Gif þu him to soðe sægst   hwylce þu selfa hæfst
bisne on breostum,   þæs þu gebod Godes
lare læstes,   he þone laðan strið,
yfel andwyrde   an forlæteð
on breost-cofan,   swa wit him bu tu
575   an sped sprecað.
   "Span þu hine georne
þæt he þine lare læste,   þy læs gyt lað Gode,
incrum waldende,   weorðan þyrfen.
Gif þu þæt angin fremest,   idesa seo betste,
forhele ic incrum herran   þæt me hearmes swa fela
580   Adam gespræc,   eargra worda.
Tyhð me untryowða,   cwyð þæt ic seo teonum georn,
gramum ambyht-secg,   nales Godes engel.
Ac ic cann ealle swa geare   engla gebyrdo,
heah heofona gehlidu;   wæs seo hwil þæs lang

44

cannot announce his message—I know that he, mighty in mind, will become enraged with you two. But if you, willing woman, will obey my words, you may be able to think of an ample solution for it.

"Consider in your heart how both of you two together 562 can ward off punishment, as I suggest. Eat of this fruit! Then your eyes will become so enlightened that you will be able to see afterward very widely across the whole world, and the throne of your master himself, and henceforth have his favor. You will be able afterward to move Adam, if you have his desire and he trusts in your words. If you truly tell him what proof you have in your own breast, because you have fulfilled God's command, his instruction, he will desist from the hateful contentiousness, the evil answer in his mind, if we two both speak skillfully to him.

"Urge him eagerly so that he follows your teaching, lest 575 you two must still become hateful to God your ruler. If you succeed at that attempt, best of women, I will conceal before your master that Adam spoke so very hurtfully to me, wicked words. He accuses me of treacheries, says that I am eager for mischief, a messenger of malice, not God's angel at all. But I know entirely well the orders of angels, the high roofs of the heavens; the time was very long in which I ea-

585   þæt ic geornlice   Gode þegnode
   þurh holdne hyge,   herran minum,
   Drihtne selfum;   ne eom ic deofle gelic."

    Lædde hie swa mid ligenum   and mid listum speon
   idese on þæt unriht,   oðþæt hire on innan ongan
590   weallan wyrmes geþeaht   —hæfde hire wacran hige
   metod gemearcod—   þæt heo hire mod ongan
   lætan æfter þam larum;   forþon heo æt þam laðan
       onfeng
   ofer Drihtnes word   deaðes beames
   weorcsumne wæstm.   Ne wearð wyrse dæd
595   monnum gemearcod!   Þæt is micel wundor
   þæt hit ece God   æfre wolde
   þeoden þolian,   þæt wurde þegn swa monig
   forlædd be þam lygenum   þe for þam larum com.

    Heo þa þæs ofætes æt,   alwaldan bræc
600   word and willan.   Þa meahte heo wide geseon
   þurh þæs laðan læn   þe hie mid ligenum beswac,
   dearnenga bedrog,   þe hire for his dædum com,
   þæt hire þuhte hwitre   heofon and eorðe,
   and eall þeos woruld wlitigre,   and geweorc Godes
605   micel and mihtig,   þeah heo hit þurh monnes geþeaht
   ne sceawode   —ac se sceaða georne
   swicode ymb þa sawle   þe hire ær þa siene onlah,
   þæt heo swa wide   wlitan meahte
   ofer heofon-rice.   Þa se forhatena spræc
610   þurh feondscipe   —nalles he hie freme lærde:
    "Þu meaht nu þe self geseon,   swa ic hit þe secgan ne
                     þearf,
   Eue seo gode,   þæt þe is ungelic

gerly served God with a loyal mind, my master, the Lord himself; I am not like a devil."

He led her on with such lies and with skill urged the lady   588 in that error, until the serpent's thought began to surge up inside her—the creator had designed a weaker mind for her—so that she began to surrender her mind to those instructions; therefore contrary to God's word she accepted the painful fruit of the tree of death from the hateful one. No worse deed was designed for human beings! It is a great wonder that the eternal God, the prince, would ever suffer that so many a servant should happen to be led astray by the lies which came before those instructions.

She ate of the fruit, broke the word and will of the ruler   599 of all. Then, by the gift of the hateful one who tricked her with lies, secretly led her astray, who had come to her for his evil deeds, she was able to see afar, so that heaven and earth seemed brighter to her, and all this world more beautiful, and God's work great and mighty, though she did not gaze upon it through human intellect—but the injurer, who had loaned her the vision, eagerly interfered within the soul, so that she was able to gaze so distantly across the kingdom of heaven. Then the detestable one spoke in his enmity—he did not teach her anything beneficial at all:

"Now you are able to see for yourself, so I have no need to   611 tell it to you, good Eve, that since you trusted in my words,

wlite and wæstmas,   siððan þu minum wordum
                             getruwodest,
læstes mine lare.   Nu scineð þe leoht fore
615   glædlic ongean   þæt ic from Gode brohte
hwit of heofonum;   nu þu his hrinan meaht.
Sæge Adame   hwilce þu gesihðe hæfst
þurh minne cime cræfta.   Gif giet þurh cuscne siodo
læst mina lara,   þonne gife ic him þæs leohtes genog
620   þæs ic þe swa godes   gegired hæbbe.
Ne wite ic him þa wom-cwidas,   þeah he his wyrðe ne
                             sie
to alætanne;   þæs fela he me laðes spræc."
    Swa hire eaforan sculon   æfter lybban:
þonne hie lað gedoð,   hie sculon lufe wyrcean,
625   betan heora hearran hearm-cwyde   ond habban his hyldo
                             forð.
Þa gieng to Adame   idesa scenost,
wifa wlitegost   þe on woruld come
—forþon heo wæs hand-geweorc   heofon-cyninges—
þeah heo þa dearnenga   fordon wurde,
630   forlæd mid ligenum,   þæt hie lað gode
þurh þæs wraðan geþanc   weorðan sceolden,
þurh þæs deofles searo   dom forlætan,
hierran hyldo,   hefon-rices þolian
monige hwile.   Bið þam men full wa
635   þe hine ne warnað   þonne he his geweald hafað.
    Sum heo hire on handum bær,   sum hire æt heortan
                             læg,
æppel unsælga,   þone hire ær forbead
drihtna Drihten,   deað-beames ofet,
and þæt word acwæð   wuldres aldor,

followed my teaching, appearances and forms are different
for you. Now the light shines pleasantly before you and up
to you, which I have brought you bright from God, from the
heavens; now you are able to grasp it. Tell Adam what skills
of perception you have by my advent. If even now he follows
my instructions in a pure way, then I will give him enough of
the light that I have given you so generously. I will not punish him for the calumnies, though he is not worthy of par-
don; he said a lot that was hurtful to me."

So must her heirs live afterward: when they do harm they   623
must make loving amends, make better the blasphemy
against their master and have his favor henceforth. Then
the brightest of ladies walked up to Adam, the most beautiful of women who should come into the world—because she
was handiwork of the king of heaven—although secretly she
had been undone then, misled by lies, so that they would become hateful to God by the plot of the hostile one, abandon
glory by the devil's devices, the support of their master, suffer the loss of the kingdom of heaven for many an age. Utterly woeful it is for the person who does not mind his guard
when he has the power to.

In her hands she carried one unblessed apple, another lay   636
beside her heart, the fruit of the tree of death that the Lord
of lords had forbidden to her, and the Father of glory had
said the word that people, his servants, did not need to suf-

640 þæt þæt micle morð   menn ne þorfton
       þegnas þolian,   ac he þeoda gehwam
       hefon-rice forgeaf,   halig Drihten,
       wid-bradne welan,   gif hie þone wæstm an
       lætan wolden   þe þæt laðe treow
645 on his bogum bær,   bitre gefylled—
       þæt wæs deaðes beam   þe him Drihten forbead.
          Forlec hie þa mid ligenum   se wæs lað Gode,
       on hete heofon-cyninges,   and hyge Euan,
   wifes wac geþoht,   þæt heo ongan his wordum truwian,
650 læstan his lare,   and geleafan nom
       þæt he þa bysene from Gode   brungen hæfde
       þe he hire swa wærlice   wordum sægde,
       iewde hire tacen   and treowa gehet,
       his holdne hyge.   Þa heo to hire hearran spræc:
655   "Adam, frea min,   þis ofet is swa swete,
       bliðe on breostum,   and þes boda sciene,
       Godes engel god,   ic on his gearwan geseo
       þæt he is ærend-secg   uncres hearran,
       hefon-cyninges.   His hyldo is unc betere
660 to gewinnanne   þonne his wiðer-medo.
       Gif þu him heo-dæg wuht   hearmes gespræce,
       he forgifð hit þeah,   gif wit him geongordom
       læstan willað.   Hwæt scal þe swa laðlic strið
       wið þines hearran bodan?   Unc is his hyldo þearf;
665 he mæg unc ærendian   to þam alwaldan,
       heofon-cyninge.
                         "Ic mæg heonon geseon
       hwær he sylf siteð   —þæt is suð and east—
       welan bewunden,   se ðas woruld gesceop;
       geseo ic him his englas   ymbe hweorfan

fer that great death, but the holy Lord had given the kingdom of heaven to each person, expansive prosperity, if they
should forgo that one fruit, which that hateful tree bore on
its boughs, full of bitterness — that was the tree of death that
the Lord forbade.

He who was hostile to God, in hatred of heaven's king, 647
deceived her with lies, and the mind of Eve, the woman's
weak intellect, so that she began to trust in his words, fulfill
his instruction, and accepted the belief that he had brought
those commands from God, which he so carefully explained
in words, revealed a sign to her, promised her his trust, and
his loyal intention. Then she spoke to her master:

"Adam, my lord, this fruit is so sweet, pleasant in the 655
breast, and this messenger is so radiant, God's good angel, I
see by his raiment that he is the ambassador of our master,
of the king of heaven. It is better for us to win his favor than
his enmity. If you spoke anything at all hurtful to him this
day, he will forgive it nevertheless, if we two give him allegiance. What will this hateful quarrel with the messenger of
our master do for you? We need his support; he is able to in-
tercede for us to the ruler of all, the king of heaven.

"From here I can see where he himself sits — that is south 666
and east — wrapped in goodness, he who created the world; I
see his angels circling about him in feather-cloaks, the great-

670   mid feðer-haman,   ealra folca mæst,
wereda wynsumast.   Hwa meahte me swelc gewit gifan,
gif hit gegnunga   God ne onsende,
heofones waldend?   Gehyran mæg ic rume
and swa wide geseon   on woruld ealle
675   ofer þas sidan gesceaft,   ic mæg swegles gamen
gehyran on heofnum.   Wearð me on hige leohte
utan and innan   siðþan ic þæs ofætes onbat.
Nu hæbbe ic his her on handa,   herra se goda;
gife ic hit þe georne.   Ic gelyfe þæt hit from Gode come,
680   broht from his bysene,   þæs me þes boda sægde
wærum wordum.   Hit nis wuhte gelic
elles on eorðan,   buton swa þes ar sægeð,
þæt hit gegnunga   from Gode come."

XIII
    Hio spræc him þicce to   and speon hine ealne dæg
685   on þa dimman dæd   þæt hie Drihtnes heora
willan bræcon.   Stod se wraða boda,
legde him lustas on   and mid listum speon,
fylgde him frecne;   wæs se feond full neah
þe on þa frecnan fyrd   gefaren hæfde
690   ofer langne weg;   leode hogode
on þæt micle morð   men forweorpan,
forlæran and forlædan,   þæt hie læn Godes,
ælmihtiges gife   an forleten,
heofen-rices geweald.   Hwæt, se hell-sceaða
695   gearwe wiste   þæt hie Godes yrre
habban sceoldon   and hell-geþwing,
þone nearwan nið   niede onfon,
siððan hie gebod Godes   forbrocen hæfdon,

est of all legions, most joyful of hosts. Who could give me such understanding, if God, the ruler of heaven, had not sent it directly? I am able to hear fully and see so widely across the whole world, across this broad creation, I am able to hear celestial rejoicing in the heavens. My intellect became enlightened inside and outside after I bit into that fruit. Now I have some of it here in my hand, good master; I give it to you eagerly. I believe that it comes from God, brought by his command, as his messenger explained to me in trustworthy words. It is not at all like anything else on earth, but as this messenger says, it has come directly from God."

XIII
She spoke to him without ceasing and all day urged him 684
to that dark deed, that they break their Lord's wish. The cruel messenger stood there, placed desires in them and urged with skills, pursued them fiercely; the fiend, who had traveled over a long road on that dangerous campaign, was very near; he intended to cast down human beings into the great death, deceive and mislead, so that they should set aside God's gift, the grace of the Almighty, the rule of the kingdom of heaven.

Indeed, hell's ravager readily knew that they should have 694
God's anger and hell's torment, necessarily receive the strict enmity, after they had shattered God's commandment,

þa he forlærde   mid ligen-wordum
700   to þam unræde   idese sciene,
wifa wlitegost,   þæt heo on his willan spræc,
wæs him on helpe   hand-weorc Godes
to forlæranne.

       Heo spræc ða to Adame   idesa sceonost
705   ful þiclice,   oð þam þegne ongan
his hige hweorfan,   þæt he þam gehate getruwode
þe him þæt wif   wordum sægde.
Heo dyde hit þeah þurh holdne hyge,   nyste þæt þær
                                      hearma swa fela,
fyren-earfeða,   fylgean sceolde
710   monna cynne,   þæs heo on mod genam
þæt heo þæs laðan bodan   larum hyrde,
ac wende þæt heo hyldo   heofon-cyninges
worhte mid þam wordum   þe heo þam were swelce
tacen oðiewde   and treowe gehet,
715   oðþæt Adame   innan breostum
his hyge hwyrfde   and his heorte ongann
wendan to hire willan.

                He æt þam wife onfeng
helle and hinn-sið   —þeah hit nære haten swa
ac hit ofetes noman   agan sceolde—
720   hit wæs þeah deaðes swefn   and deofles gespon,
hell and hinn-sið   and hæleða forlor,
menniscra morð,   þæt hie to mete dædon,
ofet unfæle.   Swa hit him on innan com,
hran æt heortan,   hloh þa and plegode
725   boda bitre gehugod,   sægde begra þanc
hearran sinum:

when he led astray the brilliant lady to that mistake with lying words, the most beautiful of women, so that she spoke according to his will, was a help to him in deceiving God's handiwork.

The most brilliant of ladies then spoke to Adam with- 704
out ceasing until the nobleman began to change his mind, so that he trusted in the promise that the woman spoke to him in words. However, she did it with a loyal intention, did not know that so many hurts, sinful sorrows, should follow there for humankind, because she accepted in mind what she heard in the instructions of the hateful messenger, but rather she thought that she was securing the favor of the king of heaven with the words because she offered the man such signs and promised good faith, until within Adam's breast his mind changed and his heart began to turn to her purpose.

He received hell and death from the woman—though it 717
was not called that but rather it should have the name of fruit—nevertheless it was death's sleep and the devil's bond, hell and death and the damnation of men, the murder of humanity, the infidel fruit, which they made their food. As it entered inside him and touched his heart, the bitter-minded messenger then laughed and clapped, and said thanks to his master for two things:

"Nu hæbbe ic þine hyldo me
witode geworhte,   and þinne willan gelæst
to ful monegum dæge.   Men synt forlædde,
Adam and Eue.   Him is unhyldo
730   waldendes witod,   nu hie word-cwyde his,
lare forleton.   Forþon hie leng ne magon
healdan heofon-rice,   ac hie to helle sculon
on þone sweartan sið.   Swa þu his sorge ne þearft
beran on þinum breostum,   þær þu gebunden ligst,
735   murnan on mode,   þæt her men bun
þone hean heofon,   þeah wit hearmas nu,
þrea-weorc þoliað,   and þystre land,
and þurh þin micle mod   monig forleton
on heofon-rice   heah-getimbro,
740   godlice geardas.

"Unc wearð God yrre
forþon wit him noldon   on heofon-rice
hnigan mid heafdum   halgum Drihtne
þurh geongordom;   ac unc gegenge ne wæs
þæt wit him on þegn-scipe   þeowian wolden.
745   Forþon unc waldend wearð   wrað on mode,
on hyge hearde,   and us on helle bedraf,
on þæt fyr fylde   folca mæste,
and mid handum his   eft on heofon-rice
rihte rodor-stolas   and þæt rice forgeaf
750   monna cynne.

"Mæg þin mod wesan
bliðe on breostum,   forþon her synt bu tu gedon:
ge þæt hæleða bearn   heofon-rice sculon
leode forlætan   and on þæt lig to þe
hate hweorfan;   eac is hearm Gode,

"Now certainly I have gained your favor for myself, and 726
carried out your desire for very many a day. Adam and Eve,
the human beings, are led astray. The ruler's disfavor for
them is certain, now that they have abandoned his teaching, his spoken word. Therefore they can no longer keep
the kingdom of heaven, but now they must go to hell on the
dark journey. So you need to bear no sorrow about it in your
breast, where you lie bound, mourning in mind, that people
may occupy the high heaven here, though we two now suffer injuries and punishment, and the land of darkness, and
through your great pride many have abandoned the tall
buildings, the pleasant courts.

"God became angry with us two because we did not wish 740
to bow our heads in servitude to the holy Lord in heaven's
kingdom; but it was not acceptable to us two that we two
should serve him as attendants. Therefore the ruler became
angry in mind with us two, hardened in heart, and drove us
into hell, knocked the greatest of hosts down into the fire,
and by his hands afterward restored the celestial thrones
and granted that kingdom to humankind.

"Your mind can be happy in your breast, because both 750
things have been accomplished here: both that people, the
children of men, must abandon the kingdom of heaven and
turn toward you in the hot flame; also a hurt, sorrow at
heart, has been done to God. Whatever deathly injury we

755 mod-sorg gemacod.   Swa hwæt swa wit her morðres
                                                    þoliað,
    hit is nu Adame   eall forgolden
    mid hearran hete   and mid hæleða forlore,
monnum mid morðes cwealme.   Forþon is min mod
                                                    gehæled,
  hyge ymb heortan gerume,   ealle synt uncre hearmas
                                                    gewrecene
760 laðes þæt wit lange þoledon.   Nu wille ic eft þam lige near,
    Satan ic þær secan wille;   he is on þære sweartan helle
    hæft mid hringa gesponne."
                              Hwearf him eft niðer
    boda bitresta;   sceolde he þa bradan ligas
      secan helle gehliðo,   þær his hearra læg
765   simon gesæled.   Sorgedon ba twa,
    Adam and Eue,   and him oft betuh
    gnorn-word gengdon;   Godes him ondredon,
    heora herran hete,   heofon-cyninges nið
    swiðe onsæton;   selfe forstodon
770   his word onwended.   Þæt wif gnornode,
    hof hreowig-mod   —hæfde hyldo Godes,
    lare forlæten—   þa heo þæt leoht geseah
    ellor scriðan   þæt hire þurh untreowa
    tacen iewde   se him þone teonan geræd,
775   þæt hie helle-nið   habban sceoldon,
    hynða unrim;   forþam him hige-sorga
    burnon on breostum.
                              Hwilum to gebede feollon
    sin-hiwan somed,   and Sige-Drihten
    godne gretton   and God nemdon,
780   heofones waldend,   and hine bædon

two suffer here, it has now all been recompensed in Adam, with his master's hate and with the damnation of men, in human beings with the contagion of death. Therefore my mind is salved, the thoughts about my heart set free, all of our hurts have been avenged for the hate that we two have long endured. Now I wish again to approach the flame, I will seek Satan there; he is imprisoned in the dark hell with a bond of chains."

The bitterest of messengers returned back below; he had   762
to seek out the broad flames, hell's chasms, where his master lay bound in chains. Both those two, Adam and Eve, sorrowed, and between them anxious words often passed; they dreaded the hate of God their master, were very apprehensive of the hostility of the king of heaven; they understood his disregarded command. The woman grieved, lamented sad in heart—she had abandoned God's favor and teaching—when she saw the light slip away, the sign that he who had advised them to the disaster had showed her in perfidy, so that they must have hell's torment, innumerable humiliations; therefore heart-sorrows burned in their breasts.

At times the wedded couple fell down in prayer, and   777
spoke to the good victorious Lord and called on God, the ruler of heaven, and begged him that they should have, read-

þæt hie his hearm-sceare   habban mosten,
georne fulgangan,   þa hie Godes hæfdon
bodscipe abrocen.   Bare hie gesawon
heora lic-haman;   næfdon on þam lande þa giet
785   sælða gesetena,   ne hie sorge wiht
weorces wiston,   ac hie wel meahton
libban on þam lande,   gif hie wolden lare Godes
forweard fremman.   Þa hie fela spræcon
sorh-worda somed,   sin-hiwan twa.
790   Adam gemælde   and to Euan spræc:
"Hwæt, þu Eue, hæfst   yfele gemearcod
uncer sylfra sið.   Gesyhst þu nu þa sweartan helle
grædige and gifre.   Nu þu hie grimman meaht
heonane gehyran.   Nis heofon-rice
795   gelic þam lige,   ac þis is landa betst,
þæt wit þurh uncres hearran þanc   habban moston,
þær þu þam ne hierde   þe unc þisne hearm geræd,
þæt wit waldendes   word forbræcon,
heofon-cyninges.   Nu wit hreowige magon
800   sorgian for þis siðe,   forþon he unc self bebead
þæt wit unc wite   warian sceolden,
hearma mæstne.   Nu slit me hunger and þurst
bitre on breostum,   þæs wit begra ær
wæron orsorge   on ealle tid.
805   "Hu sculon wit nu libban   oððe on þys lande wesan,
gif her wind cymð,   westan oððe eastan,
suðan oððe norðan?   Gesweorc up færeð,
cymeð hægles scur   hefone getenge,
færeð forst on gemang,   se byð fyrnum ceald.
810   Hwilum of heofnum   hate scineð,
blicð þeos beorhte sunne,   and wit her baru standað,

ily undergo, a punishment, as they had broken God's commandment. They noticed their naked bodies; they did not yet have established dwellings in the land, nor did they know anything at all of the misery of work, but they were able to live well in that land, had they been willing to carry out God's instruction in the first place. They spoke many sorrowful words together, the wedded pair.

Adam spoke and said to Eve: "Oh indeed, Eve, you have 790 planned an evil journey for the two of us. Do you now see the dark hell, greedy and gaping? Now you can hear it roaring from here. The kingdom of heaven is not like that flame, rather this is the best of lands, which we could have had by the grace of our master, if you had not listened to him who counseled us to this hurt, so that we two shattered the commandment of the ruler, heaven's king. Now we two can sadly grieve this event, because he himself commanded us two that we should beware of punishment, the greatest of hurts. Now hunger and thirst cut bitterly at my breast, about both of which we had not a care for all time.

"How shall we two now live or be in this land, if a wind 805 comes here, from west or east, south or north? A cloud will rise up, a shower of hail will come pressing from the sky, will come mingled with frost, which will be sinfully cold. At times the bright sun will shine, blaze hot from the heavens, and we two will stand here naked, unprotected by clothes.

unwered wædo.   Nys unc wuht beforan
to scur-sceade,   ne sceattes wiht
to mete gemearcod,   ac unc is mihtig God,
815   waldend wrað-mod.   To hwon sculon wit weorðan nu?
Nu me mæg hreowan   þæt ic bæd heofnes God,
waldend þone godan,   þæt he þe her worhte to me
of liðum minum,   nu þu me forlæred hæfst
on mines herran hete.   Swa me nu hreowan mæg
820   æfre to aldre   þæt ic þe minum eagum geseah."
XIV
       Ða spræc Eue eft,   idesa scienost,
wifa wlitegost;   hie wæs geweorc Godes,
þeah heo þa on deofles cræft   bedroren wurde:
"Þu meaht hit me witan,   wine min Adam,
825   wordum þinum;   hit þe þeah wyrs ne mæg
on þinum hyge hreowan   þonne hit me æt heortan deð."
       Hire þa Adam   andswarode:
"Gif ic waldendes   willan cuðe,
hwæt ic his to hearm-sceare   habban sceolde,
830   ne gesawe þu no sniomor,   þeah me on sæ wadan
hete heofones God   heonone nu þa,
on flod faran,   nære he firnum þæs deop,
mere-stream þæs micel,   þæt his o min mod getweode,
ac ic to þam grunde genge,   gif ic Godes meahte
835   willan gewyrcean.   Nis me on worulde niod
æniges þegnscipes,   nu ic mines þeodnes hafa
hyldo forworhte,   þæt ic hie habban ne mæg.
Ac wit þus baru ne magon   bu tu ætsomne
wesan to wuhte.   Uton gan on þysne weald innan
840   on þisses holtes hleo."

There is nothing at all covering us two as a protection against the storm, nor any goods at all planned as our food, but rather mighty God, the ruler, is furious with the two of us. What must become of us two now? Now I can regret that I asked the God of heaven, the good ruler, that he made you here for me from my limbs, now that you have misguided me into my master's hate. So now I can regret forever after that I laid eyes on you."

^{XIV}

Then Eve spoke in response, the most brilliant of ladies, 821 most beautiful of women; she was God's creature, though she had been ruined then by the devil's skill: "You can punish me for it, Adam my friend, with your words, though you cannot regret it worse in your mind than I do in my heart."

Adam then answered her: "If I knew the ruler's desire, 827 what I should have from him as a penalty, even if heaven's God should command me now to journey hence on the sea, to travel on the current, it would never be too wickedly deep, the great ocean stream, that I would ever flinch in my mind, you would never see anything quicker, but I would go into the abyss, if I could fulfill God's desire. For me there is no obligation of loyal service in the world, now I have undone my prince's favor, so that I cannot have it. But there is no way we two can be naked together; let us go inside this forest, under the protection of this wood."

Hwurfon hie ba twa,
togengdon gnorngende   on þone grenan weald,
sæton onsundran,   bidan selfes gesceapu
heofon-cyninges,   þa hie þa habban ne moston
þe him ær forgeaf   ælmihtig God.

845 Þa hie heora lic-homan   leafum beþeahton,
weredon mid ðy wealde   —wæda ne hæfdon;
ac hie on gebed feollon   bu tu ætsomne
morgena gehwilce,   bædon mihtigne
þæt hie ne forgeate   God ælmihtig,

850 and him gewisade   waldend se goda,
hu hie on þam leohte forð   libban sceolden.

GENESIS A

Þa com feran   Frea ælmihtig
ofer midne dæg,   mære þeoden,
on neorxna-wang   neode sine;

855 wolde neosian   nergend usser,
bilwit fæder,   hwæt his bearn dyde;
wiste forworhte   þam he ær wlite sealde.
Gewitan him þa gangan   geomer-mode
under beam-sceade   blæde bereafod,

860 hyddon hie on heolstre,   þa hie halig word
Drihtnes gehyrdon,   and ondredon him.
Þa sona ongann   swegles aldor
weard ahsian   woruld-gesceafta,
het him recene to   rice þeoden

865 his sunu gangan.   Him þa sylfa oncwæð,
hean hleoðrade   hrægles þearfa:
"Ic wreo me her   wæda leasne,

They both turned away, walked lamenting into the green 840
forest, sat apart, then awaited the decree of the king of
heaven himself, when they were not able to keep what almighty God had earlier given them. Then they covered their
bodies with leaves, protected themselves with branches—
they did not have clothes; but together they both fell into
prayers each morning, begged the powerful one that God
almighty should not forget them, and that the good ruler
should show them how they could live henceforth in that
light.

Genesis A

Then after midday the Lord almighty, the famous prince, 852
came to walk in paradise at his leisure; our savior, the merciful Father, wished to find out what his children might be doing; he knew that those to whom he had earlier given beauty
were undone. Depressed, they went scurrying away under
the shadow of trees, deprived of glory, they hid in the darkness, when they heard the Lord's holy words, and dreaded
him. Then immediately the Lord of the sky began to ask
for the custodian of worldly creatures, the powerful prince
commanded his son to come to him at once. Then he spoke
to him, the abject man in need of clothing said: "I conceal

Lif-Frea min,   leafum þecce.

Scyldfull mine   sceaðen is me sare,

870 frecne on ferhðe;   ne dear nu forð gan

for ðe andweardne.   Ic eom eall eall nacod."

xv

   Him ða ædre God   andswarede:

"Saga me þæt, sunu min,   for hwon secest ðu

sceade sceomiende?   Þu sceonde æt me

875 furðum ne anfenge,   ac gefean eallum.

For hwon wast þu wean   and wrihst sceome,

gesyhst sorge,   and þin sylf þecest

lic mid leafum,   sagast lif-ceare

hean hyge-geomor,   þæt þe sie hrægles þearf,

880 nymþe ðu æppel   ænne byrgde

of ðam wudu-beame   þe ic þe wordum forbead?"

Him þa Adam eft   andswarode:

"Me ða blæda on hand   bryd gesealde,

freolucu fæmne,   Frea-Drihten min,

885 ðe ic þe on teonan geþah.   Nu ic þæs tacen wege

sweotol on me selfum.   Wat ic sorga ðy ma."

   Ða ðæs Euan frægn   ælmihtig God:

"Hwæt druge þu, dohtor,   dugeþa genohra,

niwra gesceafta   neorxna-wanges,

890 growendra gifa,   þa þu gitsiende

on beam gripe,   blæda name

on treowes telgum,   and me on teonan

æte þa unfreme,   Adame sealdest

wæstme þa inc wæron   wordum minum

895 fæste forbodene?"   Him þa freolecu mæg,

ides æwisc-mod   andswarode:

"Me nædre beswac   and me neodlice

66

myself here without clothes, my life Lord, I am covered with leaves. A sinful conscience has painfully, terribly damaged my spirit; now I do not dare go forward before your presence. I am completely and utterly naked."

God quickly answered him: "Tell me, my son, why is it that you, shamed, seek the shadow? In the beginning you received no shame from me, but utter joy. How do you know woe, and clothe your shame, see sorrow, and cover your body with leaves, speak of life's anxiety, abject and sad minded, say that you are in need of clothing, unless you have tasted an apple from the tree which I forbade to you in words?" Then Adam answered him in reply: "The bride, the elegant lady, gave it into my hand, my noble Lord, which I consumed as an offense against you. Now I carry the clear sign of it on myself. Because of that I know sorrow the more."

Then almighty God asked Eve about it: "Daughter, what 887 did you accomplish with the plentiful benefits of the new creations of paradise, the flourishing gifts, which you covetously grabbed from the tree, seized fruit from the tree's branches, and as an offense against me ate the harmful thing, gave to Adam the fruits that by my words were firmly forbidden to you two?" Then the elegant kinswoman, answered him ashamed: "The snake deceived me and desper-

to forsceape scyhte   and to scyld-frece,
fah wyrm þurh fægir word,   oðþæt ic fracoðlice
900   feond-ræs gefremede,   fæhðe geworhte,
and þa reafode,   swa hit riht ne wæs,
beam on bearwe   and þa blæda æt."

    Þa nædran sceop   nergend usser,
Frea ælmihtig   fagum wyrme
905   wide siðas   and þa worde cwæð:
"þu scealt wide-ferhð   werig þinum
breostum bearm tredan   bradre eorðan,
faran feðeleas,   þenden þe feorh wunað,
gast on innan.   Þu scealt greot etan
910   þine lif-dagas.   Swa þu laðlice
wrohte onstealdest,   þe þæt wif feoð,
hatað under heofnum   and þin heafod tredeð
fah mid fotum sinum.   Þu scealt fiersna sætan
tohtan niwre;   tuddor bið gemæne
915   incrum orlegnið   a þenden standeð
woruld under wolcnum.   Nu þu wast and canst,
lað leod-sceaða,   hu þu lifian scealt."

XVI
    Ða to Euan God   yrringa spræc:
"Wend þe from wynne!   Þu scealt wæpned-men
920   wesan on gewealde,   mid weres egsan
hearde genearwad,   hean þrowian
þinra dæda gedwild,   deaðes bidan,
and þurh wop and heaf   on woruld cennan
þurh sar micel   sunu and dohtor."

925   Abead eac Adame   ece Drihten,
lifes leoht-fruma,   lað ærende:
"Þu scealt oðerne   eðel secean,

ately encouraged me to that destruction and greediness, the gaudy serpent by fair words, until I shamefully carried out that hasty betrayal, committed the crime, and then plundered the tree in the grove and ate the fruit, which was not right."

Then our savior, the almighty Lord, ordained wide wanderings for the snake, the cursed serpent, and then made this speech: "Accursed, you shall always walk the bosom of the broad earth on your belly, go footless while life dwells in you, the spirit within. In your life days you shall eat dirt. As you hatefully initiated enmity, the woman will avenge herself on you, hate you under the heavens and crush your guilty head with her feet. You shall lie in wait for her heels, for a new battle; the offspring of you two will share a common enmity forever while the world stands under the clouds. Hateful enemy of men, now you know and understand how you shall live." 903

Then God spoke angrily to Eve: "Turn yourself away from joy! You shall be under male rule, tightly restricted in awe of a man, and abject you shall suffer the error of your ways, await death, and in weeping and lamentation give birth to sons and daughters in the world through great sorrow." The eternal Lord, source of light, also announced a hateful message to Adam: "You shall seek out another homeland, a less XVI 918

wynleasran wic,　and on wræc hweorfan
nacod nied-wædla,　neorxna-wanges
930　dugeðum bedæled;　þe is gedal witod
lices and sawle.　Hwæt, þu laðlice
wrohte onstealdest;　forþon þu winnan scealt
and on eorðan þe　þine andlifne
selfa geræcan,　wegan swatig hleor,
935　þinne hlaf etan,　þenden þu her leofast,
oðþæt þe to heortan　hearde gripeð
adl unliðe　þe þu on æple ær
selfa forswulge;　forþon þu sweltan scealt."
　Hwæt, we nu gehyrað　hwær us hearm-stafas
940　wraðe onwocan　and woruld-yrmðo.
Hie þa wuldres weard　wædum gyrede,
scyppend usser;　het heora sceome þeccan
Frea frum-hrægle;　het hie from hweorfan
neorxna-wange　on nearore lif.
945　Him on laste beleac　liðsa and wynna
hihtfulne ham　halig engel
be Frean hæse　fyrene sweorde;
ne mæg þær inwitfull　ænig geferan
wom-scyldig mon,　ac se weard hafað
950　miht and strengðo,　se þæt mære lif
dugeðum deore　Drihtne healdeð.
　No hwæðre ælmihtig　ealra wolde
Adame and Euan　arna ofteon,
fæder æt frymðe,　þeah þe hie him from swice,
955　ac he him to frofre let　hwæðere forð wesan
hyrstedne hrof　halgum tunglum
and him grund-welan　ginne sealde;
het þam sin-hiwum　sæs and eorðan

happy dwelling, and as a naked drifter you shall wander in exile, deprived of the benefits of paradise; the sundering of soul and body is ordained for you. Indeed, you hatefully initiated enmity; therefore you shall toil and provide your own nourishment on the earth, bear a sweaty brow, eat your own loaf, while you live here, until unpleasant illness, which earlier you yourself had swallowed in the apple, firmly grips you around the heart; for that reason you shall die."

Listen! We hear now where the sorrows and worldly mis-   939
ery cruelly awoke for us. The guardian of glory, our creator, then dressed them in garments; the Lord commanded them to cover their shame with the first clothes; he commanded them to turn away from paradise into a more limited life. Behind them, at the Lord's behest, a holy angel with a fiery sword closed the joy-filled home of leisure and pleasure; no wicked person guilty of sin can journey there, but the warden has might and strength, he who for the Lord guards that glorious life, desirable for its benefits.

However, from the beginning the almighty Father did not   952
at all wish to strip Adam and Eve of favors, though they had cheated him, but for their comfort he nevertheless let the sky continue, decorated with the holy stars, and gave them the broad bountiful land; he commanded each fecund spe-

tuddor-teondra   teohha gehwilcre
960   to woruld-nytte   wæstmas fedan.
Gesæton þa æfter synne   sorgfulre land,
eard and eðyl   unspedigran
fremena gehwilcre   þonne se frum-stol wæs
þe hie æfter dæde of   adrifen wurdon.
965   Ongunnon hie þa   be Godes hæse
bearn astrienan,   swa him metod bebead.
Adames and Euan   aforan wæron
freolicu twa   frum-bearn cenned,
Cain and Abel.   Us cyðað bec,
970   hu þa dæd-fruman   dugeþa stryndon,
welan and wiste,   will-gebroðor.
Oðer his to eorðan   elnes tilode—
se wæs ærboren;   oðer æhte heold
fæder on fultum,   oðþæt forð gewat
975   dæg-rimes worn.   Hie þa Drihtne lac
begen brohton.   Brego engla beseah
on Abeles gield   eagum sinum,
cyning eall-wihta   — Caines ne wolde
tiber sceawian.   Þæt wæs torn were
980   hefig æt heortan.   Hyge-wælm asteah
beorne on breostum,   blatende nið,
yrre for æfstum.
He þa unræden
folmum gefremede,   freo-mæg ofsloh,
broðor sinne,   and his blod ageat,
985   Cain Abeles.   Cwealm-dreore swealh
þæs middan-geard,   monnes swate.
Æfter wæl-swenge   wea wæs ar-æred,
tregena tuddor.   Of ðam twige siððan
ludon laðwende   —leng swa swiðor—

cies of sea and earth to offer fruits to the married pair for their worldly need. Then after the sin they settled the sorrowful land, a country and homeland less productive of every sustenance than the ancient seat had been which they were driven from after the deed. At God's behest they then began to produce children, as the creator had commanded them.

From Adam and Eve offspring were begotten, the first 967 two noble children, Cain and Abel. Books make known to us how these doers of deeds, friendly brothers, produced prosperity, wellbeing and sustenance. The one by his zeal tilled the earth—he was the first-born; the other kept the livestock as a help to his father, until a count of many days had passed. Then they both brought a sacrifice to the Lord. The prince of angels, king of all things, beheld Abel's offering with his eyes—Cain's oblation he would not look at. To the man that was an insult heavy at heart. Passion surged in the man's breast, livid hate, an envious rage.

Then he did an ill-advised deed with his hands, killed his 982 close kinsmen, his brother, and Cain spilled Abel's blood. This middle-earth swallowed up the gore of the killing, a man's blood. After the deathblow woe was raised up, a progeny of injuries. Afterward, malignant and cruel fruit grew from that shoot—the longer the more vigorous. The

990 reðe wæstme.   Ræhton wide
geond wer-þeoda   wrohtes telgan,
hrinon hearm-tanas   hearde and sare
drihta bearnum   —doð gieta swa—
of þam brad blado   bealwa gehwilces
995 sprytan ongunnon.   We þæt spell magon,
wæl-grimme wyrd,   wope cwiðan,
nales holunge;   ac us hearde sceod
freolecu fæmne   þurh forman gylt
þe wið metod æfre   men gefremeden,
1000 eorð-buende,   siððan Adam wearð
of Godes muðe   gaste eacen.

XVII
    Ða worde frægn   wuldres aldor Cain,
hwær Abel   eorðan wære.
Him ða se cystleasa   cwealmes wyrhta
1005 ædre æfter þon   andswarode:
"Ne can ic Abeles   or ne fore,
hleo-mæges sið,   ne ic hyrde wæs
broðer mines."   Him þa brego engla,
god-spedig gast   gean þingade:
1010 "Hwæt, befealdest þu   folmum þinum
wraðum on wæl-bedd   wærfæstne rinc,
broðor þinne,   and his blod to me
cleopað and cigeð.   Þu þæs cwealmes scealt
wite winnan   and on wræc hweorfan,
1015 awyrged to widan aldre.   Ne seleð þe wæstmas eorðe
wlitige to woruld-nytte,   ac heo wæl-dreore swealh
halge of handum þinum;   forþon heo þe hroðra oftihð,
glæmes grene folde.   Þu scealt geomor hweorfan,
arleas of earde þinum,   swa þu Abele wurde

74

branches of that enmity reached distantly throughout the nations of men, harmful offshoots struck the children of men sorely and hard—they still do—and from those fat fruits each and every blight began to sprout. Not at all in vain can we lament that story with weeping, the slaughterous fate; but the elegant woman hurt us hard by that first crime that people ever committed against the creator, earth dwellers, after Adam was given life by the spirit of God's mouth.

Then the ruler of glory asked Cain in a word where on earth Abel might be. Then the worthless creator of murder hastily answered him: "I don't know about Abel's coming or going, the dear kinsman's journey, nor was I my brother's keeper." Then the prince of angels, the spirit rich in goodness, again inquired: "Listen, with your hostile hands you've tucked the faithful man, your brother, into a bed of slaughter, and his blood calls and cries out to me. For this murder you shall gain torment and turn away into exile, accursed into the distant ages. The earth will not fairly yield fruits for your worldly need, rather she has swallowed the holy slaughter-gore from your hands; therefore she will withhold her comforts from you, the radiance of the green earth. You shall wander, sad, without favor, from your country, because

1020   to feorh-banan;   forþon þu flema scealt
        wid-last wrecan,   wine-magum lað."
        Him þa ædre Cain   andswarode:
        "Ne þearf ic ænigre   are wenan
        on woruld-rice,   ac ic forworht hæbbe,
1025   heofona heah-cyning,   hyldo þine,
        lufan and freode;   forþon ic lastas sceal
        wean on wenum   wide lecgan,
        hwonne me gemitte   man-scyldigne,
        se me feor oððe neah   fæhðe gemonige,
1030   broðor-cwealmes.   Ic his blod ageat,
        dreor on eorðan.   Þu to dæge þissum
        ademest me fram duguðe   and adrifest from
        earde minum.   Me to aldor-banan
        weorðeð wraðra sum.   Ic awyrged sceal,
1035   þeoden, of gesyhðe   þinre hweorfan."
        Him þa selfa oncwæð   sigora Drihten:
        "Ne þearft ðu þe ondrædan   deaðes brogan,
        feorh-cwealm nu giet,   þeah þu from scyle
        freo-magum feor   fah gewitan.
1040   Gif þe monna hwelc   mundum sinum
        aldre beneoteð,   hine on cymeð
        æfter þære synne   seofon-feald wracu,
        wite æfter weorce."   Hine waldend on,
        tirfæst metod,   tacen sette,
1045   freoðo-beacen Frea,   þy læs hine feonda hwilc
        mid guð-þræce   gretan dorste
        feorran oððe nean.   Heht þa from hweorfan
        meder and magum   man-scyldigne,
        cnosle sinum.   Him þa Cain gewat
1050   gongan geomor-mod   Gode of gesyhðe,

you became Abel's murderer; therefore you shall roam distant tracks, a fugitive hateful to friendly kinsmen."

Then Cain quickly answered him: "I need expect no favor in the kingdom of this world, rather I have undone your protection, love, and friendship, high king of the heavens; therefore I must set out my tracks afar, in expectation of trouble, when someone meets me, the culprit, one who far or near may remind me of my fratricide. I spilled his blood, the gore on the earth. Today you banish me for this from prosperity and drive me out from my country. One of the aggrieved will become my slayer. I shall turn away, prince, accursed from your sight." 1022

Then the Lord of victories himself said to him: "You need not dread yet the terror of death or murder, though you must go, guilty, far from your free kinsmen. If any man deprives you of life by his hands, a sevenfold vengeance will come upon him after the sin, punishment after the act." The ruler, the glorious creator and Lord, set a sign on him, a peace-token, lest any enemy from near or far dared to greet him with violence. Then he commanded the culprit to turn away from his mother, kinsmen and family. Then Cain, downhearted, went walking from the sight of God, a friend- 1036

wine-leas wrecca,   and him þa wic geceas
east-landum on,   eðel-stowe
fæder-geardum feor,   þær him freolecu mæg,
ides æfter æðelum   eaforan fedde.
1055   Se æresta wæs   Enos haten,
frum-bearn Caines.   Siððan fæsten ongon
mid þam cneo-magum   ceastre timbran;
þæt wæs under wolcnum   weall-fæstenna
ærest ealra   þara þe æðelingas,
1060   sweord-berende,   settan heton.
Þanon his eaforan   ærest wocan,
bearn from bryde,   on þam burh-stede.
Se yldesta wæs   Iared haten,
sunu Enoses.   Siððan wocan,
1065   þa þæs cynnes   cneow-rim icton,
mæg-burg Caines.   Malalehel wæs
æfter Iarede   yrfes hyrde
fæder on laste,   oðþæt he forðgewat.
    Siððan Mathusal   magum dælde,
1070   bearn æfter bearne   broðrum sinum
æðelinga gestreon,   oðþæt aldor-gedal
frod fyrn-dagum   fremman sceolde,
lif oflætan.   Lameh onfeng
æfter fæder dæge   flet-gestealdum,
1075   botl-gestreonum.   Him bryda twa,
idesa on eðle   eaforan feddon,
Ada and Sella;   þara anum wæs
Iabal noma,   se þurh gleawne geþanc
her-buendra   hearpan ærest
1080   handum sinum   hlyn awehte,
swinsigende sweg,   sunu Lamehes.

less exile, and then chose a dwelling place for himself in the
eastern lands, a homeland far from his father's courts, where
an elegant woman, a lady raised heirs with noble lineage
for him.

The first was called Enoch, Cain's first son. Later they   1055
began to build a fortress, a city, with the next generations;
that was the first of all the ramparts which sword-bearing
princes commanded to be established. After that his heirs
first arose, children from the bride, in that city. The eldest
was called Jared, son of Enoch. Afterward arose the house of
Cain, who increased the count of the nation's generations.
Mahalalel was the keeper of the inheritance after Jared in
his father's wake, until he passed on.

Afterward Methuselah shared out the treasure of princes   1069
with the kinsmen, son after son with his brothers, until wise
in ancient days he had to go through death, to forsake life.
Lamech seized the establishment and household treasures
after the father's death day. Two brides, Adah and Zillah, ladies in the homeland, raised heirs for him; the name of one
of them was Jabal, son of Lamech, who by wise thought first
among those dwelling here awoke music from the harp by
his hands, a melodious sound.

    Swylce on ðære mægðe   maga wæs haten
on þa ilcan tid   Tubal Cain,
se þurh snytro sped   smið-cræftega wæs,
1085   and þurh modes gemynd   monna ærest,
sunu Lamehes,   sulh-geweorces
fruma wæs ofer foldan,   siððan folca bearn
æres cuðon   and isernes,
burh-sittende,   brucan wide.
1090   Þa his wifum twæm   wordum sægde
Lameh seolfa,   leofum gebeddum,
Adan and Sellan   unarlic spel:
    "Ic on morðor ofsloh   minra sumne
hylde-maga;   honda gewemde
1095   on Caines   cwealme mine,
fylde mid folmum   fæder Enoses,
ord-banan Abeles,   eorðan sealde
wæl-dreor weres.   Wat ic gearwe
þæt þam lic-hryre   on last cymeð
1100   soð-cyninges   seofon-feald wracu,
micel æfter mane.   Min sceal swiðor
mid grimme gryre   golden wurðan
fyll and feorh-cwealm,   þonne ic forð scio."
    Þa wearð Adame   on Abeles gyld
1105   eafora on eðle   oþer feded,
soð-fæst sunu,   þam wæs Seth noma.
Se wæs eadig   and his yldrum ðah
freolic to frofre,   fæder and meder,
Adames and Euan,   wæs Abeles gield
1110   on woruld-rice.   Þa word acwæð
ord mon-cynnes: "Me ece sealde

Also, in that family at the same time a man was called Tubal-cain, son of Lamech, who through wise skill was a master smith, and by his mind's intelligence was the inventor of farming tools, the first among men over the earth; afterward the children of the nations, townsfolk, have known widely how to use brass and iron. Then Lamech himself told his two wives, beloved bedfellows, Adah and Zillah, a miserable story in words:

"Murderously I killed my own close kinsman, stained my hands in Cain's murder, cut down with my hands the father of Enoch, Abel's assassin, gave the man's gore to the earth. I readily know that the sevenfold vengeance of the true king will follow in the wake of that slaying, great after the crime. My demise and killing shall be paid back more powerfully with grim terror, when I pass on."

Then for Adam another heir was raised in the homeland in compensation for Abel, a righteous son whose name was Seth. He was blessed, the noble one thrived as a solace to his elders, to father and mother, to Adam and Eve, he was Abel's compensation in the kingdom of this world. Then the origin of humankind spoke a word: "The eternal ruler

1093

1104

sunu selfa   sigora waldend,
lifes aldor   on leofes stæl,
þæs þe Cain ofsloh,   and me cear-sorge
1115   mid þys mago-timbre   of mode asceaf
þeoden usser.   Him þæs þanc sie!"

   Adam hæfde,   þa he eft ongan
him to eðel-stæfe   oðres strienan
bearnes be bryde,   beorn ellen-rof,
1120   XXX and C   þisses lifes,
wintra on worulde.   Us gewritu secgað
þæt her eahta-hund   iecte siððan
mægðum and mæcgum   mæg-burg sine
Adam on eorðan;   ealra hæfde
1125   nigen-hund wintra
and XXX eac,   þa he þas woruld
þurh gast-gedal   ofgyfan sceolde.

   Him on laste Seth   leod weardode,
eafora æfter yldrum;   eþel-stol heold
1130   and wif begeat.   Wintra hæfde
fif and hundteontig   þa he furðum ongan
his mæg-burge   men geicean
sunum and dohtrum.   Sethes eafora
se yldesta wæs   Enos haten;
1135   se nemde God   niðþa bearna
ærest ealra,   siððan Adam stop
on grene græs   gaste geweorðad.
Seth wæs gesælig;   siððan strynde
seofon winter her   suna and dohtra
1140   ond eahta-hund.   Ealra hæfde
XII and nigon-hund,   þa seo tid gewearð
þæt he frið-gedal   fremman sceolde.

of victories, life's Father, himself has given me a son in place
of the beloved, whom Cain killed, and in this successor our
prince has driven the heartbreak from my mind. To him be
thanks!"

When he then began to raise with his bride another son 1117
for himself as a support for the homeland, Adam, that heroic man, had one hundred and thirty years in the world.
The scriptures tell us that Adam increased his house here
on earth with maidens and youths for eight hundred years
afterward; altogether he was nine hundred and thirty years
old when he had to give up this world through the parting of
the spirit.

In his wake Seth watched over the people, the heir after 1128
his parents, held the native seat and got a wife. He was one
hundred and five years old when he first began to increase
his house with sons and daughters. Seth's eldest son was
called Enosh; since the time Adam stepped onto the green
grass, honored in spirit, he first of all of the children of men
called on God's name. Seth was blessed; afterward he begot
sons and daughters here for eight hundred and seven years.
In all he had nine hundred and twelve, when the time came
that he must complete the parting from life.

Him æfter heold,   þa he of worulde gewat,
Enos yrfe,   siððan eorðe swealh
1145 sæd-berendes   Sethes lice.
He wæs leof Gode   and lifde her
wintra hund-nigontig   ær he be wife her
þurh gebedscipe   bearn astrynde;
him þa cenned wearð   Cainan ærest
1150 eafora on eðle.   Siððan eahta-hund
and fiftyno   on friðo Drihtnes
gleaw-ferhð hæleð   geogoðe strynde,
suna and dohtra;   swealt, þa he hæfde,
frod fyrn-wita,   V and nigon-hund.
1155 Þære cneorisse wæs   Cainan siððan
æfter Enose   aldor-dema,
weard and wisa.   Wintra hæfde
efne hund-seofontig   ær him sunu woce.
Þa wearð on eðle   eafora feded,
1160 mago Cainanes   Malalehel wæs haten.
Siððan eahta-hund   æðelinga rim
and feowertig eac   feorum geicte
Enoses sunu.   Ealra nigon-hund
wintra hæfde   þa he woruld ofgeaf
1165 and tyne eac,   þa his tid-dæge
under rodera rum   rim wæs gefylled.

XVIIII

Him on laste heold   land and yrfe
Malalehel siððan   missera worn.
Se frum-gara   fif and sixtig
1170 wintra hæfde   þa he be wife ongann
bearna strynan.   Him bryd sunu
meowle to monnum brohte.   Se maga wæs

84

After him, when he went from the world, Enosh held   1143
the inheritance, after earth swallowed the body of the seed-
bearing Seth. He was dear to God and lived here for ninety
years before he begot children here with a wife by inter-
course; Kenan was born first to them, an heir in the homeland. After eight hundred and fifteen years in the peace of
the Lord the hero wise in heart begot young ones, sons and
daughters; when he had lived nine hundred and five years,
the wise old mentor died.

Then, after Enosh, Kenan was the senior ruler of the gen-   1155
eration, the guardian and guide. He had seventy years before
a son was born to him. Then in the homeland an heir was
raised, Kenan's kinsman was called Mahalalel. After eight
hundred and forty years Enosh's son increased in life the
number of princes. In all he had lived nine hundred and ten
years when he gave up the world, when his lifetime under
the space of the skies was fulfilled.

  XVIIII

Afterward in his wake Mahalalel held the land and in-   1167
heritance for many years. The chieftain had lived sixty-five
years when he began to produce children with his wife. The
bride brought him a son, the woman to the human race. The

on his mægðe,   mine gefræge,
guma on geogoðe,   Iared haten.
1175 Lifde siððan   and lissa breac
Malalehel lange,   mon-dreama her,
woruld-gestreona.   Wintra hæfde
fif and hund-nigontig,   þa he forð gewat,
and eahta-hund;   eaforan læfde
1180 land and leod-weard.   Longe siððan
Geared gumum   gold brittade.
Se eorl wæs æðele,   æfæst hæleð,
and se frum-gar his   freo-magum leof.
   Fif and hundteontig   on fyore lifde
1185 wintra gebidenra   on woruld-rice
and syxtig eac   þa seo sæl gewearð
þæt his wif sunu   on woruld brohte;
se eafora wæs   Enoc haten,
freolic frum-bearn.   Fæder her þa gyt
1190 his cynnes forð   cneo-rim icte,
eaforan eahta-hund;   ealra hæfde
V and syxtig,   þa he forð gewat,
and nigon-hund eac   niht-gerimes,
wine frod wintres,   þa he þas woruld ofgeaf
1195 and Geared þa   gleawum læfde
land and leod-weard,   leofum rince.
   Enoch siððan   ealdor-dom ahof,
freoðo-sped folces wisa,   nalles feallan let
dom and drihtscipe,
1200 þenden he hyrde wæs   heafod-maga.
Breac blæd-daga,   bearna strynde
þreo-hund wintra.   Him wæs þeoden hold,
rodera waldend.   Se rinc heonon

kinsman in his youth was called Jared, so I have heard. Afterward, Mahalalel lived for a long time, and enjoyed happiness here, human joys, worldly wealth. He lived for eight hundred and ninety-five years, then he passed on, left land and guardianship of the people to the heir. For a long time afterward Jared shared out the gold with men. The man was noble, a righteous hero, and the chieftain was beloved to his free kinsmen.

He had attained one hundred and sixty-five years, lived   1184
life in the kingdom of this world when the time came about that his wife brought a son into the world; the heir was called Enoch, a noble first son. The father then lived here still for eight hundred years, increased the count of the generations of his nation, of sons; in all he had nine hundred and sixty five years by reckoning of days when he passed on, the lord wise in years, when he gave up this world and Jared then wisely left land and guardianship of the people to the beloved man.

Then Enoch, the guide of the people, assumed dominion,   1197
the peace and prosperity, he did not at all let their glory and lordship diminish while he was shepherd of his close kinsmen. He enjoyed glory days, begot children for three hundred years. The prince, the ruler of the skies, was gracious to him. The man sought happiness elsewhere in his body, with

on lic-homan   lisse sohte,

1205   Drihtnes duguðe,   nales deaðe swealt
middan-geardes   —swa her men doþ,
geonge and ealde,   þonne him God heora
æhta and æt-wist,   eorðan gestreona
on genimeð   and heora aldor somed—

1210   ac he cwic gewat   mid cyning engla
of þyssum lænan   life feran
on þam gearwum   þe his gast onfeng
ær hine to monnum   modor brohte.

He þam yldestan   eaforan læfde

1215   folc, frum-bearne;   V and syxtig
wintra hæfde   þa he woruld ofgeaf,
and eac III hund.   Þrage siððan
Mathusal heold   maga yrfe,
se on lic-homan   lengest þissa

1220   woruld-dreama breac.   Worn gestrynde
ær his swylt-dæge   suna and dohtra;
hæfde frod hæle,   þa he from sceolde
niþþum hweorfan,   nigon-hund wintra
and hund-seofontig to.   Sunu æfter heold,

1225   Lamech leod-geard,   lange siððan
woruld bryttade.   Wintra hæfde
twa and hundteontig   þa seo tid gewearð
þæt se eorl ongan   æðele cennan,
sunu and dohtor.

Siððan lifde

1230   fif and hund-nigontig,   frea moniges breac
wintra under wolcnum,   werodes aldor,
and V hund eac;   heold þæt folc teala,
bearna strynde,   him byras wocan,

the Lord's company, not at all did he die a death in middle-earth—as people do here, young and old, when their God takes them away from possessions and earthly existence, from the treasures of the earth and their life as well—but rather from this borrowed life he went traveling while alive with the king of angels in the form which his spirit received before his mother bore him among people.

He left the nation to the eldest son, to the first-born; 1214 three hundred and sixty-five years he had lived when he gave up the world. Methuselah kept the family inheritance for a time afterward, he who longest enjoyed the joys of this world in the body. Before his death day he begot a multitude of sons and daughters; when he had to pass away from men, the wise hero had lived nine hundred and seventy years. His son Lamech held the guardianship of the people afterward, then for a long time he governed the world. He had lived one hundred and two years when the time came about that the man began to produce noble offspring, sons and daughters.

Afterward the lord of many enjoyed five hundred and 1229 ninety-five years under the clouds; he ruled the nation well, begot children, sons and ladies arose as heirs for him. He

eaforan and idesa.   He þone yldestan
1235   Noę nemde,   se niððum ær
land bryttade   siððan Lamech gewat.
Hæfde æðelinga   aldor-wisa
V hund wintra   þa he furðum ongan
bearna strynan,   þæs þe bec cweðaþ.
1240   Sem wæs haten   sunu Noes,
se yldesta,   oðer Cham,
þridda Iafeth.   Þeoda tymdon
rume under roderum,   rim miclade
monna mægðe   geond middan-geard
1245   sunum and dohtrum.   Ða giet wæs Sethes cynn,
leofes leod-fruman   on lufan swiðe
Drihtne dyre   and dom-eadig;

xx
oðþæt bearn Godes   bryda ongunnon
on Caines   cynne secan,
1250   wergum folce,   and him þær wif curon
ofer metodes est   monna eaforan,
scyldfulra mægð   scyne and fægere.
Þa reordade   rodora waldend
wrað mon-cynne   and þa worde cwæð:
1255   "Ne syndon me on ferhðe freo   from gewitene
cneorisn Caines,   ac me þæt cynn hafað
sare abolgen.   Nu me Sethes bearn
torn niwiað   and him to nimað
mægeð to gemæccum   minra feonda;
1260   þær wifa wlite   onwod grome,
idesa ansien,   and ece feond
folc-driht wera,   þa ær on friðe wæron."
Siððan hund-twelftig   geteled rime

named the eldest Noah, who ruled the land for the people after the time Lamech departed. The governor of princes had lived five hundred years when he first began to produce children, as the books say. The eldest son of Noah was called Shem, the second Ham, the third Japheth. The people teemed widely under the heavens, the number of the race of men multiplied across middle-earth with sons and daughters. Then the nation of Seth, the dear leader of the people, was still greatly loved, dear to the Lord and blessed with glory;

until God's children began to seek brides among the na- XX 1248 tion of Cain, the accursed folk, and without the creator's blessing the sons of men chose their wives, radiant and beautiful, in that culpable family. Then the ruler of the skies, angry with mankind, spoke and said these words: "The generations of Cain did not go from my mind free-born, but that nation has sorely enraged me. Now the children of Seth renew the anger in me and are taking to themselves women as their mates from among my foes; there the beauty of the women, the appearance of the ladies, and the eternal fiend have malevolently insinuated themselves into the nation of men who were previously in peace."

After one hundred and twenty years were counted in the 1263

wintra on worulde   wræce bisgodon
1265   fæge þeoda,   hwonne Frea wolde
on wær-logan   wite settan
and on deað slean   dædum scyldige
gigant-mæcgas,   Gode unleofe,
micle man-sceaðan,   metode laðe.
1270   Þa geseah selfa   sigoro waldend
hwæt wæs monna   manes on eorðan
and þæt hie wæron   womma ðriste,
inwitfulle.   He þæt unfægere
wera cneorissum   gewrecan þohte,
1275   forgripan gum-cynne   grimme and sare,
heardum mihtum.
                            Hreaw hine swiðe
þæt he folc-mægþa   fruman aweahte,
æðelinga ord,   þa he Adam sceop,
cwæð þæt he wolde   for wera synnum
1280   eall aæðan   þæt on eorðan wæs,
forleosan lica gehwilc   þara þe lifes gast
fæðmum þeahte.   Eall þæt Frea wolde
on ðære toweardan   tide acwellan
þe þa nealæhte   niðða bearnum.
1285   Noe wæs god,   nergende leof,
swiðe gesælig,   sunu Lameches,
domfæst and gedefe.
                            Drihten wiste
þæt þæs æðelinges   ellen dohte
breost-gehygdum;   forðon him brego sægde,
1290   halig æt hleoðre,   helm all-wihta,
hwæt he fah werum   fremman wolde;
geseah unrihte   eorðan fulle,

world, the doomed people busied themselves in exile, when the Lord wished to impose a punishment on those covenant breakers, and strike down giant-kinsmen in death, guilty in their deeds, unloved by God, the great criminals, hateful to the creator. The ruler of victories himself saw what wickedness of men there was on the earth and that they were daring in iniquity and full of guile. He meant to punish the generations of men hideously for that, to seize upon the human race grimly and sorely with unbending powers.

The origin of princes greatly regretted that he had awoken the first of nations, when he created Adam, he said that he wished to destroy everything that was on earth because of the sins of men, annihilate each body that contained life's spirit in its bosom. The Lord wished to kill everything in the approaching hour, which then converged on the children of men. Noah the son of Lamech was good, loved by the savior, very blessed, righteous and worthy.　　　1276

The Lord knew that the courage of this prince would avail in his inner thoughts; therefore the holy prince and protector of all things said to him in conversation, what he, so angered, would do to men; he saw the earth full of unrigh-　　　1287

side sæl-wongas   synnum gehladene,
widlum gewemde.   Þa waldend spræc,
1295   nergend usser,   and to Noe cwæð:
"Ic wille mid flode   folc acwellan
and cynna gehwilc   cucra wuhta,
þara þe lyft and flod   lædað and fedað,
feoh and fuglas.   Þu scealt frið habban
1300   mid sunum þinum,   ðonne sweart wæter,
wonne wæl-streamas   werodum swelgað,
sceaðum scyldfullum.

                    "Ongyn þe scip wyrcan,
mere-hus micel.   On þam þu monegum scealt
reste geryman,   and rihte setl
1305   ælcum æfter agenum   eorðan tudre.
Gescype scylfan   on scipes bosme.
Þu þæt fær gewyrc   fiftiges wid,
ðrittiges heah   and þreo-hund lang
eln-gemeta,   and wið yða gewyrc
1310   gefeg fæste.   Þær sceal fæsl wesan
cwic-lifigendra   cynna gehwilces
on þæt wudu-fæsten   wocor gelæded
eorðan tudres;   earc sceal þy mare."

    Noe fremede   swa hine nergend heht,
1315   hyrde þam halgan   heofon-cyninge,
ongan ofostlice   þæt hof wyrcan,
micle mere-cieste.   Magum sægde
þæt wæs þrealic þing   þeodum toweard,
reðe wite.   Hie ne rohton þæs.
1320   Geseah þa ymb wintra worn   wærfæst metod
geofon-husa mæst   gearo hlifigean,
innan and utan   eorðan lime

94

teousness, the broad plains heaped up with sins, marred by pollution. Then the ruler, our savior, spoke and said to Noah: "I will kill with a flood the people and every kind of living thing which air and water propagate and feed, cattle and birds. You shall have security with your sons when the dark water, the gloomy slaughter-streams, swallow the multitudes, destroy the culprits.

"Begin making yourself a ship, a great sea-house. You shall   1302
make space in it for the repose of many, and a proper berth for each of earth's offspring, according to its own kind. Create a deck in the ship's bosom. Build that vessel fifty ell-lengths wide, thirty high and three hundred long, and firmly make joints against the waves. There into that wooden fortress shall be led the offspring and issue of each kind of living creature, the progeny of the earth; for this the ark must be the greater."

Noah carried out what the savior commanded him,   1314
obeyed the holy king of heaven, quickly began to construct that building, the great sea-chest. He told his relatives that a calamitous event, a cruel punishment, was imminent for the people. They took no account of that. Then after many a year the creator, faithful to his pledge, saw the greatest of

gefæstnod wið flode,   fær Noes,
þy selestan.   Þæt is syndrig cynn;
1325 symle bið þy heardra   þe hit hreoh wæter,
swearte sæ-streamas   swiðor beatað.

XXI

Ða to Noe cwæð   nergend usser:
"Ic þe þæs mine,   monna leofost,
wære gesylle,   þæt þu weg nimest
1330 and feora fæsl   þe þu ferian scealt
geond deop wæter   dæg-rimes worn
on lides bosme.   Læd, swa ic þe hate,
under earce bord   eaforan þine,
frum-garan þry,   and eower feower wif.
1335 Ond þu seofone genim   on þæt sund-reced
tudra gehwilces   geteled rimes,
þara þe to mete   mannum lifige,
and þara oðerra   ælces twa.

"Swilce þu of eallum   eorðan wæstmum
1340 wiste under wæg-bord   werodum gelæde,
þam þe mid sceolon   mere-flod nesan.
Fed freolice   feora wocre
oð ic þære lafe   lago-siða eft
reorde under roderum   ryman wille.
1345 Gewit þu nu mid hiwum   on þæt hof gangan,
gasta werode.   Ic þe godne wat,
fæst-hydigne;   þu eart freoðo wyrðe,
ara mid eaforum.   Ic on andwlitan
nu ofor seofon niht   sigan læte
1350 wæll-regn ufan   widre eorðan.
Feowertig daga   fæhðe ic wille
on weras stælan   and mid wæg-þreate

ocean houses towering in readiness, Noah's vessel, perfectly sealed inside and outside against the flood with earth-lime. That is a special type: it always becomes harder when rough waters, dark streams, beat more vigorously against it.

Then our savior said to Noah: "Most beloved of men, I give you my pledge of this, that you will get under way, and you must transport the beasts' offspring across deep water in the ship's bosom for a great many days. Lead under the deck of the ark, as I command you, your heirs, the three chieftains, and your four wives. And take into that sea-hall seven carefully counted of each species that should live as food for people, and two of each of the others. XXI 1327

"Also lead under the wave-board provisions from all the earth's fruits for the hosts who must escape the sea-flood with you. Freely feed the progeny of living things until I wish again to spread food under the heavens for the remnant after the sea-journey. Now get going with your companions into the building, with the troop of souls. I know you to be good and resolute; you are worthy of protection, of grace with your heirs. After seven nights I will release a slaughter-rain from above on the broad face of the earth. For forty days I will prosecute vengeance on men and with 1339

æhta and agend   eall acwellan
þa beutan beoð   earce bordum
1355   þonne sweart racu   stigan onginneð."
　　Him þa Noe gewat,   swa hine nergend het,
under earce bord   eaforan lædan,
weras on wæg-þæl   and heora wif somed;
and eall þæt to fæsle   Frea ælmihtig
1360   habban wolde   under hrof gefor
to heora ætgifan,   swa him ælmihtig
weroda Drihten   þurh his word abead.
Him on hoh beleac   heofon-rices weard
mere-huses muð   mundum sinum,
1365   sigora waldend,   and segnade
earce innan   agenum spedum
nergend usser.   Noe hæfde,
sunu Lameches,   syx-hund wintra
þa he mid bearnum   under bord gestah,
1370   gleaw mid geogoðe,   be Godes hæse,
dugeðum dyrum.   Drihten sende
regn from roderum   and eac rume let
wille-burnan   on woruld þringan
of ædra gehwære,   egor-streamas
1375   swearte swogan.
　　　　　　　　Sæs up stigon
ofer stæð-weallas.   Strang wæs and reðe
se ðe wætrum weold;   wreah and þeahte
man-fæhðu bearn   middan-geardes
wonnan wæge,   wera eðel-land;
1380   hof hergode,   hyge-teonan wræc
metod on monnum.   Mere swiðe grap
on fæge folc   feowertig-daga,

the wave-troop obliterate the goods and their owners that are outside the boards of the ark when the dark storm begins to mount."

Noah then went, as the savior commanded him, leading his children under the deck of the ark, men onto the vessel, together with their wives; and all that the Lord almighty wished to have for propagation went under the roof to their caretaker, as the almighty Lord of hosts had commanded them by his word. The guardian of the kingdom of heaven, ruler of victories, sealed the mouth of the sea house behind them with his hands, and our savior blessed those inside the ark with his own success. Noah, the son of Lamech, had lived six hundred years when he climbed under the deck with his sons, the wise one with the youths, with the precious riches, by God's command. The Lord sent rain from the skies and also let the vast cataracts rush from their channels everywhere into the world, let the torrents roar. 1356

The seas climbed up over the shore-walls. He who wielded the waters was strong and fierce; he covered and hid the children of the feud of middle-earth, the homeland of men, with a dark wave; the creator destroyed buildings, malevolently inflicted revenge on humanity. The sea quickly grasped at the doomed people for forty days, and also by night. The 1375

nihta oðer swilc.   Nið wæs reðe,
wæll-grim werum;   wuldor-cyninges
1385   yða wræcon   arleasra feorh
of flæsc-homan.

Flod ealle wreah,
hreoh under heofonum   hea beorgas
geond sidne grund   and on sund ahof
earce from eorðan   and þa æðelo mid,
1390   þa segnade   selfa Drihten,
scyppend usser,   þa he þæt scip beleac.
Siððan wide rad   wolcnum under
ofer holmes hrincg   hof seleste,
for mid fearme.   Fære ne moston
1395   wæg-liðendum   wætres brogan
hæste hrinon,   ac hie halig God
ferede and nerede.   Fiftena stod
deop ofer dunum   se drence-flod
monnes elna   —þæt is mæro wyrd!
1400   Þam æt niehstan   wæs nan to gedale,
nymþe heof wæs ahafen   on þa hean lyft,
þa se egor-here   eorðan tuddor
eall acwealde   —buton þæt earce bord
heold heofona Frea—   þa hine halig God
1405   ece upp forlet   ed-modne flod
streamum stigan,   stið-ferhð cyning.

XXII
Þa gemunde God   mere-liðende,
sigora waldend   sunu Lameches
and ealle þa wocre   þe he wið wætre beleac,
1410   lifes leoht-fruma,   on lides bosme.
Gelædde þa wigend   weroda Drihten

hate was fierce, slaughter-grim for men; the king of glory's waves drove out the life of the graceless ones from the body.

The flood, fierce under the heavens, completely covered   1386
the high mountains across the wide earth and on the sea lifted up the ark from the earth, and the noble family with it, which the Lord himself, our creator, had blessed when he sealed the ship. Then the most excellent craft rode widely under the clouds across the expanse of the sea, traveled with the cargo. The terror of the water could not violently buffet the wave-tossed ship, but holy God steered and saved them. The drowning flood stood fifteen human ell-measures deep over the mountains—that is an amazing fate! Soon there was no one among them to be killed, nor was a lament raised into the high air, when the sea army had killed all the offspring of earth—except that heavens' Lord preserved the wooden ark—when holy eternal God, the resolute king, caused the obedient flood, to climb high in torrents.

XXII

Then God, the ruler of victories, remembered the seafar-   1407
ing son of Lamech and all the offspring that he, the bright source of life, had sealed up against the water in the ship's bosom. The Lord of hosts then led the warrior by his word

worde ofer wid-land.　Will-flod ongan
lytligan eft.　Lago ebbade,
sweart under swegle.　Hæfde soð metod
1415　eaforum eg-stream　eft gecyrred,
torhtne ryne,　regn gestilled.
For famig scip　L and C
nihta under roderum,　siððan nægled-bord,
fær seleste,　flod up ahof,
1420　oðþæt rim-getæl　reðre þrage
daga forðgewat.　Ða on dunum gesæt
heah mid hlæste　holm-ærna mæst,
earc Noes,　þe Armenia
hatene syndon.
　　　　　　　Þær se halga bad,
1425　sunu Lameches,　soðra gehata
lange þrage,　hwonne him lifes weard
Frea ælmihtig　frecenra siða
reste ageafe,　þæra he rume dreah
þa hine on sunde　geond sidne grund
1430　wonne yða　wide bæron.
Holm wæs heononweard;　hæleð langode,
wæg-liðende,　swilce wif heora,
hwonne hie of nearwe　ofer nægled-bord
ofer stream-staðe　stæppan mosten
1435　and of enge ut　æhta lædan.
　　Þa fandode　forðweard scipes,
hwæðer sincende　sæ-flod þa gyt
wære under wolcnum.　Let þa ymb worn daga
þæs þe heah hlioðo　horde onfengon
1440　(and æðelum eac　eorðan tudres)
sunu Lameches　sweartne fleogan

across the broad land. Afterward, the surging flood began
to recede. The sea ebbed, gloomy under the sky. The true
creator had turned back the ocean current again, its bright
course, quieted the rain, for his children. The foamy ship
journeyed one hundred and fifty nights under the skies, after the flood lifted up the riveted planks, the most excellent
vessel, until the total count of the cruel days had passed.
Then Noah's ark, the greatest of sea halls, set down high on
the mountains that are called Armenia.

There the holy son of Lamech, waited a long time for the   1424
true commands, when life's protector, the Lord almighty,
should give him rest from the perilous journeys, which he
had endured abroad when the dark waves had carried him
far on the ocean over the wide ground. The sea was with-
drawing. The hero, the wave-travelers and also their wives
longed for when they might step out from their constraint
over the nailed boards and across the stream-shore, and
bring their possessions out from confinement.

Then the ship's navigator tested whether the sea-flood   1436
was yet sinking under the clouds, when, many days after
the high peaks had received the treasure (and also the noble
families of earth's offspring), the son of Lamech let fly out of

hrefn ofer heah-flod   of huse ut.
Noe tealde   þæt he on neod hine,
gif he on þære lade   land ne funde,
1445   ofer sid wæter   secan wolde
on wæg-þele.   Eft him seo wen geleah,
ac se feond gespearn   fleotende hreaw;
salwig-feðera   secan nolde.

He þa ymb seofon-niht   sweartum hrefne
1450   of earce forlet   æfter fleogan
ofer heah wæter   haswe culufran
on fandunga   hwæðer famig sæ
deop þa gyta   dæl ænigne
grenre eorðan   ofgifen hæfde.
1455   Heo wide hire   willan sohte
and rume fleah.   Nohweðere reste fand,
þæt heo for flode   fotum ne meahte
land gespornan   ne on leaf treowes
steppan for streamum,   ac wæron steap hleoðo
1460   bewrigen mid wætrum.   Gewat se wilda fugel
on æfenne   earce secan
ofer wonne wæg,   werig sigan,
hungri to handa   halgum rince.

Ða wæs culufre eft   of cofan sended
1465   ymb wucan wilde.   Seo wide fleah
oðþæt heo rum-gal   reste-stowe
fægere funde   and þa fotum stop
on beam hyre;   gefeah bliðe-mod
þæs þe heo gesittan   swiðe werig
1470   on treowes telgum   torhtum moste.
Heo feðera onsceoc,   gewat fleogan eft
mid lacum hire,   liðend brohte

the house a dark raven over the high flood. Noah reckoned that if it could not find land on that excursion, in its need it would seek the wave-plank across the wide water. Afterward this hope deceived him, as the enemy perched on a floating corpse; the dark-feathered one did not wish to seek further.

Then after seven nights he let fly a gray dove from the ark across the high water, after the dark raven, to discover whether the deep foamy sea as yet had yielded up any part of the green earth. At large she sought her desire and flew widely. However she found no resting place, so that she could not perch on the land with her feet because of the flood, could not set foot on the tree's leaf because of the currents, but the steep cliffs were enwrapped by waters. In the evening, the wild bird went seeking the ark across the gloomy wave, sinking weary and hungry into the holy man's hands. 1449

Then after a week the wild dove was sent again from the ark. She flew widely until, exulting in freedom, she found a fair resting place and then stepped with her feet on a branch; she rejoiced contented, because she, very weary, was able to sit on the tree's bright twigs. She shook her feathers, went flying back again with her offering, brought the sailor a sin- 1464

ele-beames twig   an to handa,
grene blædæ.   Þa ongeat hraðe
1475 flot-monna frea   þæt wæs frofor cumen,
earfoð-siða bot.   Þa gyt se eadega wer
ymb wucan þriddan   wilde culufran
ane sende.   Seo eft ne com
to lide fleogan,   ac heo land begeat,
1480 grene bearwas;   nolde gladu æfre
under salwed bord   syððan ætywan
on þell-fæstenne,   þa hire þearf ne wæs.

XXIII
      Þa to Noe spræc   nergend usser,
heofon-rices weard,   halgan reorde:
1485 "Þe is eðel-stol   eft gerymed,
lisse on lande,   lago-siða rest
fæger on foldan.   Gewit on freðo gangan
ut of earce,   and on eorðan bearm
of þam hean hofe   hiwan læd þu
1490 and ealle þa wocre   þe ic wæg-þrea on
liðe nerede   þenden lago hæfde
þrymme geþeahtne   þridda eðyl."
He fremede swa   and Frean hyrde,
stah ofer stream-weall,   swa him seo stefn bebead,
1495 lustum miclum,   and alædde þa
of wæg-þele   wraðra lafe.
      Þa Noe ongan   nergende lac
rædfæst reðran,   and recene genam
on eallum dæl   æhtum sinum,
1500 ðam ðe him to dugeðum   Drihten sealde,
gleaw to þam gielde,   and þa Gode selfum
torht-mod hæle   tiber onsægde,

gle twig of an olive tree, a green shoot. Then the lord of the
sailors quickly sensed that comfort had come, consolation
for their distressing voyage. Yet again after the third week
the blessed man sent out a single wild dove. She did not
come flying back to the ship, but she found land, green
groves; not gladly would she ever again show herself under
the dark deck in the planked fortress, when she had no
need.

Then our savior, the guardian of the kingdom of heaven, **XXIII**
1483
spoke to Noah, in a holy voice: "A native seat is again opened
up for you, delight on land, rest from the voyage, fair upon
the earth. Go walking safely out of the ark, and from the tall
building lead your household onto the earth's lap, and all
the offspring that I kindly saved from the wave attack while
the sea triumphantly devoured the third homeland." He did
so and obeyed the Lord, with great eagerness climbed over
the current-wall, as the voice commanded him, and then led
from the vessel the survivors of the rages.

Then Noah, the prudent one, prepared a sacrifice, and 1497
from all his possessions that the Lord had given the wise
man for his benefit, he quickly took a portion as an offering,
and then the bright-minded man dedicated the oblation to

cyninge engla. Huru cuð dyde
nergend usser, þa he Noe
1505 gebletsade and his bearn somed,
þæt he þæt gyld on þanc agifen hæfde
and on geogoðhade godum dædum
ær geearnod þæt him ealra wæs
ara este ælmihtig God,
1510 domfæst dugeþa. Þa gyt Drihten cwæð,
wuldris aldor word to Noe:
"Tymað nu and tiedrað, tires brucað,
mid gefean fryðo; fyllað eorðan,
eall geiceað. Eow is eðel-stol
1515 and holmes hlæst and heofon-fuglas
and wildu deor on geweald geseald,
eorðe ælgrene and eacen feoh.
    "Næfre ge mid blode beod-gereordu
unarlice eowre þicgeað,
1520 besmiten mid synne sawl-dreore.
Ælc hine selfa ærest begrindeð
gastes dugeðum þæra þe mid gares orde
oðrum aldor oðþringeð. Ne ðearf he þy edleane gefeon
mod-geþance, ac ic monnes feorh
1525 to slagan sece swiðor micle,
and to broðor banan, þæs þe blod-gyte,
wæll-fyll weres wæpnum gespedeð,
morð mid mundum. Monn wæs to Godes
anlicnesse ærest gesceapen.
1530 Ælc hafað mag-wlite metodes and engla
þara þe healdan wile halige þeawas.
    "Weaxað and wridað, wilna brucað,
ara on eorðan; æðelum fyllað

God himself, the king of the angels. Indeed our savior made it known when he blessed Noah together with his sons that he had given that tribute in thanks and that in his youth he had merited by good deeds that almighty God was generous with graces for him, righteous with blessings. Then the Lord, the ruler of glory, still spoke a word to Noah: "Multiply and propagate, enjoy glory with cheerful peace; fill the earth, increase all things. Into your power is given dominion and the holdings of the sea, birds of the heaven and wild beasts, the earth all green and fecund cattle.

"You must never disgracefully eat food with blood at your feast, polluted with sin by the soul-blood. Anyone first deprives himself of the benefits of the spirit, who with the spear's point forces the life out from another. Nor need he rejoice in contemplation of the reward, for I will seek out the human life from the killer more powerfully, and from the brother-slayer, for bloodshed, carried out with weapons, a murder with hands, seek the slaying of a man. Man was first made in God's likeness. Everyone who will keep holy customs will have the appearance of the Lord and of the angels.   1518

"Increase and multiply, enjoy the good things, favors on earth; in your noble lineage fill the plains of the earth with   1532

eowre from-cynne   foldan sceatas,
1535 teamum and tudre.   Ic eow treowa þæs
mine selle,   þæt ic on middan-geard
næfre egor-here   eft gelæde,
wæter ofer widland.   Ge on wolcnum þæs
oft and gelome   andgiet-tacen
1540 magon sceawigan   þonne ic scur-bogan
minne iewe,   þæt ic monnum þas
wære gelæste   þenden woruld standeð."

Ða wæs se snotra   sunu Lamehes
of fere acumen   flode on laste
1545 mid his eaforum þrim,   yrfes hyrde
(and heora feower wif;
nemde wæron   Percoba, Olla,
Olliua, Olliuani),
wærfæst metode,   wætra lafe.
1550 Hæleð hyge-rofe   hatene wæron,
suna Noes   Sem and Cham,
Iafeð þridda.   From þam gum-rincum
folc geludon   and gefylled wearð
eall þes middan-geard   monna bearnum.

XXIIII
1555 Ða Noe ongan   niwan stefne
mid hleo-magum   ham staðelian
and to eorðan him   ætes tilian;
won and worhte,   win-geard sette,
seow sæda fela,   sohte georne
1560 þa him wlite-beorhte   wæstmas brohte,
gear-torhte gife,   grene folde.
Ða þæt geeode   þæt se eadega wer
on his wicum wearð   wine druncen,

your descendants and offspring. I give you my pledge of this, that never again will I lead the flood-army, the waters over the wide land. You may ever and always see a meaningful token of this in the clouds when I reveal my rainbow, so that I will keep this covenant with people while this world stands."

Then the wise son of Lamech, the keeper of the inheri- 1543 tance, had come from the ship in the wake of the flood, with his three sons (and their four wives; they were named Percoba, Olla, Olliva, Ollivani), faithful to the covenant with the creator, the survivors of the waters. The courageous men, sons of Noah, were called Shem and Ham, Japheth the third. From those warriors sprang nations, and all this middle earth became filled with the children of men.

XXIIII
Then Noah began once again to establish a homestead 1555 with his close relatives and to till the earth for their food; he toiled and worked, planted a vineyard, sowed many a seed, foraged eagerly when the green earth brought him beautiful fruits, spring gifts. Then it happened that the blessed man got drunk on wine in his dwelling, slept weary with feasting,

swæf symbel-werig,   and him selfa sceaf
1565   reaf of lice.   Swa gerysne ne wæs,
læg þa lim-nacod.   He lyt ongeat
þæt him on his inne   swa earme gelamp,
þa him on hreðre   heafod-swima
on þæs halgan hofe   heortan clypte.
1570   Swiðe on slæpe   sefa nearwode
þæt he ne mihte   on gemynd drepen
hine handum self   mid hrægle wryon
and sceome þeccan,   swa gesceapu wæron
werum and wifum,   siððan wuldres þegn
1575   ussum fæder and meder   fyrene sweorde
on laste beleac   lifes eðel.
Þa com ærest   Cam in siðian,
eafora Noes,   þær his aldor læg,
ferhðe forstolen.   Þær he freondlice
1580   on his agenum fæder   are ne wolde
gesceawian,   ne þa sceonde huru
hleo-magum helan,   ac he hlihende
broðrum sægde,   hu se beorn hine
reste on recede.
                            Hie þa raðe stopon,
1585   heora andwlitan   in bewrigenum
under loðum listum,   þæt hie leofum men
geoce gefremede;   gode wæron begen,
Sem and Iafeð.   Ða of slæpe onbrægd
sunu Lamehes,   and þa sona ongeat
1590   þæt him cyne-godum   Cham ne wolde,
þa him wæs are þearf,   ænige cyðan
hyldo and treowa.   Þæt þam halgan wæs
sar on mode,   ongan þa his selfes bearn

and pushed the covering from his body. He then lay naked, which was improper. He little understood what so wretchedly happened within his dwelling, when in his mind the swimming head called to his heart in that holy building.

Indeed, in sleep the mind was very constricted so that   1570
he could not remember to cover himself in clothing with his hands, protect his shame, as genitals had been for men and women, after the prince of glory locked life's homeland behind our father and mother with a fiery sword. Then Ham came journeying in first, Noah's heir, where his parent lay, robbed of his mind. He would not show grace there, amicably to his own father, nor indeed remedy the disgrace for the close kinsmen, but laughing he told his brothers how the man rested himself in the hall.

Then they quickly approached, their faces covered under   1584
the hems of cloaks, so that they might provide help for the dear man; Shem and Japheth were both good. Then the son of Lamech emerged from sleep, and then immediately realized that Ham would not manifest for him any honorable affection or loyalty, when he was in need of a favor. For the holy one that was a sorrow at heart; he began to curse his

wordum wyrgean, cwæð, he wesan sceolde
1595 hean under heofnum, hleo-maga þeow,
Cham on eorþan; him þa cwyde syððan
and his from-cynne frecne scodon.

Þa nyttade Noe siððan
mid sunum sinum sidan rices
1600 ðreo-hund wintra þisses lifes,
freo-men æfter flode, and fiftig eac, þa he forðgewat.
Siððan his eaforan ead bryttedon,
bearna stryndon; him wæs beorht wela.

Þa wearð Iafeðe geogoð afeded,
1605 hyhtlic heorð-werod heafod-maga,
sunu and dohtra. He wæs selfa til,
heold a rice, eðel-dreamas,
blæd mid bearnum, oðþæt breosta hord,
gast ellor-fus gangan sceolde
1610 to Godes dome. Geomor siððan
fæder flett-gesteald freondum dælde,
swæsum and gesibbum, sunu Iafeðes;
þæs teames wæs tuddor gefylled
unlytel dæl eorðan gesceafta.

1615 Swilce Chames suno cende wurdon,
eaforan on eðle; þa yldestan
Chus and Chanan hatene wæron,
ful freolice feorh, frum-bearn Chames.
Chus wæs æðelum heafod-wisa,
1620 wilna brytta and woruld-dugeða
broðrum sinum, botl-gestreona,
fæder on laste, siððan forð gewat
Cham of lice, þa him cwealm gesceod.
Se mago-ræswa mægðe sinre

own son with words, said that he, Ham, should be abject under the heavens, the servant of his close kinsmen on the
earth; the utterance has since fallen terribly on him and his
descendants.

Then Noah enjoyed the broad kingdom with his sons for   1598
three hundred and fifty years of this life, the freemen after
the flood, when he passed on. Afterward his heirs shared out
the wealth, produced children; their prosperity was bright.
Then for Japheth a family was raised, a hopeful hearth-troop
of close kinsmen, sons and daughters. He himself was good,
ever kept the realm, the joys of the homeland, glory amongst
his children, until the treasure in his breast, the spirit eager
to be elsewhere, had to depart to God's judgment. Afterward Gomer the son of Japheth shared his father's establishment with the friends, with dear ones and relatives; a great
part of the created earth was filled with the offspring of that
tribe.

Likewise, Ham's sons were born, heirs in the homeland;   1615
the eldest were called Cush and Canaan, very noble in life,
the firstborn of Ham. Cush was the chief among the princes,
dispenser of goods and worldly benefits to his brothers, the
household wealth in the wake of his father, after Ham went
forth from his body, when death fell to him.

The head of the family gave the judgments for his tribe,   1624

1625 domas sægde,   oðþæt his dogora wæs
rim aurnen.   Þa se rinc ageaf
eorð-cunde ead,   sohte oðer lif,
fæder Nebroðes.   Frum-bearn siððan
eafora Chuses   yrfe-stole weold,
1630 wid-mære wer,   swa us gewritu secgeað,
þæt he mon-cynnes   mæste hæfde
on þam mæl-dagum   mægen and strengo.
Se wæs Babylones   brego-rices fruma,
ærest æðelinga;   eðel-ðrym onhof,
1635 rymde and rærde.   Reord wæs þa gieta
eorð-buendum   an gemæne.

XXV
    Suilce of Cames   cneorisse woc
wer-mægða fela;   of þam wid-folce
cneo-rim micel   cenned wæron.
1640 Þa wearð Seme   suna and dohtra
on woruld-rice   worn afeded,
freora bearna,   ær ðon frod cure
wintrum wæl-reste   werodes aldor.
On þære mægðe   wæron men tile—
1645 þara an wæs   Eber haten,
eafora Semes;   of þam eorle woc
unrim þeoda,   þa nu æðelingas,
ealle eorð-buend,   Ebrei hatað.
    Gewiton him þa eastan   æhta lædan,
1650 feoh and feorme.   Folc wæs an-mod;
rofe rincas   sohton rumre land,
oðþæt hie becomon   corðrum miclum,
folc ferende,   þær hie fæstlice
æðelinga bearn,   eard genamon.

until the count of his days was run. Then the warrior, Nimrod's father, gave up earthly wealth, sought another life. Afterward the firstborn of the heirs of Cush ruled the ancestral seat, the widely famous man, as the scriptures tell us, so that he had the greatest power and strength of mankind in those days. He was the first of the princes of the empire of Babylon; he lifted the glory of the homeland, expanded and exalted it. At that time there was still one common language for all earth-dwellers.

XXV
1637

Similarly, from the generations of Ham many descendents arose; a great count of relatives was born from that widely disseminated people. Then a multitude of sons and daughters, of noble children, were raised for Shem in the kingdom of the world, before the wise leader of the troop chose his deathbed after those years. Men were good in that tribe—one of them was called Eber, Shem's heir; from that man awoke an uncountable tribe, which princes, all dwellers on the earth, now call Hebrews.

1649

Then they departed to the east, leading their possessions, cattle and goods. That folk was resolute; brave warriors sought a more spacious land, until the migrating people arrived in great multitudes, where they, the children of princes, seized the territory. Then the leaders of the people

1655 Gesetton þa Sennar   sidne and widne
leoda ræswan;   leofum mannum
heora geardagum   grene wongas,
fægre foldan,   him forðwearde
on ðære dæg-tide   duguðe wæron,
1660 wilna gehwilces   weaxende sped.
    Ða þær mon mænig   be his mæg-wine,
æðeling an-mod,   oðerne bæd
þæs hie him to mærðe   —ær seo mengeo eft
geond foldan bearm   tofaran sceolde
1665 leoda mægðe   on land-socne—
burh geworhte   and to beacne torr
up arærde   to rodor-tunglum.
    Þæs þe hie gesohton   Sennera feld,
swa þa fore-meahtige   folces ræswan,
1670 þa yldestan   oft and gelome
liðsum gewunedon;   larum sohton
weras to weorce   and to wrohtscipe,
oðþæt for wlence   and for won-hygdum
cyðdon cræft heora,   ceastre worhton
1675 and to heofnum up   hlædræ rærdon,
strengum stepton   stænenne weall
ofer monna gemet,   mærða georne,
hæleð mid honda.
                        Þa com halig God
wera cneorissa   weorc sceawigan,
1680 beorna burh-fæsten,   and þæt beacen somed,
þe to roderum up   ræran ongunnon
Adames eaforan,   and þæs unrædes
stið-ferhð cyning   steore gefremede,
þa he reðe-mod   reorde gesette

118

settled Shinar, broad and wide; in their ancient days they were green fields for dear men, at that time a beautiful earth for the troop, henceforth an increasing abundance of each good thing for them.

Then many a man with his close relative, resolute prince, 1661 suggested there to the other that for their glory—before the multitudes later should move away across the earth's bosom, the tribes of people in search of land—a city should be built and a tower raised upwards to the stars of the sky as a beacon. For that they sought out the field of Shinar, because the most powerful leaders of the nation, the most senior, dwelled happily there for a long time; with instructions, the men endeavored with work and with bickering, until by pride and by recklessness, men eager for glory manifested their skill with their hands, built a city and raised ladders upwards to the heavens, strongly erected a stone wall beyond human measure.

Then the holy God came to examine the work of the 1678 generations of men, the fortress of men, and that beacon as well, which Adam's heirs had begun to raise upwards to the skies, and the stern-minded king carried out the correction of that ill-advised deed, when, angry in mind, he established

1685   eorð-buendum   ungelice,
            þæt hie þære spæce   sped ne ahton.
            Þa hie gemitton   mihtum spedge,
            teoche æt torre,   getalum myclum,
            weorces wisan,   ne þær wer-mægða
1690   ænig wiste   hwæt oðer cwæð.

            Ne meahte hie gewurðan   weall stænenne
            up forð timbran,   ac hie earmlice
            heapum tohlocon,   hleoðrum gedælde;
            wæs oðere   æghwilc worden
1695   mæg-burh fremde,   siððan metod tobræd
            þurh his mihta sped   monna spræce.
            Toforan þa   on feower wegas
            æðelinga bearn   ungeþeode
            on land-socne.   Him on laste bu
1700   stiðlic stan-torr   and seo steape burh
            samod samworht   on Sennar stod.
            Weox þa under wolcnum   and wriðade
            mæg-burh Semes,   oðþæt mon awoc
            on þære cneorisse,   cyne-bearna rim,
1705   þancol-mod wer,   þeawum hydig.

            Wurdon þam æðelinge   eaforan acende,
            in Babilone   bearn afeded
            freolicu tu,   and þa frum-garan,
            hæleð hige-rofe,   hatene wæron
1710   Abraham and Aaron;   þam eorlum wæs
            Frea engla bam   freond and aldor.
            Ða wearð Aarone   eafora feded,
            leoflic on life,   ðam wæs Loth noma.
            Ða mago-rincas   metode geþungon,
1715   Abraham and Loth,   unforcuðlice,

different languages for the dwellers of the earth, so that they did not possess a means of conversation. When they encountered multitudes with mighty ability at the tower, leaders of the work in great teams, none of the tribes there knew what the other said.

They were not able to advance the building of the stone 1691 wall any farther, but they wretchedly divided into groups, separated by their languages; each tribe had become foreign to the other, after the creator split the languages of human beings by his mighty ability. The disunited sons of princes scattered into four directions in search of land. In their wake stood both the erect stone tower and the lofty city, partly finished together at Shinar. The tribe of Shem increased and multiplied under the clouds, until one arose in that generation, the number of royal children, a thoughtful man, mindful of customs.

Heirs were born to this prince, two noble sons raised in 1706 Babylon, and these chieftains, valiant warriors, were called Abraham and Haran; the Lord of angels was a friend and father to both these men. Then an heir was raised for Haran, dear in life, whose name was Lot. The warrior kinsmen, Abraham and Lot, prospered honorably under the creator,

swa him from yldrum   æðelu wæron
on woruld-rice;   forðon hie wide nu
dugeðum demað   driht-folca bearn.

XXVI

    Þa þæs mæles wæs   mearc agongen
1720 þæt him Abraham   idese brohte,
wif to hame,   þær he wic ahte,
fæger and freolic.   Seo fæmne wæs
Sarra haten,   þæs þe us secgeað bec.
Hie þa wintra fela   woruld bryttedon,
1725 sinc ætsomne,   sibbe heoldon
geara mengeo.   Nohwæðre gifeðe wearð
Abrahame þa gyt   þæt him yrfe-weard
wlite-beorht ides   on woruld brohte,
Sarra Abrahame,   suna and dohtra.

1730   Gewat him þa mid cnosle   ofer Caldea folc
feran mid feorme   fæder Abrahames;
snotor mid gesibbum   secean wolde
Cananea land.   Hine cneow-mægas,
metode gecorene   mid siðedon
1735 of þære eðel-tyrf,   Abraham and Loth.
Him þa cyne-gode   on Carran
æðelinga bearn   eard genamon,
weras mid wifum.   On þam wicum his
fæder Abrahames   feorh gesealde,
1740 wærfæst hæle;   wintra hæfde
twa hundteontig,   geteled rime,
and fife eac,   þa he forð gewat
misserum frod   metod-sceaft seon.

    Ða se halga spræc,   heofon-rices weard,
1745 to Abrahame,   ece Drihten:

because there were noble qualities in them from their elders
in the worldly kingdom; therefore now the sons of great nations widely praise them for their great works.

Then the appointed time had come and gone that Abra- 1719
ham brought the lady, beautiful and noble, a wife to the
home where he possessed a dwelling place. The woman was
called Sarah, as books tell us. Then they shared the world for
many seasons, and the treasure together, maintained peace
for many years. Nevertheless, it was not yet granted to Abraham that the beautiful lady brought heirs for him in the
world, Sarah for Abraham, sons and daughters.

Then the father of Abraham departed with his household 1730
from among the people of Chaldea, traveling with provisions; the wise man wished to seek the land of the Canaanites with his relatives. Abraham and Lot, his descendents
chosen by the creator, traveled with him from that native
land. Then the noble children of princes, the men with the
women, seized a homeland for themselves in Haran. In
those dwellings the father of Abraham, the man faithful to
the covenant, gave up his life; the number of years he had
counted was two hundred and five, when he passed on wise
in years to see his destiny.

Then the holy guardian of the kingdom of heaven, the 1744
eternal Lord, spoke to Abraham: "Depart now on a journey,

"Gewit þu nu feran   and þine fare lædan,
ceapas to cnosle.   Carram ofgif,
fæder eðel-stol.   Far, swa ic þe hate,
monna leofost,   and þu minum wel
1750 larum hyre,   and þæt land gesec
þe ic þe ælgrene   ywan wille,
brade foldan.   Þu gebletsad scealt
on mund-byrde   minre lifigan.

"Gif ðe ænig   eorð-buendra
1755 mid wean greteð,   ic hine wergðo on
mine sette   and mod-hete,
longsumne nið;   lisse selle,
wilna wæstme   þam þe wurðiað.
Þurh þe eorð-buende   ealle onfoð,
1760 folc-bearn freoðo   and freond-scipe,
blisse minre   and bletsunge
on woruld-rice.   Wriðende sceal
mægðe þinre   mon-rim wesan
swiðe under swegle   sunum and dohtrum,
1765 oðþæt from-cyme   folde weorðeð,
þeod-lond monig   þine gefylled."

Him þa Abraham gewat   æhte lædan
of Egipta   eðel-mearce,
gum-cystum god,   golde and seolfre
1770 swið-feorm and gesælig,   swa him sigora weard,
waldend usser   þurh his word abead,
ceapas from Carran;   sohton Cananea
lond and leod-geard.   Þa com leof Gode
on þa eðel-turf   idesa lædan,
1775 swæse gebeddan   and his suhtrian
wif on willan.
            Wintra hæfde

124

and take your freight, your possessions for your offspring.
Give up Haran, your father's native seat. Travel, as I command you, dearest of men, and obey my instructions well,
and seek that land which I wish to reveal to you, the broad
earth all-green. You shall live blessed under my surety.

"If any of the dwellers on earth greets you with evil, I shall   1754
set on him my curse and hatred, enduring hostility; to those
who honor you I shall give an abundance of good things.
Through you all dwellers on the earth, sons of the nations,
shall receive peace and friendship, my bliss and blessing in
the kingdom of the world. The number of your tribe shall
teem with sons and daughters, far under the sun, until many
a nation on earth is filled with your offspring."

Then Abraham, the most excellent man, departed as the   1767
guardian of victories, our ruler commanded him by his word,
leading his possessions near the border of the Egyptians'
homeland, happy and rich in gold and silver, his goods from
Haran; they sought the land and territory of the Canaanites.
Then the one dear to God came leading his lady, his tender
bedfellow, and the wife of his brother's son in his charge,
onto that native soil.

He was seventy-five years old when he had to travel,   1776

fif and hund-seofontig   ða he faran sceolde,
Carran ofgifan   and cneow-magas.

Him þa feran gewat   fæder ælmihtiges
1780   lare gemyndig   land sceawian
geond þa folc-sceare   be Frean hæse
Abraham wide,   oðþæt ellen-rof
to Sicem com   siðe spedig,
cynne Cananeis.   Þa hine cyning engla
1785   Abrahame   iewde selfa,
domfæst wereda   and Drihten cwæð:
"Þis is seo eorðe   þe ic æl-grene
tudre þinum   torhte wille
wæstmum gewlo   on geweald don,
1790   rume rice."   Þa se rinc Gode
wi-bed worhte   and þa waldende
lifes leoht-fruman   lac onsægde
gasta helme.   Him þa gyt gewat
Abraham eastan   eagum wlitan
1795   on landa cyst   —lisse gemunde
heofon-weardes gehat,   þa him þurh halig word
sigora self-cyning   soð gecyðde—
oðþæt driht-weras   duguþum geforan
þær is botl-wela,   Bethlem haten.
1800   Beorn bliðe-mod   and his broðor sunu
forð oferforan   folc-mæro land
eastan mid æhtum,   æfæste men
weall-steapan hleoðu,   and him þa wic curon
þær him wlite-beorhte   wongas geþuhton.
XXVII (A)
1805   Abraham þa   oðere siðe
wi-bed worhte.   He þær wordum God

forsake Haran and his relatives. Then Abraham set out to travel, mindful of the instructions of the Father almighty, to look widely across the country by the command of the Lord, until the courageous man, successful on the journey, arrived at Shechem, in the nation of Canaan. Then the king of angels, the glorious Lord of hosts, revealed himself to Abraham and said:

"This is the all-green earth, bright and adorned with 1787
fruits, a spacious kingdom, which I will give into the rule of your descendants." Then the warrior built an altar to God and offered sacrifice to the ruler, source of life and light, protector of souls. Then Abraham traveled still further to the east to look with his eyes on the best of lands—he remembered the favors, the promise of the guardian of heaven, which the same king of victories had truthfully made known by holy word—until the companions with their goods reached the place called Bethel, where there is a rich dwelling place. The glad-hearted man and his brother's son proceeded into the famous land from the east with their possessions, men faithful to the law on the precipitous slopes, and chose a dwelling for themselves where the plains seemed beautiful to them.

XXVII (A)
Then on a second occasion Abraham made an altar. There 1805
he called on God with clear words, offered an oblation to

torhtum cigde,   tiber onsægde
his Lif-Frean   —him þæs lean ageaf
nalles hneawlice   þurh his hand metend—
1810   on þam gled-styde   gum-cystum til.
Ðær ræs-bora   þrage siððan
wicum wunode   and wilna breac,
beorn mid bryde,   oðþæt broh-þrea
Cananea wearð   cynne getenge,
1815   hunger se hearda,   ham-sittendum,
wæl-grim werum.   Him þa wis-hydig
Abraham gewat   on Egypte,
Drihtne gecoren,   drohtað secan,
fleah wærfæst wean;   wæs þæt wite to strang.
1820   Abraham maðelode   —geseah Egypta
horn-sele hwite   and hea byrig
beorhte blican—   ongan þa his bryd frea,
wis-hydig wer,   wordum læran:
"Siððan Egypte   eagum moton
1825   on þinne wlite wlitan   wlance monige,
þonne æðelinga   eorlas wenað,
mæg ælf-scieno,   þæt þu min sie
beorht gebedda,   þe wile beorna sum
him geagnian.   Ic me onegan mæg
1830   þæt me wraðra sum   wæpnes ecge
for freond-mynde   feore beneote.
    "Saga þu, Sarra,   þæt þu sie sweostor min,
lices mæge,   þonne þe leod-weras
fremde fricgen   hwæt sie freond-lufu
1835   ell-ðeodigra   uncer twega,
feorren cumenra.   Þu him fæste hel
soðan spræce;   swa þu minum scealt
feore gebeorgan,   gif me freoðo Drihten

his life Lord—the one who measures gave him a reward for
that by his own hand, not at all stingily—superbly good in
the place of the holocaust. There the counselor dwelt in that
home for a while afterward and enjoyed good things, the
man with the bride, until fearful calamity began to oppress
the nation of the Canaanites, the hard hunger against the
householders, lethal for men. Then wise-minded Abraham,
chosen by the Lord, departed into Egypt to seek a new life,
the one faithful to the covenant fled misery; the torment
was too severe.

Abraham made a speech—he saw the radiant gabled halls   1820
and lofty cities of the Egyptians shining brightly—then the
husband, the wise-minded man, began to instruct his bride
in words: "When many proud men in Egypt have gazed with
their eyes on your face, then the princely men will think,
woman of elven beauty, that you are my radiant bedfellow,
who some man wishes to have for himself. Then I might fear
that some hostile man will deprive me of life by the weapon's edge because of his sexual desire.

"Sarah, say that you are my sister, a blood relative, when   1832
the alien men of this country enquire what the relationship might be between us two foreigners, arriving from afar.
Firmly conceal the true explanation from them; thus you
shall save my life, if the Lord of peace, our ruler, allows me

on woruld-rice,   waldend usser,
1840   an ælmihtig,   swa he ær dyde,
lengran lifes.   Se us þas lade sceop,
þæt we on Egiptum   are sceolde
fremena friclan   and us fremu secan."
    Þa com ellen-rof   eorl siðian,
1845   Abraham mid æhtum   on Egypte,
þær him folc-weras   fremde wæron,
wine uncuðe.   Wordum spræcon
ymb þæs wifes wlite   wlonce monige,
dugeðum dealle;   him drihtlicu mæg,
1850   on wlite modgum   mænegum ðuhte,
cyninges þegnum.   Hie þæt cuð dydon
heora folc-frean   and fægerro lyt
for æðelinge   idese sunnon,
ac hie Sarran   swiðor micle,
1855   wynsumne wlite   wordum heredon,
oðþæt he lædan heht   leoflic wif to
his selfes sele.
                 Sinces brytta,
æðelinga helm   heht Abrahame
duguðum stepan.   Hwæðere Drihten wearð,
1860   Frea Faraone   fah and yrre
for wif-myne;   þæs wraðe ongeald
hearde mid hiwum   hæg-stealdra wyn.
Ongæt hwæðere   gumena aldor
hwæt him waldend wræc   wite-swingum;
1865   heht him Abraham to   egesum geðreadne
brego Egipto,   and his bryd ageaf,
wif to gewealde;   heht him wine ceosan,
ellor æðelingas,   oðre dugeðe.

longer life in the kingdom of this world, the one almighty, as he did before. He ordained this journey for us, that we should desire welfare, seek mercy and help among the Egyptians."

Then the courageous man went journeying, Abraham 1844 with his possessions, into Egypt, where the countrymen were alien to him, friends unknown. Many proud men, resplendent in wealth, spoke in words about his wife's beauty; it seemed to many of them, to the king's attendants, that the woman was noble in bearing. They made that known to their nation's lord and before the prince, that they accounted for few women fairer, but Sarah much more so, they praised her beautiful countenance with words, until he summoned the lovely woman to his own hall.

The protector of princes, the giver of treasure, com- 1857 manded Abraham to be ennobled with wealth. However, the Lord God became angered and wrathful against Pharaoh because of his sexual desire; the bachelors' pleasure paid harshly for that among his household. However, the leader of men perceived that the ruler somehow punished him with chastisements; pressed by terror, the prince of Egypt summoned Abraham to him, and gave him his bride, the wife into his authority; he commanded him to choose friends elsewhere, princes in other society.

Abead þa þeod-cyning   þegnum sinum,
1870   ombiht-scealcum,   þæt hie hine arlice
ealles onsundne   eft gebrohten
of þære folc-sceare,   þæt he on friðe wære.
Ða Abraham   æhte lædde
of Egypta   eðel-mearce;
1875   hie ellen-rofe   idese feredon,
bryd and begas,   þæt hie to Bethlem
on cuðe wic   ceapas læddon,
eadge eorð-welan   oðre siðe,
wif on willan   and heora woruld-gestreon.
1880   Ongunnon him þa bytlian   and heora burh ræran
and sele settan,   salo niwian.
Weras on wonge   wi-bed setton
neah þam þe Abraham   æror rærde
his waldende   þa westan com.
1885   Þær se eadga eft   ecan Drihtnes
niwan stefne   noman weorðade;
til-modig eorl   tiber onsægde
þeodne engla,   þancode swiðe
lifes leoht-fruman   lisse and ara.

1890   Wunedon on þam wicum,   hæfdon wilna geniht
Abraham and Loth.   Ead bryttedon,
oðþæt hie on þam lande   ne meahton leng somed
blædes brucan   and heora begra þær
æhte habban,   ac sceoldon arfæste,
1895   þa rincas þy   rumor secan
ellor eðel-seld.   Oft wæron teonan
wærfæstra wera   weredum gemæne,

Then the nation's king ordered his attendants, his stew- 1869
ards, that they then should conduct him in full safety away
from that territory, so that he might be in peace. Then Abraham led his possessions across the border of the Egyptians'
homeland; the courageous men transported the ladies, the
brides and rings, so that they led their property to Bethel, to
a familiar dwelling, blessed earthly goods on a second journey, the women in their charge and their worldly treasures.

Then they began to build and raise their city and estab- 1880
lish a hall, rebuild a residence. The men established an altar
on the plain near the one that Abraham earlier had raised
for his ruler when he had come to the west. There again the
blessed one honored the name of the eternal Lord with renewed voice; the good-minded man offered an oblation to
the prince of angels, greatly thanked the source of life and
light for favors and graces.

XXVII (B)

Abraham and Lot remained in those dwellings, had an 1890
abundance of goods. They shared happiness until in that
land they were no longer able to enjoy prosperity together,
and both of them have possessions there, but for this reason
the virtuous warriors had to seek a more spacious domain
elsewhere. There were frequent quarrels among the herds-

heardum hearm-plega.   Þa se halga ongan
ara gemyndig   Abraham sprecan
1900   fægre to Lothe:
                    "Ic eom fædera þin
sib-gebyrdum,   þu min suhterga.
Ne sceolon unc betweonan   teonan weaxan,
wroht wriðian   —ne þæt wille God!
Ac wit synt gemagas;   unc gemæne ne sceal
1905   elles awiht,   nymþe eall tela
lufu langsumu.   Nu þu, Loth, geþenc
þæt unc modige   ymb mearce sittað,
þeoda þrymfæste   þegnum and gesiððum,
folc Cananea   and Feretia,
1910   rofum rincum.
                    "Ne willað rumor unc
land-riht heora;   forðon wit lædan sculon,
teon of þisse stowe,   and unc staðol-wangas
rumor secan.   Ic ræd sprece,
bearn Arones,   begra uncer,
1915   soðne secge.   Ic þe selfes dom
life, leofa.   Leorna þe seolfa
and geþanc-meta   þine mode
on hwilce healfe   þu wille hwyrft don,
cyrran mid ceape,   nu ic þe cyst abead."
1920   Him þa Loth gewat   land sceawigan
be Iordane,   grene eorðan.
Seo wæs wætrum weaht   and wæstmum þeaht,
lago-streamum leoht,   and gelic Godes
neorxna-wange,   oðþæt nergend God
1925   for wera synnum   wylme gesealde
Sodoman and Gomorran,   sweartan lige.

men of the faithful men, with severe strife. Then the holy
Abraham began to speak fairly to Lot:

"I am your father's sibling, you the son of my brother. 1900
Quarrels should not grow between us, nor turmoil sprout—
let God not wish that! But we are relatives; between us shall
be nothing else except all happiness, long lasting love. Now,
Lot, think that around our borders sit proud men, triumphant nations with noblemen and their followers, the people of Canaan and Pherezite, with stout warriors.

"They do not wish for us a more spacious right to their 1910
land; therefore we two should take our quarrel from this
place, and seek more ample ranges for ourselves. I speak a
counsel, a true saying, for both of us, son of Haran. Dear
one, I give you yourself the choice. Study yourself and consider in your mind the direction in which you wish to move,
turn with your possessions, now I offer you the choice."

Then Lot departed to survey land by the Jordan, the 1920
green earth. It was made fertile by water and flourished with
produce, shimmering with streams and pools, and was like
God's paradise, until the saving God gave Sodom and Gomorrah to destruction by the dark flame because of men's

Him þa eard geceas   and eðel-setl
sunu Arones   on Sodoma byrig,
æhte sine   ealle lædde,
1930 beagas from Bethlem   and botl-gestreon,
welan, wunden gold.   Wunode siððan
be Iordane   geara mænego.
    Þær folc-stede   fægre wæron—
men arlease,   metode laðe.
1935 Wæron Sodomisc cynn   synnum þriste,
dædum gedwolene;   drugon heora selfra
ecne unræd.   Æfre ne wolde
þam leod-þeawum   Loth onfon,
ac he þære mægðe   mon-wisan fleah
1940 —þeah þe he on þam lande   lifian sceolde—
facen and fyrene,   and hine fægre heold,
þeawfæst and geþyldig   on þam þeodscipe,
emne þon gelicost,   lara gemyndig,
þe he ne cuðe   hwæt þa cynn dydon.
1945 Abraham wunode   eðel-eardum
Cananea forð.   Hine cyning engla,
metod mon-cynnes   mund-byrde heold,
wilna wæstmum   and woruld-dugeðum,
lufum and lissum;   forþon his lof secgað
1950 wide under wolcnum   wera cneorisse,
full-wona bearn.   He Frean hyrde
estum on eðle,   ðenden he eardes breac,
halig and hige-frod.   Næfre hleow-lora
æt edwihtan   æfre weorðeð
1955 feorh-berendra   forht and acol,
mon for metode,   þe him æfter a
þurh gemynda sped   mode and dædum,

sins. The son of Haran chose a domain and native seat in the
city of Sodom, led there all his possessions, rings and household wealth from Bethel, goods and twisted gold. For many
years afterward he dwelt by the Jordan.

The people's settlements there were beautiful—the men
without honor, hateful to the creator. The Sodomite race
were shameless in their sins, perverse in their deeds; they
brought about their own eternal detriment. Lot never
wished to take up the people's customs, but he recoiled from
the men's ways, the stain and the crime—though he had to
live in that land—and kept himself unblemished, virtuous
and patient among that nation, just as though, mindful of
doctrine, he did not know what that race did.

Abraham continued to dwell on the lands of the Canaan-
ite nation. The king of angels, creator of the human race,
kept him in his protection, with an abundance of good
things and worldly benefits, with love and favors; therefore
the generations of men, the children of baptism, tell his
praise widely under the clouds. Holy and wise, he obeyed
the Lord gladly in the homeland, while he enjoyed use of the
land. No mortal need at any time become fearful or terrified
of the loss of protection, ever at all, the man before the creator, who until his death should desire to gain favor for him-

1933

1945

worde and gewitte,   wise þance,
oð his ealdor-gedal   oleccan wile.

Ða ic aldor gefrægn   Elamitarna
fromne folc-togan,   fyrd gebeodan,
Orlahomar;   him Ambrafel
of Sennar   side worulde
for on fultum.   Gewiton hie feower þa
1965   þeod-cyningas   þrymme micle
secan suð ðanon   Sodoman and Gomorran.
Þa wæs guð-hergum   be Iordane
wera eðel-land   wide geondsended,
folde feondum.   Sceolde forht monig
1970   blac-hleor ides   bifiende gan
on fremdes fæðm;   feollon wergend
bryda and beaga,   bennum seoce.

        Him þa togeanes   mid guð-þræce
fife foran   folc-cyningas
1975   sweotum suðon,   woldon Sodome burh
wraðum werian.   Þa wintra XII
norð-monnum ær   niede sceoldon
gombon gieldan   and gafol sellan,
oðþæt þa leode   leng ne woldon
1980   Elamitarna   aldor swiðan
folc-gestreonum,   ac him from swicon.
Foron þa tosomne   —francan wæron hlude—
wraðe wæl-herigas.   Sang se wanna fugel
under deoreð-sceaftum,   deawig-feðera,
1985   hræs on wenan.

                    Hæleð onetton
on mægen-corðrum,   modum þryðge,
oðþæt folc-getrume   gefaren hæfdon

self forever and always by speedy recollection in mind and deeds, with word and intelligence, in wise thought.

Then I discovered that the ruler of the Elamites, Chedor-laomer, the brave leader of the nation, summoned an army; Amraphel of Shinar set out to support him across the wide world. Then four peoples' kings set out with a great force to seek Sodom and Gomorrah south from there. Then the homeland of the men by Jordan was fully occupied by armies, the land by enemies. Many a blanched maiden had to go fearful, trembling into a foreigner's embrace; the defenders of the brides and the rings had fallen, sick with wounds.

Then with violence five kings of the people set out against them with armies from the south, they wished to defend the city of Sodom against the invaders. For the twelve previous years they had been compelled to yield tribute and pay a tax to the northmen, until the people no longer wished to empower the Elamites from their national wealth, but they rebelled against them. Then the angry slaughter-armies came together—the lances were loud. The dark bird sang under the spear shafts, dewy-feathered, in hope of a corpse.

The warriors hastened in battalions with forceful courage, until the national armies had come together widely

sid tosomne   suðan and norðan,
helmum þeahte.   Þær wæs heard plega,
1990   wæl-gara wrixl,   wig-cyrm micel,
hlud hilde-sweg.   Handum brugdon
hæleð of scæðum   hring-mæled sweord,
ecgum dihtig.   Þær wæs eað-fynde
eorle orleg-ceap,   se ðe ær ne wæs
1995   niðes genihtsum.   Norð-men wæron
suð-folcum swice;   wurdon Sodom-ware
and Gomorre,   goldes bryttan,
æt þæm lind-crodan   leofum bedrorene,
fyrd-gesteallum.   Gewiton feorh heora
2000   fram þam folc-styde   fleame nergan,
secgum ofslegene;   him on swaðe feollon
æðelinga bearn,   ecgum ofþegde,
will-gesiððas.
               Hæfde wig-sigor
Elamitarna   ordes wisa,
2005   weold wæl-stowe.   Gewat seo wæpna laf
fæsten secan.   Fynd gold strudon,
ahudan þa mid herge   hord-burh wera,
Sodoman and Gomorran,   þa sæl ageald,
mære ceastra.   Mægð siðedon,
2010   fæmnan and wuduwan,   freondum beslægene,
from hleow-stole.   Hettend læddon
ut mid æhtum   Abrahames mæg
of Sodoma byrig.   We þæt soð magon
secgan furður,   hwelc siððan wearð
2015   æfter þæm gehnæste,   here-wulfa sið,
þara þe læddon Loth   and leoda god,
suð-monna sinc,   sigore gulpon.

from south and north, protected by helmets. There was hard contact, an exchange of slaughter-spears, a great roar of war, loud battle-noise. With their hands the warriors drew ring-decorated swords from their sheaths, bold in their blades. Plunder was easily discovered there by the man who had not found the slaughter satisfying enough. The northmen out-witted the southerners; the people of Sodom and Gomor-rah, the givers of gold, were deprived of their beloved com-rades in arms at the shield-clash. They departed from the battlefield to save their life by flight, from killing by men; in their wake the sons of princes fell, allies were destroyed by blades.

The general of the Elamites' vanguard had victory in war, he controlled the battlefield. The survivors of the weap-ons departed to seek a refuge. Then the enemy plundered gold, robbed with looting the treasuries of the men of So-dom and Gomorrah, then was the time of payback for the great cities. Their lovers slain, the maidens, wives and wid-ows journeyed from the protecting throne. The hostile ones led Abraham's kinsman away from the city of Sodom with the loot. We are able to explain the truth further, what came about later after the slaughter, the experience of the army-wolves, those who led away Lot and the people's goods, the treasure of the southerners, who boasted of victory. 2003

Him þa secg hraðe   gewat siðian
—an gara laf,   se ða guðe genæs—
2020   Abraham secan.   Se þæt orleg-weorc
þam Ebriscan   eorle gecyðde—
forslegen swiðe   Sodoma folc,
leoda duguðe   and Lothes sið.
Þa þæt inwit-spell   Abraham sægde
2025   freondum sinum;   bæd him fultumes
wærfæst hæleð   will-geðoftan,
Aner and Manre,   Escol þriddan,
cwæð þæt him wære   weorce on mode,
sorga sarost,   þæt his suhtriga
2030   þeow-nyd þolode.   Bæd him þræc-rofe
þa rincas þæs   ræd ahicgan,
þæt his hylde-mæg   ahreded wurde,
beorn mid bryde.
                        Him þa broðor þry
æt spræce þære   spedum miclum
2035   hældon hyge-sorge   heardum wordum,
ellen-rofe,   and Abrahame
treowa sealdon,   þæt hie his torn mid him
gewræcon on wraðum,   oððe on wæl feollan.
Þa se halga heht   his heorð-werod
2040   wæpna onfon.   He þær wigena fand,
æsc-berendra,   XVIII
and CCC eac   þeoden-holdra,
þara þe he wiste   þæt meahte wel æghwylc
on fyrd wegan   fealwe linde.
2045   Him þa Abraham gewat   and þa eorlas þry
þe him ær treowe sealdon   mid heora folce getrume;

Then a warrior—one survivor of the spears who escaped the battle—quickly departed on a journey to look for Abraham. He made known to the Hebrew man the work of strife—the great blow against the nation of Sodom, the people's welfare, and Lot's journey. Then Abraham told the evil tiding to his friends; the faithful man asked for the support of his comrades, Aner and Mamre, the third was Eshcol, he said that it was painful in his heart, the sorest of sorrows, that his brother's son suffered enslavement. He asked the courageous warriors to think of some advice for him, so that his close kinsman could be freed, the man with his wife.

The three brothers, famous for their courage, healed his heart-sorrow with great success by their tough words at that deliberation, and gave Abraham a pledge, that they would avenge his injury on his enemies, or fall in the slaughter. Then the saint commanded his hearth-companions to take up their weapons. He found there three hundred and eighteen spear-bearers loyal to their prince, each of whom he knew could well carry a tawny shield in the army.

Then Abraham set out with the three men who had earlier given him the pledge, together with their people's force;

wolde his mæg huru,
Loth alynnan   of laðscipe.
Rincas wæron rofe,   randas wægon
2050   forð fromlice   on fold-wege.
Hilde-wulfas   here-wicum neh
gefaren hæfdon.   Þa he his frum-garan,
wis-hydig wer,   wordum sægde,
Þares afera,   him wæs þearf micel
2055   þæt hie on twa healfe
grimme guð-gemot   gystum eowdon
heardne hand-plegan;   cwæð þæt him se halga,
ece Drihten,   eaðe mihte
æt þam spere-niðe   spede lænan.
2060   Þa ic neðan gefrægn   under niht-scuwan
hæleð to hilde.   Hlyn wearð on wicum
scylda and sceafta,   sceotendra fyll,
guð-flana gegrind;   gripon unfægre
under sceat werum   scearpe garas,
2065   and feonda feorh   feollon ðicce,
þær hlihende   huðe feredon
secgas and gesiððas.   Sigor eft ahwearf
of norð-monna   nið-geteone,
æsc-tir wera.   Abraham sealde
2070   wig to wedde,   nalles wunden gold,
for his suhtrigan,   sloh and fylde
feond on fitte.   Him on fultum grap
heofon-rices weard.   Hergas wurdon
feower on fleame,   folc-cyningas,
2075   leode ræswan.
            Him on laste stod
hihtlic heorð-werod,   and hæleð lagon,

indeed, he wished to rescue his kinsman Lot from his distress. The warriors were tough, and boldly carried their shields forward on the road. The battle-wolves had nearly reached their encampment. Then the wise-minded man, Terah's heir, spoke words to his generals: it was his great need that they advance on two fronts into the grim battle meeting with their guests, for the difficult encounter; the holy one said that the eternal Lord could easily grant them success in the spear-hate.

I have heard that then the warriors dared to go into battle   2060
under the shadow of night. The noise of shields and shafts was in the encampment, the fall of archers, the rasp of battle-arrows; sharp spears lodged in men hideously under the bosom, and the life of enemies fell thickly, where the men and comrades, laughing, carried off the plunder. Afterward, victory, the spear-glory of men, turned away from the northmen in the battle. Abraham gave war as a ransom for his brother's son, not at all twisted gold, he struck and felled the enemy in the division. The guardian of the kingdom of heaven took part to help him. The four armies were put to flight, the people-kings, the leaders of the nation.

In their wake stood the jubilant hearth-troop, and war-   2075

on swaðe sæton,   þa þe Sodoma
and Gomorra   golde berofan,
bestrudon stig-witum.   Him þæt stiðe geald
2080 fædera Lothes.   Fleonde wæron
Elamitarna   aldor-duguðe
dome bedrorene,   oðþæt hie Domasco
unfeor wæron.   Gewat him Abraham ða
on þa wigrode   wiðer-trod seon
2085 laðra monna.   Loth wæs ahreded,
eorl mid æhtum,   idesa hwurfon,
wif on willan.   Wide gesawon
freora feorh-banan   fuglas slitan
on ecg-wale.   Abraham ferede
2090 suð-monna eft   sinc and bryda,
æðelinga bearn,   oðle nior,
mægeð heora magum.   Næfre mon ealra
lifigendra her   lytle werede
þon wurðlicor   wig-sið ateah,
2095 þara þe wið swa miclum   mægne geræsde.
xxx
     Þa wæs suð þanon   Sodoma folce
guð-spell wegen,   hwelc gromra wearð
feonda from-lad.   Gewat him frea leoda,
eorlum bedroren,   Abraham secan,
2100 freonda fea-sceaft.   Him ferede mid
Solomia   sinces hyrde;
þæt wæs se mæra   Melchisedec,
leoda bisceop.   Se mid lacum com
fyrd-rinca fruman   fægre gretan,
2105 Abraham arlice,   and him on sette
Godes bletsunge,   and swa gyddode:

riors lay dead, laid out on the track, those who had looted
Sodom and Gomorrah of gold, robbed the stewards. Lot's
paternal uncle paid them hard for that. The nobility of the
Elamites were put to flight, deprived of glory, until they were
near Damascus. Then Abraham set out on the warpath to
see the retreat of the hated men. Lot was rescued, the man
with the possessions, the ladies returned, wives in delight.
They saw birds abroad, tearing at the killers of free men in
the sword-slaughter. Abraham carried back again the treasure and brides of the southerners, the sons of princes,
nearer to their homes, and the maidens to their kinsmen.
Never did anyone of all those living here achieve a more
worthy war venture, who rushed against so great a force
with such a small troop.

Then the dispatch was carried south from there to the
nation of Sodom, about how the rout of the grim enemies
had come about. The lord of the nation, deprived of warriors and bereft of friends, went out to look for Abraham.
He brought with him the keeper of the treasure of Salem;
that was the famous Melchizedek, the bishop of the people.
He came to greet fairly the leader of the company of warriors, graciously greet Abraham, and place God's blessing
upon him, and intoned thus:

XXX
2096

"Wæs ðu gewurðod   on wera rime
for þæs eagum   þe ðe æsca tir
æt guðe forgeaf.   Þæt is God selfa:
2110   se ðe hettendra   herga þrymmas
on geweald gebræc,   and þe wæpnum læt
ranc-stræte forð   rume wyrcan,
huðe ahreddan   and hæleð fyllan
—on swaðe sæton—   ne meahton sið-werod
2115   guðe spowan,   ac hie God flymde,
se ðe æt feohtan   mid frum-garum
wið ofer-mægnes   egsan sceolde
handum sinum,   and halegu treow,
seo þu wið rodora weard   rihte healdest."
2120   Him þa se beorn   bletsunga lean
þurh hand ageaf,   and þæs here-teames
ealles teoðan sceat   Abraham sealde
Godes bisceope.   Þa spræc guð-cyning,
Sodoma aldor,   secgum befylled,
2125   to Abrahame—   him wæs ara þearf:
"Forgif me mennen   minra leoda,
þe þu ahreddest   herges cræftum
wera wæl-clommum!   Hafa þe wunden gold
þæt ær agen wæs   ussum folce,
2130   feoh and frætwa!   Læt me freo lædan
eft on eðel   æðelinga bearn,
on weste wic   wif and cnihtas,
earme wydewan!   Eaforan syndon deade,
folc-gesiðas,   nymðe fea ane,
2135   þe me mid sceoldon   mearce healdan."
Him þa Abraham   andswarode
ædre for eorlum,   elne gewurðod,

148

"Be honored among the number of men in the sight of   2107
him who granted you the glory of spears in the battle. That
is God himself: he who shattered the forces of the hateful
army in his power, and allowed you to clear a spacious and
bold road forward, rescued the plunder and felled the warriors—they remained by the way—the marching army could
not succeed in battle, but God, who alongside the princes
protected you with his hands from terror against a superior
force in battle, and the holy covenant, which you rightly
keep with the guardian of the heavens, put them to flight."

Then the man granted him a reward of blessings by his   2120
own hand, and Abraham gave altogether a tenth part of the
army's booty to God's bishop. Then the war-king, the leader
of the Sodomites, bereft of his men, spoke to Abraham—
he was needful of favor: "Return to me the handmaidens of
my nation, whom you have rescued from the army's deadly
bonds by your skill! Keep the twisted gold that was formerly
the property of our nation, the cattle and the treasure! Allow me to lead again the children of princes, free to the
homeland, wives and boys and the wretched widows to the
desolate dwelling! The heirs, comrades are dead, all but a
few, who had to keep the borders with me."

Then Abraham answered him quickly in the presence of   2136
the men, honored by courage, by glory and victory, he spoke

dome and sigore,   drihtlice spræc:
"Ic þe gehate,   hæleða waldend,
2140 for þam halgan,   þe heofona is
and þisse eorðan   Agend-Frea,
wordum minum,   nis woruld-feoh,
þe ic me agan wille,
sceat ne scilling,   þæs ic on sceotendum,
2145 þeoden mæra,   þines ahredde,
æðelinga helm,   þy læs þu eft cweðe
þæt ic wurde,   will-gesteallum,
eadig on eorðan   ær-gestreonum
Sodoma rices;   ac þu selfa most heonon
2150 huðe lædan,   þe ic þe æt hilde gesloh,
ealle buton dæle   þissa driht-wera,
Aneres and Mamres   and Escoles.

    "Nelle ic þa rincas   rihte benæman,
ac hie me fulleodon   æt æsc-þræce,
2155 fuhton þe æfter frofre.   Gewit þu ferian nu
ham hyrsted gold   and heals-mægeð,
leoda idesa.   Þu þe laðra ne þearft
hæleða hild-þræce   hwile onsittan,
norð-manna wig;   ac ne-fuglas
2160 under beorh-hleoþum   blodige sittað,
þeod-herga wæle   þicce gefylled."

    Gewat him þa se healdend   ham siðian
mid þy here-teame   þe him se halga forgeaf,
Ebrea leod   arna gemyndig.
2165 Þa gen Abrahame   eowde selfa
heofona heah-cyning   halige spræce,
trymede til-modigne   and him to reordode:
"Meda syndon micla þina!   Ne læt þu þe þin mod asealcan,

nobly: "I promise you by my words, ruler of the warriors, before the holy one who is the sustaining Lord of this earth and the heavens, there is no worldly wealth I wish to have, shot nor shilling, of yours great ruler, protector of princes, that I rescued from the bowmen, lest you should later say that I became rich, happy on earth, by the treasure and old wealth of the kingdom of Sodom; but you yourself can lead the loot from here, that I won for you at battle, all but a share for these noble men, Aner and Mamre and Eshcol.

"I do not wish to deprive these warriors of their rights,   2153 because they went so far with me in the spear-violence, fought for your comfort. Depart now to carry home the decorated gold and dear virgins, the ladies of the people. You have no need to expect the battle-violence of the hostile warriors for a while, war from the northmen; but the carrion birds sit bloody under the bright cliffs, filled fatly with the slaughtered flesh of their national armies."

Then the keeper set out to journey home with the spoils   2162 that the holy man of the Hebrews had granted him, mindful of favors. Then again the high king of the heavens revealed himself to Abraham in a holy speech, strengthened the noble-minded man and spoke to him: "Great are your rewards! Do not let your mind be idle, oh man faithful to my

wær-fæst willan mines!   Ne þearft þu þe wiht ondrædan,
2170   þenden þu mine lare læstest,   ac ic þe lifigende her
      wið weana gehwam   wreo and scylde
      folmum minum;   ne þearft þu forht wesan."

XXXI   Abraham þa   andswarode,
      dæd-rof Drihtne sinum,   frægn hine dæg-rime frod:
2175   "Hwæt gifest þu me,   gasta waldend,
      freo-manna to frofre,   nu ic þus fea-sceaft eom?
      Ne þearf ic yrfe-stol   eaforan bytlian
      ænegum minra,   ac me æfter sculon
      mine woruld-magas   welan bryttian.
2180   Ne sealdest þu me sunu;   forðon mec sorg dreceð
      on sefan swiðe.   Ic sylf ne mæg
      ræd ahycgan.   Gæð gerefa min
      fægen freo-bearnum,   fæste mynteð
      in-geþancum   þæt me æfter sie
2185   eaforan sine   yrfe-weardas.
      Geseoð þæt me of bryde   bearn ne wocon."
      Him þa ædre God   andswarode:
      "Næfre gerefan   rædað þine
      eafora yrfe,   ac þin agen bearn
2190   frætwa healdeð,   þonne þin flæsc ligeð.
      Sceawa heofon,   and hyrste gerim,
      rodores tungel,   þa nu rume heora
      wuldorfæstne wlite   wide dælað
      ofer brad brymu   beorhte scinan—
2195   swilc bið mæg-burge   menigo þinre
      folc-bearnum frome.   Ne læt þu þin ferhð wesan
      sorgum æsæled.   Gien þe sunu weorðeð,
      bearn of bryde   þurh gebyrd cumen,

will! You do not need to fear anything at all while you fulfill my teaching, but with my own hands I will protect and
shield you against each woe, as long as you live; you need not
be afraid."

Then the illustrious Abraham answered his Lord, wise in
the count of his days, he asked him: "What do you give me,
ruler of spirits, as a comfort for free people, now that I am
so bereft? I need not build up a hereditary seat for any of
my heirs, but after me my blood relatives shall divide up my
goods. You have not given me a son; therefore sorrows af-
flict me greatly in mind. I cannot think up any counsel. My
steward goes rejoicing in his freeborn sons, firmly intends
in his inner thoughts that after me his heirs should be the
guardians of the inheritance. They see that no sons have
awoken for me from the bride."

Then God quickly answered him: "Never will your steward control the inheritance of your heirs, but your own son
will keep the treasure, when your flesh lies dead. Look at
heaven, and the number of jewels, the stars of the sky, which
now spaciously spread their glorious beauty widely across
the broad sea, shining brightly—so will be the multitude of
your tribe, stout with sons of the nation. Do not let your
heart be fettered with sorrows. Moreover, you will get a son,
a child will be born from the bride, he who later will be

XXXI
2173

2187

se ðe æfter bið   yrfes hyrde,
2200   gode mære.   Ne geomra þu!

"Ic eom se waldend   se þe for wintra fela
of Caldea   ceastre alædde,
feowera sumne,   gehet þe folc-stede
wide to gewealde.   Ic þe wære nu,
2205   mago Ebrea,   mine selle,
þæt sceal from-cynne   folde þine,
sid-land manig,   geseted wurðan,
eorðan sceatas   oð Eufraten,
and from Egypta   eðel-mearce
2210   swa mid niðas   swa Nilus sceadeð,
and eft Wendel-sæ   wide rice.
Eall þæt sculon agan   eaforan þine,
þeod-landa gehwilc,   swa þa þreo wæter
steape stan-byrig   streamum bewindað,
2215   famige flodas   folc-mægða byht."

Þa wæs Sarran   sar on mode,
þæt him Abrahame   ænig ne wearð
þurh gebedscipe   bearn gemæne,
freolic to frofre.   Ongann þa ferhð-cearig
2220   to were sinum   wordum mæðlan:
"Me þæs forwyrnde   waldend heofona,
þæt ic mæg-burge   moste þinre
rim miclian   roderum under
eaforum þinum.   Nu ic eom orwena
2225   þæt unc se eðyl-stæf   æfre weorðe
gifeðe ætgædere.   Ic eom geomor-frod.

"Drihten min,   do swa ic þe bidde!
Her is fæmne,   freolecu mæg,
ides Egyptisc,   an on gewealde.

guardian of the inheritance, the glorious property. Do not lament!

"I am the ruler who many years ago led you with a select few out of the city of the Chaldeans, promised you a wide homeland to rule. Now I will give you my covenant, prince of the Hebrews, so that many a broad land on the earth will be populated by your descendants, the regions of the earth as far as the Euphrates, and from the borders of Egypt, as many men, as wide a kingdom as the Nile separates, and back to the Mediterranean. Your heirs shall possess all that, each of the territories, as these three waters enclose the high cities of stone with currents, the foamy floods, the dwelling of the tribes." 2201

Then was Sarah sore in mind, that Abraham did not get a son by their fellowship in bed, nobly as a comfort. She began then, troubled in spirit, to speak words to her husband: "The ruler of the heavens has denied me this, that I might increase the count of your tribe under the skies with your heirs. Now I am despairing that the foundation should ever be granted to the two of us together. I am miserably old. 2216

"My lord, do as I bid you! Here is a woman, noble kinsman, an Egyptian lady, one in servitude. Quickly command 2227

2230 Hat þe þa recene   reste gestigan,
and afanda hwæðer   Frea wille
ænigne þe   yrfe-wearda
on woruld lætan   þurh þæt wif cuman."
Þa se eadega wer   idese larum
2235 geðafode,   heht him þeow-mennen
on bedd gan   bryde larum.
Hire mod astah   þa heo wæs mago-timbre
be Abrahame   eacen worden.
Ongan æfþancum   agend-frean
2240 halsfæst herian,   hige-þryðe wæg,
wæs laðwende.   Lustum ne wolde
þeowdom þolian,   ac heo þriste ongan
wið Sarran   swiðe winnan.
Þa ic þæt wif gefrægn   wordum cyðan
2245 hire man-drihtne   modes sorge,
sar-ferhð sægde   and swiðe cwæð:
"Ne fremest þu gerysnu   and riht wið me.
Þafodest þu gena   þæt me þeow-mennen,
siððan Agar ðe,   idese laste,
2250 bedd-reste gestah,   swa ic bena wæs.
Drehte dogora gehwam   dædum and wordum
unarlice.   Þæt agan sceal,
gif ic mot for þe   mine wealdan,
Abraham leofa.   Þæs sie ælmihtig,
2255 duguða Drihten,   dema mid unc twih."
Hire þa ædre   andswarode
wis-hidig wer   wordum sinum:
"Ne forlæte ic þe,   þenden wit lifiað bu,
arna lease,   ac þu þin agen most
2260 mennen ateon,   swa þin mod freoð."

her then to climb into your bed, and discover whether the Lord will let any heir come into the world for you by that woman." Then the blessed man submitted to the counsel of the lady. He commanded the serving woman to go into the bed by the bride's counsel.

Her heart exulted when she was made pregnant with a   2237
son by Abraham. The haughty one began to scorn her mistress with spite, she bore herself arrogantly, was evil-minded. According to her desires she would not endure servitude, but she began to strive with great boldness against Sarah. Then I discovered that to her husband the wife made known with words her anguished spirit, spoke of her troubled heart and earnestly said:

"You do not do what is proper and right by me. You still   2247
tolerate that serving woman, Hagar, who by a lady's path climbed into bed as I requested. Every day she has afflicted me shamefully in deeds and words. I will have that one, will rule my own, if I may, in your presence, dear Abraham. Let the almighty Lord of hosts judge between us two." Then the wise man quickly answered her with his words: "I will not allow you to be deprived of honors while we two both live, but you may deal with your possession, your servant, as your mind pleases."

Ða wearð unbliðe   Abrahames cwen,
hire worc-þeowe   wrað on mode,
heard and hreðe,   hige-teonan spræc
fræcne on fæmnan.   Heo þa fleon gewat
2265   þrea and þeowdom;   þolian ne wolde
yfel and ondlean,   þæs ðe ær dyde
to Sarrai,   ac heo on sið gewat
westen secan.   Þær hie wuldres þegn,
engel Drihtnes   an gemitte
2270   geomor-mode,   se hie georne frægn:
    "Hwider fundast þu,   fea-sceaft ides,
siðas dreogan?   Þec Sarre ah."
Heo him ædre   andswarode:
"Ic fleah wean, wana   wilna gehwilces,
2275   hlæfdigan hete,   hean of wicum,
tregan and teonan.   Nu sceal tearig-hleor
on westenne   witodes bidan,
hwonne of heortan   hunger oððe wulf
sawle and sorge   somed abregde."
2280   Hire þa se engel   andswarode:
"Ne ceara þu feor heonon   fleame dælan
som-wist incre,   ac þu sece eft,
earna þe ara,   eað-mod ongin
dreogan æfter dugeðum,   wes drihten-hold.
2285   Þu scealt, Agar,   Abrahame sunu
on woruld bringan.   Ic þe wordum nu
minum secge,   þæt se mago-rinc sceal
mid yldum wesan   Ismahel haten.
Se bið unhyre,   orlæg-gifre,
2290   and wiðer-breca   wera cneorissum,

Then Abraham's queen became hostile, angry in mind at   2261
her servant, hard and cruel, fiercely spoke insults at the
woman. She then fled punishment and servitude; she did
not desire to endure evil and retribution for what she had
done earlier to Sarah, but she set out on a journey to seek
the wilderness. A servant of glory, an angel of the Lord, met
her there, sad in mind, who eagerly asked her:

"Where do you struggle to, bereft woman, trudging the   2271
paths? Sarah owns you." She quickly answered him: "Abject,
destitute of every good thing I have fled the woe, the hate of
a mistress, vexations and harms, from the dwellings. Now I,
teary-cheeked, must await a hard fate in the wilderness, for
the moment when hunger or wolf should draw out sorrow
and the soul together from my heart."

Then the angel answered her: "Do not worry so that you   2280
cut yourself off from life together by flight, far from here,
but go back, earn favor, start again humbly to strive for favors, be loyal to your lord. Hagar, you shall bring a son into
the world for Abraham. By my words I tell you now that
the warrior kinsman shall be called Ishmael among men. He
will be fierce, hungry for his destiny and an enemy to gener-

magum sinum;   hine monige on
wraðe winnað   mid wæpen-þræce.
Of þam frum-garan   folc awæcniað,
þeod unmæte.   Gewit þu þinne eft
2295   waldend secan;   wuna þæm þe agon!"
   Heo þa ædre gewat   engles larum
hire hlafordum,   swa se halga bebead,
Godes ærend-gast,   gleawan spræce.
Þa wearð Abrahame   Ismael geboren,
2300   efne þa he on worulde   wintra hæfde
VI and LXXX.   Sunu weox and ðah,
swa se engel ær   þurh his agen word,
fæle freoðo-scealc,   fæmnan sægde.
Þa se ðeoden   ymb XIII gear,
2305   ece Drihten,   wið Abrahame spræc:
   "Leofa, swa ic þe lære,   læst uncre wel
treow-rædenne.   Ic þe on tida gehwone
duguðum stepe: wes þu dædum from
willan mines!   Ic þa wære forð
2310   soðe gelæste,   þe ic þe sealde geo
frofre to wedde,   þæs þin ferhð bemearn.
Þu scealt halgian   hired þinne
Sete sigores tacn   soð on gehwilcne
wæpned-cynnes,   gif þu wille on me
2315   hlaford habban   oððe holdne freond
þinum from-cynne.   Ic þæs folces beo
hyrde and healdend,   gif ge hyrað me
breost-gehygdum   and bebodu willað
min fullian.
               "Sceal monna gehwilc
2320   þære cneorisse   cildisc wesan

ations of men, and to his kinsmen; many a man will struggle angrily with him in combat. A nation will rise from this prince, an innumerable tribe. Now go and look for you ruler; dwell with those who own you!"

Then according to the angel's instructions she quickly set out for her masters, as God's holy messenger spirit commanded in the wise speech. Then Ishmael was born to Abraham, when he had lived exactly eighty-six years in the world. The son grew and prospered, as the angel, the faithful servant of peace, had earlier told the woman by his own words. Then, after thirteen years, the eternal Lord spoke with Abraham: 2296

"Dear one, well fulfill our covenant as I instruct you. I will always generously exalt you: be zealous for my will in your deeds! Henceforth I will truly fulfill the covenant, which I formerly gave to you, consolation as a pledge, because your heart mourned. You shall sanctify your household. Set the sign of true victory on each male, if you wish to have me as a Lord or loyal friend for your descendants. I will be the shepherd and keeper of that people, if you obey me in your inner thoughts and will fulfill my commandments. 2306

"Each male person in this line of descent, of those who 2319

wæpned-cynnes, þæs þe on woruld cymð,
ymb seofon-niht sigores tacne
geagnod me, oððe of eorðan
þurh feondscipe feor adæled,
2325 adrifen from duguðum. Doð swa ic hate!
Ic eow treowige, gif ge þæt tacen gegaþ
soð-geleafan, þu scealt sunu agan,
bearn be bryde þinre, þone sculon burh-sittende
ealle Isaac hatan. Ne þearf þe þæs eaforan sceomigan,
2330 ac ic þam mago-rince mine sylle
god-cunde gife gastes mihtum,
freond-sped fremum. He onfon sceal
blisse minre and bletsunge,
lufan and lisse. Of þam leod-fruman
2335 brad folc cumað, brego-wearda fela
rofe arisað, rices hyrdas,
woruld-cyningas wide mære."

XXXIII
Abraham ða ofestum legde
hleor on eorðan, and mid hucse bewand
2340 þa hleoðor-cwydas on hige sinum,
mod-geðance. He þæs mæl-dæges
self ne wende þæt him Sarra,
bryd blonden-feax bringan meahte
on woruld sunu; wiste gearwe
2345 þæt þæt wif huru wintra hæfde
efne C, geteled rimes.
He þa metode oncwæð missarum frod:
"Lifge Ismael larum swilce,
þeoden, þinum, and þe þanc wege,
2350 heard-rædne hyge, heortan strange,

come into the world, shall as a child, be marked for me after seven nights with the sign of victory, or else be separated far on earth by enmity, driven from good things. Do as I command! I promise you, if you wear that sign in true belief, you will have a son, a child by your bride, whom the citizens will call Isaac. You will not need to be ashamed of that heir, but I will give to the excellent warrior my divine grace, power of the spirit, an abundance of friends. He will receive my joy and my blessing, love and delight. From that patriarch a great nation will come, many a brave prince will spring from him, guardians of the kingdom, widely-famed world kings."

Then Abraham laid his cheek on the earth at once, and scoffingly turned over these prophetic utterances in his mind in contemplation. He himself did not expect that Sarah, the gray-haired bride, at that time of life could bring a son into the world; he readily knew that the woman was even then one hundred years old, carefully counted. Then, wise in years, he said to the creator: "May Ishmael live according to your commandments in such a manner, prince,

XXXIII
2338

to dreoganne   dæges and nihtes
wordum and dædum   willan þinne."

Him þa fægere   Frea ælmihtig,
ece Drihten,   andswarode:

2355 "Þe sceal wintrum frod   on woruld bringan
Sarra sunu,   soð forð gan
wyrd æfter þissum   word-gemearcum.
Ic Ismael   estum wille
bletsian nu,   swa þu bena eart

2360 þinum frum-bearne,   þæt feorh-daga
on woruld-rice   worn gebide,
tanum tudre.   Þu þæs tiða beo!
Hwæðre ic Isace,   eaforan þinum,
geongum bearne,   þam þe gen nis

2365 on woruld cumen,   willa spedum
dugeða gehwilcre   on dagum wille
swiðor stepan   and him soðe to
modes wære   mine gelæstan,
halige hige-treawa,   and him hold wesan."

2370 Abraham fremede   swa him se eca bebead,
sette friðo-tacen   be Frean hæse
on his selfes sunu,   heht þæt segn wegan
heah gehwilcne,   þe his hina wæs
wæpned-cynnes,   wære gemyndig,

2375 gleaw on mode,   ða him God sealde
soðe treowa,   and þa seolf onfeng
torhtum tacne.   A his tir metod,
domfæst cyning,   dugeðum iecte
on woruld-rice;   he him þæs worhte to,

2380 siððan he on fære   furðum meahte
his waldendes   willan fremman.

164

and bear you thanks with resolute mind, a strong heart, to carry out your will in words and deeds by day and night."

Then the Lord almighty, the eternal Lord, answered him   2353 beautifully: "Into the world Sarah will bring a son for you, wise in years, the truth will go forth, destiny from these defining words. I will now bless Ishmael with my favors, as you are the intercessor for your firstborn son, so that he may abide for many life-days in the kingdom of this world, with branches of offspring. Be guaranteed of that! However, Isaac, your heir, the young son who has not yet come into the world, I intend to exalt more greatly with an abundance of joys and each good thing in his days, and truly fulfill in him the pledge of my heart, the holy covenant, and be loyal to him."

Abraham did as the eternal one commanded him, set the   2370 sign of peace on his own son, by the Lord's decree, and ordered that each male member of his household should wear that high sign, mindful of the covenant, wise in heart, when God gave him the true pledge, then he himself received the glorious sign. The creator, the righteous king, always increased his glory with goods in the kingdom of this world; he did that for him, since he first was able to carry out the will of his ruler on the journey.

* * *

Þa þæt wif ahloh   wereda Drihtnes
—nalles glædlice—   ac heo gearum frod
þone hleoðor-cwyde   husce belegde
2385   on sefan swiðe.   Soð ne gelyfde,
þæt þære spræce   sped folgode.
Þa þæt gehyrde   heofona waldend,
þæt on bure ahof   bryd Abrahames
hihtleasne hleahtor,   þa cwæð halig God:
2390   "Ne wile Sarran   soð gelyfan
wordum minum.   Sceal seo wyrd swa þeah
forð steallian   swa ic þe æt frymðe gehet.
Soð ic þe secge,   on þas sylfan tid
of idese bið   eafora wæcned.
2395   Þonne ic þas ilcan   oðre siðe
wic gesece,   þe beoð word-gehat
min gelæsted.   Þu on magan wlitest,
þin agen bearn,   Abraham leofa."

XXXIIII
    Gewiton him þa ædre   ellor-fuse
2400   æfter þære spræce   spedum feran
of þam hleoðor-stede,   halige gastas,
lastas legdon   —him wæs Lothes mæg
sylfa on gesiððe—   oðþæt hie on Sodoman,
weall-steape burg,   wlitan meahton.
2405   Gesawon ofer since   salo hlifian,
reced ofer readum golde.   Ongan þa rodera waldend,
arfæst wið Abraham sprecan,   sægde him unlytel spell:
"Ic on þisse byrig   bearhtm gehyre,
synnigra cyrm   swiðe hludne,
2410   ealo-galra gylp,   yfele spræce

* * *

Then the woman laughed—not at all happily—at the   2382
Lord of hosts, but she, wise in years, with great scoffing set
aside the prophecy in her mind. She did not believe the
truth, that the outcome of the promise would follow. When
the ruler of the heavens heard that Abraham's bride raised
skeptical laughter in the chamber, then the holy God said:
"Sarah will not believe the truth in my words. Nevertheless,
the destiny will be accomplished in the future as I promised
you at the beginning. I tell you the truth: in the same time
will an heir be born of the bride, when I seek this dwelling
on a second journey; my multitude of promises to you will
be fulfilled. You will look on your kinsman, your own son,
beloved Abraham."

XXXIIII
Then they quickly departed eagerly after that exchange,   2399
to journey prosperously from that meeting place, the holy
spirits made tracks—Lot's kinsman was himself on a journey—until they could gaze on Sodom, the ramparted city.
They saw the palaces tower over the treasure, the halls over
the red gold. The righteous ruler of the skies began to speak
with Abraham, told him a long story: "I hear a tumult in
this city, the very loud noise of sinners, the boast of those

werod under weallum habban;   forþon wær-logona sint,
folce firena hefige.   Ic wille fandigan nu,
    mago Ebrea,   hwæt þa men don,
    gif hie swa swiðe   synna fremmað
2415   þeawum and geþancum,   swa hie on þweorh sprecað
    facen and inwit;   þæt sceal fyr wrecan,
    swefyl and sweart lig   sare and grimme,
    hat and hæste   hæðnum folce."

                    * * *

    Weras basnedon   witelaces,
2420   wean under weallum,   and heora wif somed.
    Duguðum wlance   Drihtne guldon
    god mid gnyrne,   oðþæt gasta helm,
    lifes leoht-fruma   leng ne wolde
    torn þrowigean,   ac him to sende
2425   stið-mod cyning   strange twegen
    aras sine,   þa on æfen-tid
    siðe gesohton   Sodoma ceastre.
    Hie þa æt burh-geate   beorn gemitton
    sylfne sittan   sunu Arones,
2430   þæt þam gleawan were   geonge þuhton
    men for his eagum.   Aras þa metodes þeow
    gastum togeanes,   gretan eode
    cuman cuðlice,   cynna gemunde
    riht and gerisno,   and þam rincum bead
2435   niht-feormunge.   Him þa nergendes
    æðele ærendran   andswarodon:
        "Hafa arna þanc   þara þe þu unc bude!
    Wit be þisse stræte   stille þencað
    sæles bidan,   siððan sunnan eft

drunk on ale, I hear that the troop under the walls have evil speech; therefore the sins of the covenant-breakers among the nation are heavy. Man of the Hebrews, I will now discover what the people do, if they commit sins as greatly in actions and thoughts, as they perversely utter crime and vice; fire shall sorely and grimly avenge that, brimstone and dark flame, heat and fury on the pagan people."

* * *

The men and their wives awaited punishment together, 2419 misery under the walls. Proud in riches, they repaid good from the Lord with evil, until the protector of spirits, the source of life and light would put up with their offense no longer, but the resolute king sent to them two of his strong messengers, who in the evening sought the city of Sodom on their journey. At the city gates they encountered the son of Haran, the man himself, sitting, so that they seemed like young men before the eyes of the wise man. Then the servant of the creator got up, and went toward the spirits to greet the travelers nobly, he thought their bearing right and proper, and offered the warriors hospitality for the night. The princely messengers of the savior answered him:

"Have thanks for the favors that you have offered the 2437 two of us! We intend to wait quietly by this street for the

forð to morgen   metod up forlæt."

2440

Þa to fotum Loth
þam giestum hnah,   and him georne bead
reste and gereorda   and his recedes hleow
and þegnunge.   Hie on þanc curon

2445 æðelinges est,   eodon sona,
swa him se Ebrisca   eorl wisade,
in undor edoras.   Þær him se æðela geaf,
gleaw-ferhð hæle,   giest-liðnysse
fægre on flette,   oðþæt forð gewat

2450 æfen-scima.

Þa com æfter niht
on last dæge,   lagu-streamas wreah,
þrym mid þystro   þisses lifes,
sæs and sid-land.   Comon Sodom-ware,
geonge and ealde,   Gode unleofe,

2455 corðrum miclum   cuman acsian,
þæt hie behæfdon   herges mægne
Loth mid giestum.   Heton lædan ut
of þam hean hofe   halige aras,
weras to gewealde,   wordum cwædon

2460 þæt mid þam hæleðum   hæman wolden
unscomlice   —arna ne gymden.

Þa aras hraðe   —se ðe oft ræd ongeat—
Loth on recede,   eode lungre ut;
spræc þa ofer ealle   æðelinga gedriht

2465 sunu Arones,   snytra gemyndig:
"Her syndon inne   unwemme twa
dohtor mine.   Doð, swa ic eow bidde
—ne can þara idesa   owðer gieta
þurh gebedscipe   beorna neawest—

170

time when the creator allows the sun to rise again, forward
to morning." Then Lot bowed to the feet of the guests, and
eagerly offered them beds and a meal, and the shelter and
service of his hall. They gratefully chose the prince's favor,
went immediately within his courtyards, as the Hebrew man
guided them. There the prince, the wise-minded man, gave
them fair hospitality in the hall, until the evening light departed.

Then night came afterward, in the wake of the day, cov-   2450
ered the sea streams, the glory of this life, with darkness,
the seas and the wide land. The citizens of Sodom came,
young and old, unloved by God, they came in a great band to
demand the visitors, so that they trapped Lot and his guests
with an army's strength. They commanded that he lead the
holy messengers out of the high building, the men into their
power, said in their words that wished to have sex shame-
lessly with those men—they did not care for grace.

Then Lot got up quickly in the hall—he who often per-   2462
ceived a good course of action—and went out straight away;
the son of Haran mindful of wisdom, then spoke over that
company of princes: "Here inside are my two unblemished
daughters. Do as I offer you—neither of these ladies knows
anything of the experience of men in bed—and desist from

2470 and geswicað þære synne.   Ic eow sylle þa,
ær ge sceonde   wið gesceapu fremmen,
ungifre yfel   ylda bearnum.
Onfoð þæm fæmnum,   lætað frið agon
gistas mine,   þa ic for Gode wille
2475 gemund-byrdan,   gif ic mot, for eow."
        Him þa seo mænigeo   þurh gemæne word,
arlease cyn,   andswarode:
"Þis þinceð gerisne   and riht micel,
þæt þu ðe aferige   of þisse folc-sceare.
2480 Þu þas wer-ðeode   wræccan laste
freonda fea-sceaft   feorran gesohtest,
wine-þearfende.   Wilt ðu—gif þu most—
wesan usser her   aldor-dema,
leodum lareow?"   Þa ic on Lothe gefrægn
2485 hæðne here-mæcgas   handum gripan,
faum folmum.   Him fylston wel
gystas sine,   and hine of gromra þa,
cuman arfæste,   clommum abrugdon
in under edoras,   and þa ofstlice
2490 anra gehwilcum   ymbstandendra
folces Sodoma   fæste forsæton
heafod-siena.
            Wearð eal here sona
burh-warena blind.   Abrecan ne meahton
reðe-mode   reced æfter gistum,
2495 swa hie fundedon,   ac þær frome wæron
Godes spell-bodan.   Hæfde gist-mægen
stiðe strengeo,   styrnde swiðe
werode mid wite.   Spræcon wordum þa
fæle freoðo-scealcas   fægre to Lothe:

this sin. I give them to you, before you do shame against creation, a harmful evil against the sons of men. Take the maidens, let my guests have peace, who I will protect against you before God, if I am able."

Then the mob, the graceless race, answered him in one voice: "It seems very proper and fitting that you should depart from this territory. You sought out this nation from afar on an exile's path, bereft of friends, needing friends. Do you now wish—if you can—to be our chief judge here, the teacher of the people?" Then I heard that the pagan mob grabbed at Lot with their hands, with hostile fists. His guests helped him well, and the righteous travelers then drew him out of the clutches of the enemies, into the courtyards, and then quickly sealed fast the eyesight of each of those besieging people of Sodom.   2476

The whole mob of the citizens immediately became blind. They were not able angrily to break into the hall after the guests as they intended, but God's messengers were busy there. The guest-force had hardy strength, was very severe with punishment on the troop. The faithful servants of peace spoke beautifully to Lot in these words: 2492

2500 "Gif þu sunu age   oððe swæsne mæg,
oððe on þissum folcum   freond ænigne
eac þissum idesum   þe we her on wlitað,
alæde of þysse leod-byrig,   þa ðe leofe sien,
ofestum miclum,   and þin ealdor nere,
2505 þy læs þu forweorðe   mid þyssum wær-logan.
Unc hit waldend heht   for wera synnum
Sodoma and Gomorra   sweartan lige,
fyre gesyllan   and þas folc slean,
cynn on ceastrum   mid cwealm-þrea
2510 and his torn wrecan.   Þære tide is
neah geþrungen.   Gewit þu nergean þin
feorh fold-wege.   Þe is Frea milde."

* * *

XXXVI
Him þa ædre Loth   andswarode:
"Ne mæg ic mid idesum   aldornere mine
2515 swa feor heonon   feðe-gange
siðe gesecan.   Git me sibb-lufan
and freondscipe   fægre cyðað,
treowe and hyldo   tiðiað me.
Ic wat hea burh   her ane neah,
2520 lytle ceastre.   Lyfað me þær
are and reste,   þæt we aldornere
on Sigor up   secan moten.
Gif git þæt fæsten   fyre willað
steape forstandan,   on þære stowe we
2525 gesunde magon   sæles bidan,
feorh generigan."
Him þa freondlice
englas arfæste   andswaredon:

174

"If you have a son or dear kinsman, or any friend among this nation, in addition to these ladies that we look at here, with great haste lead out of this capital those who are loved by you, and save your life, lest you be annihilated with these covenant-breakers. The ruler has commanded us two to give dark flame and fire to Sodom and Gomorrah because of men's sins, and slaughter the nation, the race within the fortifications, and to avenge his injury with deadly terror. The time has nearly closed in. Set out to save your life on the road. The Lord is merciful to you." 2500

* * *

Then Lot quickly answered them: "I cannot look too far from here for the saving of my life, with these ladies going by foot. You two are showing me a kinsman's love and fair friendship, and offer me a pledge and protection. I know a high city near here, a small fortress. Deliver me there with favor and respite, so that we are able to seek survival in Zoar. If you will defend that steep refuge against the fire, we can wait safely for a time in that place to save our lives." XXXVI 2513

Then the righteous angels answered him in a friendly 2526

"Þu scealt þære bene,   nu þu ymb þa burh sprycest,
tiða weorðan.   Teng recene to
2530   þam fæstenne;   wit þe friðe healdað
and mund-byrde.   Ne moton wyt
on wær-logum   wrecan torn Godes,
swebban synnig cynn,   ær ðon þu on Sægor þin
bearn gelæde   and bryd somed."
2535   Þa onette   Abrahames mæg
to þam fæstenne.   Feðe ne sparode
eorl mid idesum,   ac he ofstum forð
lastas legde,   oðþæt he gelædde
bryd mid bearnum   under burh-locan
2540   in Sægor his.   Þa sunne up,
folca frið-candel,   furðum eode,
þa ic sendan gefrægn   swegles aldor
swefl of heofnum   and sweartne lig
werum to wite,   weallende fyr,
2545   þæs hie on ær-dagum   Drihten tyndon
lange þrage.   Him þæs lean forgeald
gasta waldend.   Grap heah-þrea
on hæðen-cynn.   Hlynn wearð on ceastrum,
cirm arleasra   cwealmes on ore,
2550   laðan cynnes.
            Lig eall fornam
þæt he grenes fond   gold-burgum in,
swylce þær ymbutan   unlytel dæl
sidre foldan   geondsended wæs
bryne and brogan.   Bearwas wurdon
2555   to axan and to yslan,   eorðan wæstma,
efne swa wide   swa ða witelac
reðe geræhton   rum land wera.

way: "Now that you have mentioned that city, your request will be granted. Press on quickly to the refuge; we two will keep you in peace and under our protection. We cannot avenge God's injury on the covenant-breakers, put that sinful race to rest, before you have led your children, together with your bride, into Zoar."

Then Abraham's kinsman set out for the refuge. The man 2535 did not spare the pace for the ladies, but he quickly made tracks forward, until he led his bride with the children into the fortress of Zoar. When the sun was up, the peace-candle of the nations went forth, then, I hear tell, the ruler of the skies sent brimstone from the heavens and black flame for the punishment of men, surging fire, because in earlier days they had offended God for a long time. The ruler of spirits gave them a reward for that. A high terror gripped the pagan nation. There was tumult in the fortresses, the cry of those without grace at the onset of death, of the hated people.

The flame seized on anything green it found in the golden 2550 city, also a great part of the broad earth around there was dispatched with burning and terror. As far as the cruel punishment reached, the spacious land of the men, trees, fruits of the earth, became ashes and embers. The destroying fire,

Strudende fyr   steapes and geapes,
swogende leg,   forswealh eall geador
2560   þæt on Sodoma byrig   secgas ahton
and on Gomorra.   Eall þæt God spilde,
Frea mid þy folce.

                        Þa þæt fyr-gebræc,
leoda lif-gedal,   Lothes gehyrde
bryd on burgum,   under bæc beseah
2565   wið þæs wæl-fylles.   Us gewritu secgað
þæt heo on sealt-stanes   sona wurde
anlicnesse.   Æfre siððan
se mon-lica   —þæt is mære spell—
stille wunode,   þær hie strang begeat
2570   wite, þæs heo wordum   wuldres þegna
hyran ne wolde.   Nu sceal heard and steap
on þam wicum   wyrde bidan,
Drihtnes domes,   hwonne dogora rim,
woruld gewite.   Þæt is wundra sum,
2575   þara ðe geworhte   wuldres aldor.

XXXVII

    Him þa Abraham gewat   ana gangan
mid ær-dæge   þæt he eft gestod
þær wordum ær   wið his waldend spræc
frod frum-gara.   He geseah from foldan up
2580   wide fleogan   wæl-grimne rec.
Hie þæs wlenco onwod   and win-gedrync
þæt hie firen-dæda   to frece wurdon,
synna þriste,   soð ofergeaton,
Drihtnes domas,   and hwa him dugeða forgeaf,
2585   blæd on burgum.   Forþon him brego engla
wylm-hatne lig   to wræce sende.

the roaring flame, swallowed all things together, steep and broad, that men possessed in the cities of Sodom and Gomorrah. God the Lord destroyed all that, with that people.

When Lot's wife heard that fiery destruction, the exter- 2562 mination of the nation in the cities, she looked back toward the slaughter. Scriptures tell us that she was immediately transformed into the likeness of a salt-stone. Ever since, that human likeness—it is an amazing story—has stood there motionless, where she received the severe punishment, because she did not wish to obey the words of the ministers of glory. Now stiff and upright, she must await the Lord's judgment in that place, when the world realizes the count of its days. That is one of the miracles that the ruler of glory has done.

XXXVII

Then Abraham set out to walk alone at dawn, so that he 2576 again stood where he, the wise prince, had spoken in words with his ruler. He saw the smoke from the slaughter flying up widely from the earth. Pride and drunkenness had taken possession of them so much that they became gluttonous for sinful deeds, eager for sins, forgot the truth, the decrees of the Lord, and the one who gave them benefits, glory in the cities. Therefore the prince of angels sent them surging hot flame as a punishment. Our ruler, faithful to the cov-

Waldend usser   gemunde wærfæst þa
Abraham arlice,   swa he oft dyde
leofne mannan.   Loth generede,
2590   mæg þæs oðres,   þa seo mænegeo forwearð.
    Ne dorste þa   dæd-rof hæle
for Frean egesan   on þam fæstenne
leng eardigean,   ac him Loth gewat
of byrig gangan   and his bearn somed
2595   wæl-stowe fyrr   wic sceawian,
oðþæt hie be hliðe   heare dune
eorð-scræf fundon.   Þær se eadega Loth
wærfæst wunode,   waldende leof,
dæg-rimes worn   and his dohtor twa.

* * *

2600   Hie dydon swa;   druncnum eode
seo yldre to   ær on reste
heora bega fæder.   Ne wiste blonden-feax
hwonne him fæmnan to bryde   him bu wæron
—on ferhð-cofan   fæste genearwod
2605   mode and gemynde—   þæt he mægða sið
wine druncen   gewitan ne meahte.
Idesa wurdon eacne,   eaforan brohtan
will-gesweostor   on woruld sunu
heora ealdan fæder.   Þara æðelinga
2610   modor oðerne   Moab nemde,
—Lothes dohter,   seo on life wæs
wintrum yldre.   Us gewritu secgeað,
god-cunde bec,   þæt seo gingre
hire agen bearn   Ammon hete.
2615   Of þam frum-garum   folces unrim,
þrymfæste twa   þeoda awocon.

GEN ESIS

enant, then graciously remembered Abraham, the dear man, as he often had done. He saved Lot, the other one's kinsman, when the multitude perished.

Then for fear of the Lord the celebrated hero did not dare 2591 remain long in that fortress, but Lot departed from the city together with his children to look for a dwelling far from the place of slaughter, until they found a cave in a cliff beside the high mountain. The blessed Lot dwelled there, faithful to the covenant, dear to the ruler, for a great number of days, with his two daughters.

* * *

They did so; the older one went first into the bed, to the 2600 drunken one, the father of them both. The gray-haired one didn't know when both maidens were with him as brides — he was fast constrained in his heart, mind, and memory — so that he, drunk with wine, couldn't know about the maidens' enterprise. The ladies became pregnant, the dear sisters brought heirs into the world for their old father. The mother — Lot's daughter who was elder in the years of life — named one of these princes Moab. The scriptures, the divine books, tell us that the younger called her own son Benammi. From these princes awoke an innumerable people,

Oðre þara mægða   Moabitare
eorð-buende   ealle hatað,
wid-mære cynn;   oðre weras nemnað,
2620   æðelinga bearn,   Ammonitare.

XXXVIII
    Gewat him þa mid bryde   broðor Arones
under Abimelech   æhte lædan
mid his hiwum.   Hæleðum sægde
þæt Sarra his   sweostor wære,
2625   Abraham wordum   —bearh his aldre—
þy he wiste gearwe   þæt he wine-maga,
on folce lyt   freonda hæfde.
Þa se þeoden his   þegnas sende,
heht hie bringan   to him selfum.
2630   Þa wæs ell-þeodig   oðre siðe
wif Abrahames   from were læded
on fremdes fæðm.   Him þær fylste þa
ece Drihten,   swa he oft dyde,
nergend usser.   Com nihtes self,
2635   þær se waldend læg   wine druncen.
    Ongan þa soð-cyning   þurh swefn sprecan
to þam æðelinge   and him yrre hweop:
"Þu Abrahames   idese gename,
bryde æt beorne.   Þe abregdan sceal
2640   for þære dæde   deað of breostum
sawle þine."   Him symbel-werig
synna brytta   þurh slæp oncwæð:
"Hwæt, þu æfre,   engla þeoden,
þurh þin yrre wilt   aldre lætan
2645   heah beheowan   þæne þe her leofað
rihtum þeawum,   bið on ræde fæst,

182

the two glorious nations. One of these nations all earth-
dwellers call Moabites, a widely famed nation; men, the sons
of princes, call the other Ammonites.

Then the brother of Haran set out with his bride to lead
his possessions with his household into the land of Abimelech. Abraham told the men in speech that Sarah was his
sister—he saved his life—because he clearly knew that he
had few kinsmen or friends among that nation. Then the
prince sent his officers, commanded that they bring her to
him. That was the second occasion when Abraham's wife
was led from her husband into a stranger's embrace. Then
the eternal Lord, our savior, helped him there, as he often
did. He came himself by night, to where the ruler lay drunk
with wine.

The king of truth began to speak to the prince through a   2636
dream, and angrily threatened him: "You seized Abraham's
wife, the bride from the man. For that deed, death shall rip
out your soul from your breast." The one who shared in sins,
exhausted from the feast, said to him through his sleep: "O
high prince of angels, will you ever through your anger
let one be hacked off from life who abides here with correct
customs, who is firm in counsel, thoughtful, and who looks

mod-geþance,   and him miltse
to þe seceð?   Me sægde ær
þæt wif hire   wordum selfa
2650 unfricgendum,   þæt heo Abrahames
sweostor wære.   Næbbe ic synne wið hie
facna ænig   gefremed gena."
    Him þa ædre eft   ece Drihten,
soðfæst metod,   þurh þæt swefn oncwæð:
2655 "Agif Abrahame   idese sine,
wif to gewealde,   gif þu on worulde leng,
æðelinga helm,   aldres recce.
He is god and gleaw,   mæg self wið God sprecan,
geseon swegl-cyning.   Þu sweltan scealt
2660 mid feo and mid feorme,   gif ðu þam frum-garan
bryde wyrnest.   He abiddan mæg,
gif he ofstum me   ærendu wile
þeawfæst and geþyldig   þin abeodan,
þæt ic þe lissa   lifigendum giet
2665 on dagum læte   duguþa brucan
sinces gesundne."
                        Þa slæpe tobrægd
forht folces weard.   Heht him fetigean to
gesprecan sine;   spedum sægde
eorlum Abimeleh   —egesan geðread—
2670 waldendes word.   Weras him ondredon
for þære dæde   Drihtnes handa
sweng æfter swefne.   Heht sylf cyning
him þa Abraham to   ofstum miclum.
Þa reordode   rice þeoden:
2675 "Mago Ebrea,   þæs þu me wylle
wordum secgean,   hu geworhte ic þæt,

to you for mercy? Unasked this woman told me earlier in her own words, that she was Abraham's sister. I have not yet committed a sin, any crime, against her."

Then the eternal Lord, the righteous creator, quickly   2653
spoke to him through that dream: "Give Abraham his lady, the woman to rule, if you reckon on living long in the world, protector of princes. He is good and wise, and can person-ally speak with God, can see the radiant king. You shall die, with your wealth and your tributes, if you withhold the bride from the prince. He can pray, if he, virtuous and patient, wishes hastily to deliver your petition, so that I allow you to be living still, to enjoy the delights of good things, wealth unimpeded."

Then the guardian of the people was suddenly torn from   2666
sleep. He commanded his advisors be fetched to him; Abi-melech quickly told his men—afflicted with terror—the words of the ruler. The men dreaded after the dream the blow from the Lord's hand for that deed. The king himself then summoned Abraham to him with great haste. Then the powerful prince spoke:

"Man of the Hebrews, you will now explain to me in   2675

siððan þu usic under,   Abraham, þine
on þas eðel-turf   æhta læddest,
þæt þu me þus swiðe   searo renodest?
2680 Þu ell-þeodig   usic woldest
on þisse folc-sceare   facne besyrwan,
synnum besmitan,   sægdest wordum
þæt Sarra þin   sweostor wære
—lices mæge—   woldest laðlice
2685 þurh þæt wif on me   wrohte alecgean,
ormæte yfel.   We þe arlice
gefeormedon,   and þe freondlice
on þisse wer-þeode   wic getæhton,
land to lissum.   Þu us leanast nu,
2690 unfreondlice   fremena þancast!"

Abraham þa   andswarode:
"Ne dyde ic for facne   ne for feondscipe
ne for wihte þæs   ic þe wean uðe.
Ac ic me, gumena baldor,   guð-bordes sweng
2695 leod-magum feor   lare gebearh,
siððan me se halga   of hyrde frean,
mines fæder   fyrn alædde.
Ic fela siððan   folca gesohte,
wina uncuðra,   and þis wif mid me,
2700 freonda fea-sceaft.   Ic þæs færes a
on wenum sæt   hwonne me wraðra sum
ell-þeodigne   aldre beheowe,
se ðe him þas idese eft   agan wolde.
    "Forðon ic wig-smiðum   wordum sægde
2705 þæt Sarra min   sweostor wære,
æghwær eorðan   þær wit earda leas

speech, Abraham, when you led your possessions here to us, into this native soil, what I did that you should set such a trap for me? You, foreigner, evilly desired to trick us in this country, pollute us with sins, you said in words that Sarah was your sister—related in the flesh—you desired loathsomely to lay upon me a sin through the woman, an immeasurable evil. Honorably we cared for you, and in friendly manner offered you a dwelling place among this nation, land for enjoyment. Now you pay us back, you thank us for favors in an unfriendly way!"

Abraham then answered: "I did not do so for hostility, nor for enmity, nor that I might bring about misery for you in any way. But, prince of men, far from my kinsmen I protected myself against the clash of the shield by this counsel, after the holy one led me far from the household of the lord my father. Destitute of friends I and this woman with me have sought out many nations, unknown friends. I always remained in the expectation of the occasion when some foreign enemy would cut me off from life, one who would then wish to have this woman for himself.

"Therefore I told warriors in speech that Sarah was my sister, wherever on earth we two, deprived of a homeland,

XXXVIIII
2691

2704

mid wea-landum   winnan sceoldon.
Ic þæt ilce dreah   on þisse eðyl-tyrf,
siððan ic þina,   þeoden mæra,
2710   mund-byrde geceas.   Ne wæs me on mode cuð,
hwæðer on þyssum folce   Frean ælmihtiges
egesa wære,   þa ic her ærest com.
Forþon ic þegnum   þinum dyrnde
and sylfum þe   swiðost micle
2715   soðan spræce,   þæt me Sarran
bryde laste   bedd-reste gestah."
Þa ongan Abimæleh   Abraham swiðan
woruld-gestreonum   and him his wif ageaf.
    Sealde him to bote   þæs þe he his bryd genam
2720   gangende feoh   and glæd seolfor
and weorc-þeos.   Spræc þa wordum eac
to Abrahame   æðelinga helm:
"Wuna mid usic   and þe wic geceos
on þissum lande   þær þe leofost sie,
2725   eðel-stowe: þe ic agan sceal.
Wes us fæle freond,   we ðe feoh syllað!"
Cwæð þa eft raðe   oðre worde
to Sarrai   sinces brytta:
    "Ne þearf ðe on edwit   Abraham settan,
2730   ðin frea-drihten,   þæt þu flett-paðas,
mæg ælf-scieno,   mine træde,
ac him hyge-teonan   hwitan seolfre
deope bete.   Ne ceara incit duguða
of ðisse eðyl-tyrf   ellor secan,
2735   winas uncuðe,   ac wuniað her."
Abraham fremede   swa hine his aldor heht,
onfeng freondscipe   be frean hæse,

had to struggle against foreigners. I acted in the same way
on this native soil, great prince, after I chose your sovereign
protection. Nor was it known to me in my mind, when I
first came here, whether there was any fear of the almighty
Lord among this nation. Therefore, I kept secret the true
tale from your courtiers and most of all from you personally,
that Sarah has climbed into bed with me in the bride's way."
Then Abimelech began to enrich Abraham with worldly
treasures and gave his wife to him.

In compensation for seizing his wife he gave him grazing   2719
cattle and shining silver and servants. Then the protector of
princes spoke in words to Abraham: "Dwell with us and
choose for yourself a dwelling place in this land where it is
most dear to you: I must have you. Be a faithful friend to us,
and we will give you wealth!" Then after that, the giver of
treasure spoke another word to Sarah:

"Abraham your lord and master has no need to reproach   2729
you, elf-bright woman, that you trod my hallways, but I have
compensated him well for the intended slight with white
silver. Do not trouble yourselves to seek good things far
from this land among unknown friends, but remain here."
Abraham did as his leader commanded, accepted friendship,

lufum and lissum.　He wæs leof Gode.

Forðon he sibbe　gesælig dreah

2740　and his scippende　under sceade gefor,

hleow-feðrum þeaht,　her þenden lifde.

　Þa gien wæs yrre　God Abimelehe

for þære synne　þe he wið Sarrai

and wið Abrahame　ær gefremede,

2745　þa he gedælde　him deore twa,

wif and wæpned.　He þæs weorc gehleat,

frecne wite.　Ne meahton freo ne þeowe

heora brego-weardas　bearnum ecan

mon-rim mægeð,　ac him þæt metod forstod,

2750　oðþæt se halga　his hlaforde

Abraham ongan　arna biddan

ecne Drihten.　Him engla helm

getigðode,　tuddor-sped onleac

folc-cyninge　freora and þeowra,

2755　wera and wifa;　let weaxan eft

heora rim-getel　rodora waldend,

ead and æhta.　Ælmihtig wearð

milde on mode,　mon-cynnes weard,

Abimeleche,　swa hine Abraham bæd.

2760　　Þa com feran　Frea ælmihtig

to Sarrai,　swa he self gecwæð,

waldend user;　hæfde word-beot

leofum gelæsted　lifes Aldor

eaforan and idese.　Abrahame woc

2765　bearn of bryde,　þone brego engla

ær ðy mago-tudre　modor wære

eacen be eorle　Isaac nemde.

Hine Abraham on　mid his agene hand

love, and happiness by the lord's decree. He was dear to
God. Therefore he happily enjoyed peace and proceeded
under the shadow of his creator, protected by his wings,
while he lived here.

Then God was still angry with Abimelech because of the   2742
sin that he had committed earlier against Sarah and against
Abraham, when he separated them, the loving couple,
woman and man. He earned pain for that, a terrible punishment. Neither free woman nor slave could augment their
lords and masters, the count of the people, with children,
but the creator blocked that to them, until the holy Abraham began to pray to the eternal Lord for mercy for his lord.
The protector of angels acceded to the request, unlocked
the fertility of the free and enslaved, of men and women for
the people's king; the ruler of the skies let their population
grow again, prosperity and possessions. The almighty, the
guardian of humankind, became mild in mind toward Abimelech, as Abraham had asked him.

Then the Lord almighty came journeying to Sarah, as our   2760
ruler himself had said; the Lord of life had fulfilled his promise to the dear ones, the heir and bride. A child was born
to Abraham of the bride, whom the prince of angels had
named Isaac before the mother was pregnant with the noble offspring. After a week, Abraham set on him with his

beacen sette,   swa him bebead metod,
2770   wuldor-torht ymb wucan,   þæs þe hine on woruld
to mon-cynne   modor brohte.

XL

Cniht weox and þag,   swa him cynde wæron
æðele from yldrum.   Abraham hæfde
wintra hunteontig   þa him wif sunu
2775   on þanc gebær.   He þæs ðrage bad,
siððan him ærest   þurh his agen word
þone dæg-willan   Drihten bodode.
Þa seo wyrd gewearð   þæt þæt wif geseah
for Abrahame   Ismael plegan,
2780   ðær hie æt swæsendum   sæton bu tu,
halig on hige,   and heora hiwan eall,
druncon and drymdon.   Þa cwæð drihtlecu mæg,
bryd to beorne: "Forgif me, beaga weard,
min swæs frea,   hat siðian
2785   Agar ellor   and Ismael
lædan mid hie;   ne beoð we leng somed
willum minum,   gif ic wealdan mot.
Næfre Ismael   wið Isace,
wið min agen bearn   yrfe dæleð
2790   on laste þe,   þonne þu of lice
aldor asendest."
Þa wæs Abrahame
weorce on mode   þæt he on wræc drife
his selfes sunu,   þa com soð metod
freom on fultum,   wiste ferhð guman
2795   cearum on clommum.   Cyning engla spræc
to Abrahame,   ece Drihten:
"Læt þe aslupan   sorge of breostum,

192

own hand the radiant sign as God had commanded, on him whom the mother had brought into the world to mankind.

The boy grew and flourished, as nobility was natural in him according to his ancestry. Abraham was one hundred years old when his wife bore him a son with thanks. He had waited for a long time for that, since the Lord first promised him the joyful day by his own word. Then it happened that the woman saw Ishmael playing before Abraham, where they both sat at a meal, holy in mind, and all their household drank and rejoiced. Then said the noble kinswoman, the bride to the warrior: "Grant me this, guardian of the rings, my dear lord: command Hagar afterward to go elsewhere and lead Ishmael with her; by my wishes we will not be together long, if I may have control. Never should Ishmael share the inheritance with Isaac when you are gone, when you send your life from the body."

Then was Abraham tormented in mind because he drove his own son into exile. Then came the true God, strong in comfort. He knew the spirit of the man to be in the bonds of anxiety. The king of angels, the eternal Lord, spoke to Abraham: "Let the sorrow slip from your breast, conflict

2791

mod-gewinnan, and mægeð hire,
bryde þinre. Hat bu tu aweg
2800 Agar feran and Ismael,
cniht of cyððe. Ic his cynn gedo
brad and bresne bearna tudre,
wæstmum spedig, swa ic þe wordum gehet."
Þa se wer hyrde his waldende,
2805 draf of wicum dreorig-mod tu,
idese of earde and his agen bearn.

* * *

"Sweotol is and gesene þæt þe soð metod
on gesiððe is, swegles aldor,
se ðe sigor seleð snytrum mihtum
2810 and þin mod trymeð,
godcundum gifum. Forðon ðe giena speow,
þæs þu wið freond oððe feond fremman ongunne
wordum oððe dædum. Waldend scufeð,
Frea on forð-wegas folmum sinum
2815 willan þinne. Þæt is wide cuð
burh-sittendum. Ic þe bidde nu,
wine Ebrea, wordum minum,
þæt þu til-modig treowa selle,
wæra þina, þæt þu wille me
2820 wesan fæle freond fremena to leane,
þara þe ic to duguðum ðe gedon hæbbe,
siððan ðu fea-sceaft feorran come
on þas wer-þeode wræccan laste.
"Gyld me mid hyldo, þæt ic þe hneaw ne wæs
2825 landes and lissa. Wes þissum leodum nu
and mæg-burge minre arfæst,
gif þe alwalda, ure Drihten,

194

in the mind, and hear the woman, your bride. Command both Hagar and Ishmael to go away, the boy from home. I will make his nation broad and powerful in the progeny of its sons, prosperous in offspring, as I promised you by my words." Then the man obeyed his ruler, drove the downcast two from the dwellings, the lady and his own son from the court.

* * *

"It is clear and apparent that the true creator, the ruler of glory, is with you in companionship, he who gives you victory with wise power, and strengthens your mind with divine gifts. Therefore you have succeeded until now in what you have undertaken to do with friend or foe, in words or deeds. The ruler, the Lord, advances with his hands your desires on the way forward. That is widely known to the citizens. I ask you now by my words, lord of the Hebrews, that you, faithful one, give me a pledge, your covenant, that you will be a good friend to me in return for the good things, which I have done for your benefit, since you first came into this nation from afar, bereft on an exile's path. 2807

"Repay me with kindness, so that I will not be mean to you with land and pleasant things. Be law-abiding now among this people and great house of mine, if the ruler of 2824

scirian wille,   se ðe gesceapu healdeð,
þæt þu rand-wigum   rumor mote
2830 on ðisse folc-sceare   frætwa dælan,
modigra gestreon,   mearce settan."
Ða Abraham   Abimelehe
wære sealde   þæt he wolde swa.

XLI
　　Siððan wæs se eadega   eafora Þares
2835 in Filistea   folce eardfæst,
leod Ebrea   lange þrage,
fea-sceaft mid fremdum.   Him Frea engla
wic getæhte   þæt weras hatað
burh-sittende   Bersabea lond.
2840 Ðær se halga   heah-steap reced,
burh timbrede   and bearo sette,
weo-bedd worhte,   and his waldende
on þam glæd-stede   gild onsægde,
lac geneahe   þam þe lif forgeaf,
2845 gesæliglic   swegle under.
Þa þæs rinces   se rica ongan
cyning costigan,   cunnode georne
hwilc þæs æðelinges   ellen wære,
stiðum wordum   spræc him stefne to:
2850 　　"Gewit þu ofestlice,   Abraham, feran,
lastas lecgan   and þe læde mid
þin agen bearn.   Þu scealt Isaac me
onsecgan, sunu ðinne,   sylf to tibre.
Siððan þu gestigest   steape dune,
2855 hrincg þæs hean landes,   þe ic þe heonon getæce,
up þinum agnum fotum,   þær þu scealt ad gegærwan,
bæl-fyr bearne þinum,   and blotan sylf

all, our Lord, he who guides destinies, will decree that you might further deal out treasures, the wealth of the valiant, to warriors, and set up boundary markers in this country." Then Abraham gave Abimelech a pledge that he would do so.

Then the blessed son of Terah, the prince of the Hebrews, was resident among the nation of the Philistines for a long time, lonely among strangers. The Lord of angels informed him of a dwelling which those men, the citizens, call the land of Beer-sheba. There the holy one built a steep hall and a city, and established a grove, made an altar, and in that bright place offered a gift to his ruler, an abundant oblation to him who had given him life, blessedly under the sky. Then the mighty king began to tempt the warrior, eagerly probed what the prince's courage was, spoke hard words to him in his voice:

"Abraham, depart quickly, make tracks and take your own son with you. You yourself shall offer your son Isaac to me as a sacrifice. After you have climbed up the high hill on your own feet, the circle of the high land, which I will show you from here, there you shall prepare a pyre, a funeral fire for your son, and personally sacrifice your son with the sword's

2850

sunu mid sweordes ecge,   and þonne sweartan lige
leofes lic forbærnan   and me lac bebeodan."
2860   Ne forsæt he þy siðe,   ac sona ongann
fysan to fore.   Him wæs Frean engla
word ondrysne,   and his waldende leof.
Þa se eadga   Abraham sine
niht-reste ofgeaf.   Nalles nergendes
2865   hæse wiðhogode,   ac hine se halga wer
gyrde grægan sweorde,   cyðde þæt him gasta weardes
egesa on breostum wunode.   Ongan þa his esolas bætan
gamol-ferhð goldes brytta,   heht hine geonge twegen
men mid siðian.   Mæg wæs his agen þridda
2870   and he feorða sylf.   Þa he fus gewat
from his agenum hofe   Isaac lædan,
bearn unweaxen,   swa him bebead metod.
Efste þa swiðe   and onette
forð fold-wege,   swa him Frea tæhte
2875   wegas ofer westen,   oðþæt wuldor-torht,
dæges þriddan up   ofer deop wæter
ord aræmde.   Þa se eadega wer
geseah hlifigan   hea dune
swa him sægde ær   swegles aldor.
2880   Ða Abraham spræc   to his ombihtum:
"Rincas mine,   restað incit
her on þissum wicum.   Wit eft cumað,
siððan wit ærende   uncer twega
gast-cyninge   agifen habbað."
2885   Gewat him þa se æðeling   and his agen sunu
to þæs gemearces   þe him metod tæhte,
wadan ofer wealdas.   Wudu bær sunu,
fæder fyr and sweord.   Ða þæs fricgean ongann

edge, and then incinerate his dear body in the dark flame, and offer the oblation to me."

He did not delay the venture, but immediately began to hasten to the journey. The word of the Lord of angels was awesome to him, and he dear to his ruler. Then the blessed Abraham left his night's rest. He did not resist the savior's command at all, but the holy man girded himself with the gray sword, made known that the fear of the guardian of spirits dwelled within his breast. The gray-haired giver of gold began to harness his donkeys, commanded two young men to journey with him. His own kinsman was the third, and he himself the fourth. Then he quickly set out from his own homestead leading Isaac, the ungrown boy, as the creator had commanded him. 2860

He hurried greatly then, and hastened forward on the earthen road, as the Lord showed him the pathways across the wilderness, until the gloriously bright beginning of the third day rose up over the deep water. Then the blessed man saw the high hill towering, as the Lord of the sky had told him earlier. Then Abraham spoke to his servants: "My men, you two rest here in this place. We two will come back, after we have made our errand to the king of spirits." 2873

Then the prince and his own son went to the location that the creator showed him, walking through the woods. The son bore lumber, the father fire and sword. Then the 2885

wer wintrum geong   wordum Abraham:
2890 "Wit her fyr and sweord,   frea min, habbað—
hwær is þæt tiber   þæt þu torht Gode
to þam bryne-gielde   bringan þencest?"
Abraham maðelode   (hæfde on an gehogod
þæt he gedæde   swa hine Drihten het):
2895 "Him þæt soð-cyning   sylfa findeð,
mon-cynnes weard,   swa him gemet þinceð."

      Gestah þa stið-hydig   steape dune
up mid his eaforan,   swa him se eca bebead,
þæt he on hrofe gestod   hean landes
2900 on þære stowe   þe him se stranga to,
wærfæst metod   wordum tæhte.
Ongan þa ad hladan,   æled weccan,
and gefeterode   fet and honda
bearne sinum   and þa on bæl ahof
2905 Isaac geongne,   and þa ædre gegrap
sweord be gehiltum   —wolde his sunu cwellan
folmum sinum,   fyre sencan
mæges dreore.   Þa metodes ðegn,
ufan engla sum,   Abraham hlude
2910 stefne cygde.   He stille gebad
ares spræce   and þam engle oncwæð.
Him þa ofstum to   ufan of roderum
wuldor-gast Godes   wordum mælde:
      "Abraham leofa,   ne sleah þin agen bearn,
2915 ac þu cwicne abregd   cniht of ade,
eaforan þinne!   Him an wuldres God!
Mago Ebrea,   þu medum scealt
þurh þæs halgan hand,   heofon-cyninges,
soðum sigor-leanum   selfa onfon,

man young in years began to ask Abraham in speech: "My lord, we two have here fire and sword—where is the bright sacrifice that you mean to bring as a burnt offering for God?" Abraham spoke formally (he had resolved that he should do as the Lord commanded him): "The king of truth, the guardian of mankind, will himself find it, as it seems appropriate to him."

Resolute, he then climbed up the steep hill with his heir,   2897
as the eternal one commanded him, until he stood on the summit of the high land in the place that the strong one, the covenant-faithful creator, showed him in words. He began then to load up the pyre, give life to the fire, and fettered the feet and hands of his son, and then lifted young Isaac onto the blaze, and then quickly grabbed the sword by the hilt— he intended to kill his son with his own hands, plunge his kinsman's gore in the fire. Then the creator's officer, a certain angel from above, cried out to Abraham in loud voice. Motionless he awaited the messenger's speech and answered the angel. Then the glory-spirit of God quickly spoke to him from above, in words from the skies:

"Dear Abraham, do not slay your own child, but pull the   2914
boy, your heir, living from the fire! The God of glory is pleased with him! Prince of the Hebrews, by the holy hand of the king of heaven you personally shall receive rewards,

2920 gin-fæstum gifum.   Þe wile gasta weard
lissum gyldan   þæt þe wæs leofra his
sibb and hyldo   þonne þin sylfes bearn."
    Ad stod onæled.   Hæfde Abrahame
metod mon-cynnes,   mæge Lothes,
2925 breost geblissad,   þa he him his bearn forgeaf,
Isaac cwicne.   Ða se eadega bewlat,
rinc ofer exle,   and him þær rom geseah
unfeor þanon   ænne standan,
broðor Arones,   brembrum fæstne.
2930 Þone Abraham genam   and hine on ad ahof
ofestum miclum   for his agen bearn.
    Abrægd þa mid þy bille,   bryne-gield onhread,
reccendne weg   rommes blode,
onbleot þæt lac Gode,   sægde leana þanc
2935 and ealra þara   þe he him ær and sið,
gifena Drihten,   forgifen hæfde.

true spoils of victory, abundant gifts. The guardian of spirits will give you delights, because his peace and favor were dearer to you than your own son."

The fire continued to burn. The creator of humankind   2923 had delighted the heart of Abraham, Lot's kinsman, when he returned to him his son, the living Isaac. Then the blessed man, Haran's brother, glanced over his shoulder, and saw there a ram not far from him, standing alone, stuck in brambles. Abraham took it and lifted it onto the fire with great zeal, in place of his own son. Then he moved quickly with the sword, decorated the burnt offering, the smoking altar with the ram's blood, offered that oblation to God, said thanks for the rewards and all the gifts that the Lord had given him, both early and late.

EXODUS

Hwæt! We feor and neah   gefrigen habað
ofer middan-geard   Moyses domas,
wræclico word-riht,   wera cneorissum,
in up-rodor   eadigra gehwam
5   æfter bealu-siðe   bote lifes,
lifigendra gehwam   langsumne ræd,
hæleðum secgan.   Gehyre se ðe wille!
Þone on westenne   weroda Drihten,
soðfæst cyning,   mid his sylfes miht
10   gewyrðode,   and him wundra fela,
ece alwalda,   in æht forgeaf.
He wæs leof Gode,   leoda aldor,
horsc and hreðer-gleaw,   herges wisa,
freom folc-toga.   Faraones cyn,
15   Godes andsacan,   gyrd-wite band,
þær him gesealde   sigora waldend,
modgum mago-ræswan,   his maga feorh,
onwist eðles,   Abrahames sunum.
Heah wæs þæt hand-lean   and him hold Frea,
20   gesealde wæpna geweald   wið wraðra gryre,
ofercom mid þy campe   cneo-maga fela,
feonda folc-riht.
            Ða wæs forma sið
þæt hine weroda God   wordum nægde,

Listen! Far and near throughout the middle-earth we
have heard tell of the judgments of Moses, and of promises
in exile made to generations of men, of the reward of heavenly life for each of the blessed after the dangerous journey,
of everlasting benefit for each living person. He who will, let
him listen! The Lord of the hosts of heaven, the king firm
in truth, exalted him in the desert by his own authority, the
eternal ruler of all gave wondrous powers into his possession.

He was beloved of God, a gifted and wise leader of his   12
people, commander of the army and a bold general. He
humbled Pharaoh's nation, that enemy of God, by punishment with the rod, when the Lord of victories guaranteed it
to him, their brave teacher, the life of his compatriots, and
to the sons of Abraham a dwelling in a homeland. Divine
was the retribution of his hand, and steadfast his Lord; he
made him matchless in arms against the fury of angry foes,
and so wasted in war the might of many nations, his enemies.

That was the first time that the God of hosts spoke in   22

þær he him gesægde   soð-wundra fela—
25   hu þas woruld worhte   witig Drihten,
eorðan ymbhwyrft   and up-rodor,
gesette sige-rice,   and his sylfes naman,
ðone yldo bearn   ær ne cuðon,
frod fædera cyn,   þeah hie fela wiston.
30   Hæfde he þa geswiðed   soðum cræftum
and gewurðodne   werodes aldor,
Faraones feond,   on forð-wegas.
Þa wæs ingere   ealdum witum
deaðe gedrenced   driht-folca mæst,
35   hord-wearda hryre   —heaf wæs geniwad—
swæfon sele-dreamas   since berofene.
    Hæfde man-sceaðan   æt middere niht
frecne gefylled,   frum-bearna fela,
abrocene burh-weardas.   Bana wide scrað,
40   lað leod-hata,   land ðrysmyde
deadra hræwum;   dugoð forð gewat,
wop wæs wide,   woruld-dreama lyt.
Wæron hleahtor-smiðum   handa belocene,
alyfed lað-sið   leode gretan,
45   folc ferende.   Feond wæs bereafod,
hergas on helle   —heofon þider becom—
druron deofol-gyld.   Dæg wæs mære
ofer middan-geard   þa seo mengeo for.
Swa þæs fæsten dreah   fela missera,
50   eald-werige,   Egypta folc,
þæs þe hie wide-ferð   wyrnan þohton
Moyses magum,   (gif hie Metod lete)
on langne lust   leofes siðes.

words to him, when he told him many a wondrous truth—
how the wise Lord had created this world, the expanse of
the earth and the sky above, had founded the victorious nation, and told him his own name, which the sons of men, the
wise line of patriarchs had not known, though they knew
much. After that he strengthened and lifted up with proper
powers this leader of the host, Pharaoh's foe, on the on-
ward paths. Then a vast number of people, of the treasure-
watchers, was completely drowned in destruction and death
by ancient punishments—the lament was renewed—hall-
joys slept, deprived of wealth.

In the middle of the night he cruelly struck down the 37
wicked oppressors, the many firstborn sons, smashed the
defenders of the city. A destroyer flew far, a deadly enemy
to all, the land stank with the corpses of the dead; the company set out, there was weeping all over, and little worldly
joy. The hands of the mockers were paralyzed, the folk, the
emigrant nation, were permitted to begin the resented journey. The enemy was despoiled, and his hell-hordes—heaven
came down—the idols fell. That day was famous across the
earth when the multitude set out. So the Egyptian nation,
accursed so long, endured famine for many a season, because
they had wished (if God would have allowed it) to frustrate
the people of Moses in their long-lasting desire for the beloved journey.

Fyrd wæs gefysed,   from se ðe lædde,
55 modig mago-ræswa,   mæg-burh heora.
Oferfor he mid þy folce   fæstena worn,
land and leod-weard   laðra manna,
enge an-paðas,   uncuð gelad,
oðþæt hie on guð-myrce   gearwe bæron—
60 wæron land heora   lyft-helme beþeaht.
Mearc-hofu mor-heald   Moyses ofer þa,
fela meoringa,   fyrde gelædde.

XLIII

Heht þa ymb twa niht   tirfæste hæleð,
siððan hie feondum   oðfaren hæfdon,
65 ymbwicigean   werodes bearhtme
mid ælfere   Æthanes byrig,
mægnes mæste   mearc-landum on.
Nearwe genyddon   on norð-wegas—
wiston him be suðan   Sigel-wara land,
70 forbærned burh-hleoðu,   brune leode,
hatum heofon-colum.   Þær halig God
wið fær-bryne   folc gescylde—
bælce oferbrædde   byrnendne heofon,
halgan nette   hat-wendne lyft.
75 Hæfde weder-wolcen   widum fæðmum
eorðan and up-rodor   efne gedæled,
lædde leod-werod,   lig-fyr adranc,
hate heofon-torht.   Hæleð wafedon,
drihta gedrymost.   Dæg-scealdes hleo
80 wand ofer wolcnum;   hæfde witig God
sunnan sið-fæt   segle ofertolden,
swa þa mæst-rapas   men ne cuðon,
ne ða segl-rode   geseon meahton,

The army was prepared, fearless was the one who led   54
their people, a brave guide. With that tribe he ranged over
many natural strongholds, the land and home of hostile peoples, narrow gorges and unknown paths, until they came
carrying weapons among warlike frontier tribes — their lands
were cloaked in covering cloud. Moses led that army past
desert dwellings on sloping mountains, and many an ob-
stacle.

Two days after they had escaped their enemies the man   63
sure of glory commanded the setting up of camp near the
city of Etham, with the clamor of the army, and the whole
procession, a massive force, at the borderlands. Danger had
forced them onto a northward track—they knew that the
Ethiopians' land was to their south, lofty mountains and
brown people, scorched by the hot embers of heaven. Holy
God shielded the people there against that blasting fire — he
covered the burning heaven with a roof and the broiling sky
with a holy screen.

A billowing cloud with a broad embrace evenly divided   75
earth and sky, directed the mass of people, quenched
the flaming fire, blazing heaven-bright. The heroes were
amazed, the troop most delighted. The day-shield's shelter
moved across the clouds; the wise God had veiled the sun's

eorð-buende   ealle cræfte,
85 hu afæstnod wæs   feld-husa mæst,
siððan he mid wuldre   geweorðode
þeoden-holde.   Þa wæs þridda wic
folce to frofre.   Fyrd eall geseah
hu þær hlifedon   halige seglas,
90 lyft-wundor leoht;   leode ongeton,
dugoð Israhela,   þæt þær Drihten cwom
weroda Drihten   wic-steal metan.

Him beforan foran   fyr and wolcen
in beorht-rodor,   beamas twegen,
95 þara æghwæðer   efn-gedælde
heah-þegnunga   haliges gastes,
deor-modra sið   dagum and nihtum.
Þa ic on morgen gefrægn   modes rofan
hebban here-byman   hludan stefnum,
100 wuldres woman.   Werod eall aras,
modigra mægen,   swa him Moyses bebead,
mære mago-ræswa,   metodes folce,
fus fyrd-getrum.   Forð gesawon
lifes latþeow   lif-weg metan;
105 segl siðe weold,   sæ-men æfter
foron flod-wege.   Folc wæs on salum,
hlud herges cyrm.   Heofon-beacen astah
æfena gehwam,   oðer wundor,
syllic æfter sunnan   setl-rade beheold,
110 ofer leod-werum   lige scinan,
byrnende beam.   Blace stodon
ofer sceotendum   scire leoman;
scinon scyld-hreoðan,   sceado swiðredon,
neowle niht-scuwan   neah ne mihton

course with a sail, though in a way that people were unaware of mast-ropes, nor could the earth-dwellers, for all their skill, see how the sailyards, the mightiest tent, was tied, when he gloriously honored the loyal nation. That then was the third camp to comfort the folk. The whole army saw how the holy sails towered high, the wondrously lofty light; the people understood, Israel's old guard, that the Lord had arrived there, the Lord of hosts to set up camp.

Fire and cloud went before them in the bright-sky, the   93
two beams, each one evenly divided with the other by day and by night the brave-hearts' journey, those high-servants of the Holy Spirit. I have heard that then in the morning the courageous ones blew on their bugles with loud voice, a glorious roar. The whole host rose up, mighty in their courage, as Moses commanded them, the famous counselor, the creator's folk, the eager band of warriors. They saw life's general mark out the life-way ahead; the sail steered the journey, the sailors followed the current. The folk were delighted, loud the army's tumult. The heaven-beacon rose up each evening, the second wonder, kept its course happy behind the sun, shining over the people with flame, the burning beam. The blinding rays stood radiant over the archers; the shield covers shone, shadows diminished, the deep night-

115 heolstor ahydan;   heofon-candel barn.

　Niwe niht-weard　nyde sceolde
wician ofer weredum,　þy læs him westen-gryre,
har hæð-broga,　holmegum wederum
on fer-clamme　ferhð getwæfde.

120 Hæfde fore-genga　fyrene loccas,
blace beamas;　bell-egsan hweop
in þam here-þreate,　hatan lige,
þæt he on westenne　werod forbærnde,
nymðe hie mod-hwate　Moyses hyrde.

125 　Scean scir werod,　scyldas lixton.
Gesawon rand-wigan　rihte stræte,
segn ofer sweoton,　oðþæt sæ-fæsten
landes æt ende　leod-mægne forstod,
fus on forð-weg.　Fyrd-wic aras;

130 wyrpton hie werige,　wiste genægdon
modige mete-þegnas,　hyra mægen beton.
Bræddon æfter beorgum,　siððan byme sang,
flotan feld-husum.　Þa wæs feorðe wic,
rand-wigena ræst,　be þan Readan Sæ.

XLIIII
135 　Ðær on fyrd hyra　fær-spell becwom:
oht inlende.　Egsan stodan,
wæl-gryre weroda.　Wræc-mon gebad
laðne last-weard,　se ðe him lange ær
eðelleasum　on-nied gescraf,

140 wean witum fæst.　Wære ne gymdon,
ðeah þe se yldra cyning　ær ge . . .

　　　* * *

XLV
　Þa wearð yrfe-weard　in-gefolca,
manna æfter maðmum,　þæt he swa miceles geðah.

214

shades could not hide in the darkness; the heaven-candle burned.

A new night-watchman was needed to watch over 116 the troops, so that the wasteland-fear, the hoary heath-terror, should not put an end to life with ocean storms' sudden grasp. This scout had fiery locks, and lustrous beams of light; it threatened that army-throng with fire-terror, with hot flame so that in the wasteland it could incinerate the company, unless they, keen-spirited, obeyed Moses.

The troop shone bright, the shields glistened. The shield- 125 warriors saw the right highway, the standard over the troop, until the sea-ramparts at land's edge hindered the multitude, eager for the journey hence. Camp was set up; the weary ones revived, the victuallers provided food for the brave, restored their power. When the trumpet sang the sailors pitched campaign-houses on the hills. That then was the fourth camp, shield-warriors' rest, by the Red Sea.

XLIIII

There among their army a rumor arrived: pursuit from 135 inland. Panic spread, the host's terror of death. The exile awaited the terrible tracker, he who for some time before had enslaved those without a homeland, detained them in miserable suffering. They cared not for a treaty, even though their ancient king had previously given . . .

* * *

XLV

Then [Joseph] became protector of that native people's 142 inheritance, over the people's treasures, so that he flour-

Ealles þæs forgeton   siððan grame wurdon
145 Egypta cyn   ymb antwigða.
Heo his mæg-winum   morðor fremedon,
wroht berenedon,   wære fræton.
Wæron heaðo-wylmas   heortan getenge,
miht-mod wera   —manum treowum—
150 woldon hie þæt feorh-lean   facne gyldan,
þætte hie þæt dæg-weorc   dreore gebohte,
Moyses leode,   þær him mihtig God
on ðam spild-siðe   spede forgefe.

Þa him eorla mod   ortrywe wearð
155 siððan hie gesawon   of suð-wegum
fyrd Faraonis   forð ongangan,
eofer-holt wegan,   eored lixan,
garas trymedon,   guð hwearfode,
blicon bord-hreoðan,   byman sungon,
160 þufas þunian,   þeod mearc tredan,
on hwæl   . . .
Hreopon here-fugolas,   hilde grædige,
deawig-feðere   ofer driht-neum,
wonn wæl-ceasega.   Wulfas sungon
165 atol æfen-leoð   ætes on wenan,
car-leasan deor,   cwyld-rof beodan
on laðra last   leod-mægnes fyl.
Hreopon mearc-weardas   middum nihtum,
fleah fæge gast,   folc wæs genæged.

170   Hwilum of þam werode   wlance þegnas
mæton mil-paðas   meara bogum.
Him þær segn-cyning   wið þone segn foran,
manna þengel,   mearc-þreate rad.
Guð-weard gumena   grim-helm gespeon,

ished. The Egyptians forgot all that, when they grew angry concerning their lingering. Then they committed murder against his kinsmen, did them injury, devoured the agreement. The surges of hate, the passions of men, were tormenting their hearts—in breach of trust—they wished to return a life-debt with treachery, so that Moses's people would pay for that day's work in blood if mighty God would give the enemy success on their slaughter-journey.

Then the mind of the men turned to mistrust, when they saw on the south-way the army of Pharaoh marching forward, brandishing boar-spears, their riders radiant, lances were lifted, battle rounded on them, shields shimmered, bugles sang, banners unfurled, the nation marched on its border, on slaughter . . . A battle-fowl screeched, greedy for the skirmish, dewy-feathered, the dark slaughter-picker, over the dead warriors. Wolves sang a hideous evensong in expectation of eating, uncaring beasts, slaughter-bold, waited in the train of the enemies, the fall of the mighty nation. These border-guards howled in the midnights, the fated spirit flew, the folk was brought low.

At times from the troop proud noblemen planned the lines of battle on horseback. There in front went the flag-king with the banner, the prince of men rode with the vanguard. The warriors' war-guardian fastened his battle-

154

170

175   cyning cin-berge   —cumbol lixton—
        wiges on wenum;   wæl-hlencan sceoc.
        Het his here-ciste   healdan georne
        fæst fyrd-getrum.   Freond onsegon
        laðum eagan   land-manna cyme.
180   Ymb hine wægon   wigend unforhte,
        hare heoru-wulfas   hilde gretton,
        þurstige þræc-wiges,   þeoden-holde.
        Hæfde him alesen   leoda dugeðe
        tir-eadigra   twa þusendo,
185   þæt wæron cyningas   and cneow-magas
        on þæt ealde riht,   æðelum deore;
        forðon anra gehwilc   ut alædde
        wæpned-cynnes,   wigan æghwilcne
        þara þe he on ðam fyrste   findan mihte.
190   Wæron in-gemen   ealle ætgædere,
        cyningas on corðre.   Cuð oft gebad
        horn on heape   to hwæs hægsteald-men,
        guð-þreat gumena,   gearwe bæron.
        Swa þær eorp werod,   ecan læddon,
195   lað æfter laðum,   leod-mægnes worn,
        þusend-mælum;   þider wæron fuse.
        Hæfdon hie gemynted   to þam mægen-heapum
        to þam ær-dæge   Israhela cynn
        billum abreotan   on hyra broðor-gyld.
200   Forþon wæs in wicum   wop up ahafen,
        atol æfen-leoð,   egesan stodon
        —weredon wæl-net—   þa se woma cwom.
        Flugon frecne spel.   Feond wæs an-mod,
        werud wæs wig-blac—   oðþæt wlance forsceaf
205   mihtig engel,   se ða menigeo beheold

helmet, the king his chin-guard—the standards shone—
waiting for war; the chain-mail shook. He commanded his
select troop eagerly to hold their formation fast. The friends
looked with hateful eyes on the approach of the land-men.
Around him moved fearless fighters, hoary battle-wolves
welcomed war, loyal to the leader, thirsty for violent battle.

He himself had chosen two thousand of the battle- 183
glorious from the nobility of the people, who were kings and
near kinsmen in the ancient order, bold in their bloodlines;
consequently, each one of those men led out every warrior
he could find at the time. The countrymen were all together,
kings in the cohort. The familiar trumpets among the troop
constantly made known where the young men, the battalion
of warriors, should carry equipment. So the dark division
led reinforcements there, foe after foe, the nation's mighty
multitude by the thousand; they were keen to get there.
They had planned at dawn to exterminate the nation of Israel with swords in a great army as payback for their brothers.

Therefore in the camps a cry was raised up, a terrible 200
evensong, panic spread—slaughter-nets trapped them—
when the tumult came. Bold speeches flew away. The enemy
was single-minded, the troop was polished for battle—until
a mighty angel thrust in before the proud ones, he protected

þæt þær gelaðe mid him   leng ne mihton
geseon tosomne.   Sið wæs gedæled.
Hæfde nyd-fara   niht-langne fyrst,
þeah ðe him on healfa gehwam   hettend seomedon,
210   mægen oððe mere-stream;   nahton maran hwyrft.
Wæron orwenan   eðel-rihtes,
sæton æfter beorgum   in blacum reafum,
wean on wenum.   Wæccende bad
eall seo sib-gedriht   somod ætgædere
215   maran mægenes,   oð Moyses bebead
eorlas on uht-tid   ærnum bemum
folc somnigean,   frecan arisan,
habban heora hlencan,   hycgan on ellen,
beran beorht searo,   beacnum cigean
220   sweot sande near.   Snelle gemundon
weardas wig-leoð   —werod wæs gefysed—
brudon ofer burgum,   (byman gehyrdon),
flotan feld-husum   —fyrd wæs on ofste.

Siððan hie getealdon   wið þam teon-hete
225   on þam forð-herge   feðan twelfe
mode-rofra—   mægen wæs onhrered.
Wæs on anra gehwam   æðelan cynnes
alesen under lindum   leoda duguðe
on folc-getæl   fiftig cista;
230   hæfde cista gehwilc   cuðes werodes
gar-berendra,   guð-fremmendra,
X hund geteled,   tir-eadigra.
Þæt wæs wiglic werod.   Wace ne gretton
in þæt rinc-getæl   ræswan herges,
235   þa þe for geoguðe   gyt ne mihton
under bord-hreoðan   breost-net wera

the multitude so that the enemy could no longer see them together there. The advance was divided. The refugees had a nightlong rest, though on either side an enemy was waiting for them, the army or the sea-flood; they had no room to maneuver.

They were despairing of the promised homeland, sat 211 across the slopes, in worn-out rags, in expectation of sorrow. The band of brothers waited, watching all together, for the more powerful army, until Moses commanded the men in the dawning light to summon the nation with their brass bugles, the men to rise up, to put on their mail-coats, to consider their courage, to bear their bright war-gear, to summon the troop to the standards near the sand. Quickly the guards heeded the war-song—the troop was on the move—the sailors folded the campaign tents on the hills (they heard the trumpet)—the army was in haste.

Against the hateful malice they later marshaled the van- 224 guard into twelve divisions of the brave hearted—strength was stirred up. From each one was chosen fifty of the best under the shield of that noble nation from among the populace, from the old guard of the people; each of these had a thousand all told of the best of the experienced troop of spear-bearers, of war-makers, of the triumphant. That was a warlike host. The army's commanders did not welcome the weak into that muster, those who because of their youth could not yet protect with their hands the breast-net of men under the shield-wall against the hostile enemy, nor had yet

wið flane feond　folmum werigean,
ne him bealu-benne　gebiden hæfdon
ofer linde lærig,　lic-wunde swor,
240　gylp-plegan gares.
　　　　　　　　　　Gamele ne moston,
hare heaðo-rincas,　hilde onþeon,
gif him mod-heapum　mægen swiðrade,
ac hie be wæstmum　on wig curon,
hu in leodscipe　læstan wolde
245　mod mid aran,　eac þan mægnes cræft,
gar-beames feng.
Þa wæs hand-rofra　here ætgædere,
fus forð-wegas.　Fana up gerad,
beama beorhtost;　bidon ealle þa gen
250　hwonne sið-boda　sæ-streamum neah
leoht ofer lindum　lyft-edoras bræc.

XLVI
　　Ahleop þa for hæleðum　hilde-calla,
bald beadu-hata,　bord up ahof,
heht þa folc-togan　fyrde gestillan,
255　þenden modiges meðel　monige gehyrdon.
Wolde reordigean　rices hyrde
ofer here-ciste　halgan stefne;
werodes wisa　wurð-myndum spræc:
"Ne beoð ge þy forhtran,　þeah þe Faraon brohte
260　sweord-wigendra　side hergas,
eorla unrim.　Him eallum wile
mihtig Drihten　þurh mine hand
to dæge þissum　dæd-lean gyfan,
þæt hie lifigende　leng ne moton
265　ægnian mid yrmðum　Israhela cyn.

experienced a grievous wound across the shield's rim, the
scar of a flesh-wound, in a contest of the spear.

The old gray-haired warriors could not be useful in battle,   ²⁴⁰
if in the melee their strength weakened, but they chose the
war-group for its stature, how courage with grace would last
among the company, also for the skill of strength in holding
a spear. Then the hand-strong army was assembled, eager
for engagements. The standard rode high, the brightest of
banners; they all waited yet for the moment when the journey's herald near the sea currents, the light broke through
the sky-enclosures across the shields.

                                                                                  ^{XLVI}
Then a messenger leapt up before the heroes, the bold   ²⁵²
battle-herald lifted his shield high, commanded the officers
to silence the army while the assembly listened to the brave
one's speech. The kingdom's shepherd wished to make a
speech with holy voice before the elite troop; the army's
guide spoke honorably: "Do not be the more afraid, though
Pharaoh should bring vast armies of sword warriors, innumerable fighters. On this day the mighty Lord will give them
their wages by my hand, so that they will not be able to survive longer to scourge the nation of Israel with miseries.

"Ne willað eow andrædan   deade feðan,
fæge ferhð-locan—   fyrst is æt ende
lænes lifes.   Eow is lar Godes
abroden of breostum.   Ic on beteran ræd,
270 þæt ge gewurðien   wuldres aldor,
and eow lif-frean   lissa bidde,
sigora gesynto,   þær ge siðien.
Þis is se ecea   Abrahames God,
frum-sceafta frea,   se ðas fyrd wereð,
275 modig and mægen-rof,   mid þære miclan hand."
Hof ða for hergum   hlude stefne
lifigendra þeoden,   þa he to leodum spræc:
"Hwæt, ge nu eagum to   on lociað,
folca leofost,   fær-wundra sum,
280 hu ic sylfa sloh   and þeos swiðre hand
grene tacne   gar-secges deop.

"Yð up færeð,   ofstum wyrceð
wæter on wealfæsten.   Wegas syndon dryge,
haswe here-stræta,   holm gerymed,
285 ealde staðolas,   þa ic ær ne gefrægn
ofer middan-geard   men geferan,
fage feldas,   þa forð heonon
in ece tid   yðe þeahton,
sælde sæ-grundas.   Suð-wind fornam
290 bæð-weges blæst,   brim is areafod,
sand sæ-cir spaw.   Ic wat soð gere
þæt eow mihtig God   miltse gecyðde,
eorlas ær-glade.   Ofest is selost
þæt ge of feonda   fæðme weorðen,
295 nu se agend   up arærde
reade streamas   in rand-gebeorh.

"You will not dread dead infantry, doomed bodies — the   266
time of their borrowed life is at an end. God's counsel has
been plucked from your breasts. I offer you better advice,
that you should honor the prince of glory, and pray for grace
from the Lord of life, for health in victories, when you advance. This is the eternal God of Abraham, Lord of created
things, who will protect this army, brave and imperious, with
that great hand." Before the armies the prince of the living raised up a loud voice when he spoke to the people: "Indeed, most beloved of nations, you will now behold an in-
stant miracle with your eyes, how I myself and this right
hand have struck the deep ocean with a green emblem.

"The wave is traveling upward, quickly working the wa-   282
ter into a rampart. The pathways are dry, the gray army-
highways, the sea is cleared away, the ancient foundations,
which as far as I know, people over earth have never crossed
before, the decorated plains, the confined sea-beds, which
hereafter the waves will overspread into eternity. The south
wind has taken away the bath-way's blast, the sea is drawn
back, the undertow has spewed sand. I very well know the
truth, that mighty God has made known mercy to you, men
who once were happy. Speed is best, so that you get out of
the enemies' grasp, now that the owner has lifted up the red
streams as a protecting shield. The outer walls are neatly

Syndon þa fore-weallas   fægre gestepte,
wrætlicu wæg-faru,   oð wolcna hrof."
   Æfter þam wordum   werod eall aras,
300 modigra mægen.   Mere stille bad.
Hofon here-cyste   hwite linde,
segnas on sande.   Sæ-weall astah,
uplang gestod   wið Israhelum
an-dægne fyrst.   Wæs seo eorla gedriht
305 anes modes,
fæstum fæðmum   freoðo-wære heold.
Nalles hige gehyrdon   haliges lare,
siððan leofes leoþ   læste near
sweg swiðrode   and sances bland.
310   Þa þæt feorðe cyn   fyrmest eode,
wod on wæg-stream,   wigan on heape,
ofer grenne grund;   Iudisc feða
on onette   uncuð gelad
for his mæg-winum.   Swa him mihtig God
315 þæs dæg-weorces   deop lean forgeald,
siððan him gesælde   sigor-worca hreð,
þæt he ealdordom   agan sceolde
ofer cyne-ricu,   cneow-maga blæd.

XLVII

   Hæfdon him to segne,   þa hie on sund stigon,
320 ofer bord-hreoðan   beacen aræred
in þam gar-heape,   gyldenne leon—
driht-folca mæst,   deora cenost.
Be þam here-wisan   hynðo ne woldon
be him lifigendum   lange þolian,
325 þonne hie to guðe   gar-wudu rærdon
ðeoda ænigre.   Þracu wæs on ore,

terraced, an ingenious thoroughfare up to the roof of the clouds."

After these words the troop all rose up, the force of brave ones. The sea remained still. The elite troop lifted the white shields, their standards on the sand. The seawall ascended, stood upright for the Israelites for the space of a day. The company of men was of one mind, kept the covenant firm in their hearts. Not at all did they despise the teaching of the holy one, when closer behind the hymn of life, the sound and blending of song, grew stronger.   299

Then the fourth tribe went foremost, walked into the wave-stream, warriors in a group, across the green ground; a soldier of Judah hastened onto the unknown path before his tribesmen. So mighty God gave him a deep reward for that day's work, when the glory of victorious works was given to him, so that he should have dominion over kingdoms, an abundance of descendants.   310

They had as their standard, when they climbed onto the sea, a beacon raised up over the shield formation, a golden lion among the stand of spears — the greatest of lordly peoples, the keenest of wild beasts. Beside that battle-leader they did not wish to endure humiliation for themselves for a long time by surviving, when they lifted spear-shafts in war against any nation. There was a surge in the vanguard,   XLVII
319

heard hand-plega,   hæg-steald modige
wæpna wæl-slihtes,   wigend unforhte,
bil-swaðu blodige,   beadu-mægnes ræs,
330   grim-helma gegrind,   þær Iudas for.
   Æfter þære fyrde   flota modgade,
Rubenes sunu.   Randas bæron
sæ-wicingas   ofer sealtne mersc,
manna menio;   micel an-getrum
335   eode unforht.   He his ealdordom
synnum aswefede,   þæt he siðor for
on leofes last.   Him on leod-sceare
frum-bearnes riht   freo-broðor oðþah,
ead and æðelo;   he wæs gearu swa þeah.
340   Þær forð æfter him   folca þryðum
sunu Simeones   sweotum comon;
þridde þeod-mægen   —þufas wundon
ofer gar-fare—   guð-cyste onþrang
deawig sceaftum.   Dæg-woma becwom
345   ofer gar-secge,   Godes beacna sum,
morgen mære-torht;   mægen forð gewat.
   Þa þær folc-mægen   for æfter oðrum,
isern-hergum.   An wisode
mægen-þrymmum mæst   —þy he mære wearð—
350   on forðwegas   folc æfter wolcnum,
cynn æfter cynne.   Cuðe æghwilc
mæg-burga riht,   swa him Moises bead,
eorla æðelo.   Him wæs an fæder,
leof leod-fruma,   land-riht geþah,
355   frod on ferhðe,   freo-magum leof.

hard combat hand-to-hand, brave young fighters, warriors
unafraid of deadly cuts of weapons, bloody sword wounds,
the rush of a fighting force, the crash of grim helmets, wherever Judah went.

After that battalion the sea-force paraded, the sons of 331
Ruben. The sea-marauders bore shields across the salt
marsh, many a man; the great cohort went unafraid. He had
diminished his seniority with sins, so that he went further
back in the train of the beloved. His noble brother had
taken over his right as firstborn in the national division,
wealth and nobility; he was ready nonetheless. After them
the sons of Simeon with hosts of people advanced there,
with their troops; the third tribal force—banners flapped
over the marching spears—the dewy spear-shafts pressed
on in a company. Daybreak came over the sea, God's special
beacon, the morning splendidly bright; the force went on.

Then advanced there one division after the other, in 347
armies of iron. One man guided that greatest of glorious
forces on the paths ahead, the nation under the clouds, tribe
after tribe—for that he became famous. Each one knew his
tribal right, as Moses had instructed them, the lineage of
noblemen. For them there was one father, beloved origin of
the people, he received the land-right, wise in spirit, dear to
noble kinsmen.

Cende cneow-sibbe cenra manna
heah-fædera sum, halige þeode,
Israela cyn, onriht Godes,
swa þæt orþancum ealde reccað
360 þa þe mæg-burge mæst gefrunon,
frum-cyn feora, fæder-æðelo gehwæs.
Niwe flodas Noe oferlað,
þrymfæst þeoden, mid his þrim sunum,
þone deopestan drence-floda
365 þara ðe gewurde on woruld-rice.
Hæfde him on hreðre halige treowa;
forþon he gelædde ofer lagu-streamas
maðm-horda mæst, mine gefræge.
On feorh-gebeorh foldan hæfde
370 eallum eorð-cynne ece lafe,
frum-cneow gehwæs, fæder and moder
tuddor-teondra, geteled rime
missenlicra þonne men cunnon,
snottor sæ-leoda. Eac þon sæda gehwilc
375 on bearm scipes beornas feredon,
þara þe under heofonum hæleð bryttigað.
Swa þæt wise men wordum secgað
þæt from Noe nigoða wære
fæder Abrahames on folc-tale.
380 Þæt is se Abraham se him engla God
naman niwan asceop; eac þon neah and feor
halige heapas in gehyld bebead,
wer-þeoda geweald; he on wræce lifde.
Siððan he gelædde leofost feora
385 haliges hæsum, heah-lond stigon
sib-gemagas, on Seone beorh.

A certain one of the patriarchs begot a generation of   356
brave men, a holy people, the nation of Israelites, the upright of God, just as the elders recount skillfully, those who
have most studied the distant tribal origin, the noble pedi-
gree, of each great house. Noah journeyed over new floods,
the glorious chieftain, with his three sons, the deepest of
drowning-floods that ever had happened in the kingdom of
the world. He had the holy covenant in his heart; therefore
he led the greatest of treasure-hoards over the ocean currents, so I've heard.

He had in life-protection the everlasting remnant of all   369
land creatures of the world, the first generation of each, the
father and mother of those offspring-makers, the wise sailor
counted a more diverse number than men know. Also the
men carried in the bosom of the ship each seed that heroes
enjoy under the heavens. Thus wise people say in words, that
Abraham was the ninth father from Noah in the line of descendents. That is the Abraham for whom the God of angels
created a new name; furthermore, near and far holy multitudes were given into his protection, the power of the nations; he lived in exile.

After that, by holy God's commands, he led the most be-   384
loved of living things, the close kinsmen climbed the upland,
onto Mount Zion. There they discovered a pledge, saw glory,

Wære hie þær fundon,   wuldor gesawon,
halige heah-treowe,   swa hæleð gefrunon.
Þær eft se snottra   sunu Dauides,
390   wuldorfæst cyning,   witgan larum
getimbrede   tempel Gode,
alh haligne,   eorð-cyninga
se wisesta   on woruld-rice,
heahst and haligost,   hæleðum gefrægost,
395   mæst and mærost   þara þe manna bearn,
fira æfter foldan   folmum geworhte.
To þam meðel-stede   magan gelædde
Abraham Isaac.   Ad-fyr onbran;
fyrst ferhð-bana   no þy fægenra wæs.
400   Wolde þone last-weard   lige gesyllan,
in bæl-blyse   beorna selost,
his swæsne sunu   to sige-tibre,
angan ofer eorðan   yrfe-lafe,
feores frofre   —ða he swa forð gebad—
405   leodum to lafe,   langsumne hiht.
He þæt gecyðde,   þa he þone cniht genam
fæste mid folmum   —folc-cuð geteag
ealde lafe,   ecg grymetode—
þæt he him lif-dagas   leofran ne wisse
410   þonne he hyrde   heofon-cyninge.
Up aræmde   Abraham þa;
se eorl wolde slean   eaferan sinne
unweaxenne,   eagum reodan,
magan mid mece,   gif hine metod lete.
415   Ne wolde him beorht Fæder   bearn æt niman,
halig tiber,   ac mid handa befeng.
Þa him styran cwom   stefn of heofonum,
wuldres hleoðor,   word æfter spræc:

a holy solemn covenant, as men have heard. Later at that place the wise son of David, the glorious king, by the instructions of the prophet built a temple for God, a sacred shrine, the wisest of earth's kings in worldly dominion, highest and holiest, best known to men, greatest and most famous of those which the sons of men, people across the earth, made with their hands. To that meeting place Abraham led his son Isaac. He lit a fire; the foremost soul-slayer was none the happier for that.

He was willing to give the heir to the flame, the best of 400 sons into the blaze of the pyre, his sweet son as a victory holocaust, his only successor on earth, his life's comfort—as from that time he so experienced—a legacy to his people, an enduring hope. He made that known, when he seized the boy firmly in his hands—the illustrious one drew the ancient heirloom, the blade rasped loudly—that he did not consider the boy's life-days dearer to him than obeying the king of heaven. Then Abraham rose up; the man was willing to kill his stripling heir, with reddened eyes, the son with the sword, if the creator would allow it. The bright Father did not wish to deprive him of his son, a holy offering, but grabbed him by the hands. Then to restrain him a voice came from the heavens, the sound of glory, spoke words about it:

"Ne sleh þu, Abraham,   þin agen bearn,
420 sunu mid sweorde!   Soð is gecyðed,
nu þin cunnode   cyning alwihta,
þæt þu wið waldend   wære heolde,
fæste treowe,   seo þe freoðo sceal
in lif-dagum   lengest weorðan,
425 awa to aldre   unswiciendo.
Hu þearf mannes sunu   maran treowe?
Ne behwylfan mæg   heofon and eorðe
his wuldres word,   widdra and siddra
þonne befæðman mæge   foldan sceattas,
430 eorðan ymbhwyrft   and up-rodor,
gar-secges gin   and þeos geomre lyft.

"He að swereð,   engla þeoden,
wyrda waldend   and wereda God,
soðfæst sigora,   þurh his sylfes lif
435 þæt þines cynnes   and cneow-maga,
rand-wiggendra   rim ne cunnon,
yldo ofer eorðan,   ealle cræfte
to gesecgenne   soðum wordum,
nymðe hwylc þæs snottor   in sefan weorðe
440 þæt he ana mæge   ealle geriman
stanas on eorðan,   steorran on heofonum,
sæ-beorga sand,   sealte yða;
ac hie gesittað   be sæm tweonum
oð Egipte   in-geðeode
445 land Cananea,   leode þine,
freo-bearn fæder,   folca selost."

* * *

Folc wæs afæred,   flod-egsa becwom
gastas geomre,   geofon deaðe hweop.

"Abraham, do not slaughter your own child, your son with   419
the sword! The truth is made known, now that the king of
all things has tested you, that you keep your covenant with
the ruler, which will become an enduring peace-pledge for
you in your life-days, unfailingly forever to the ages. How
could a son of man need more of a pledge? Heaven and earth
cannot overarch his glorious word, wider and broader than
the surfaces of the earth could encompass, the circuit of
the earth and vault above, the abyss of the ocean and this
gloomy sky.

"He, the prince of angels, ruler of fates, and God of hosts,   432
righteous in victories, swears an oath on his own life, that
men across the earth will not be able with all their skill,
to count in true words your people, generations of descendants, of shield-bearing warriors, unless someone become
so wise in mind that he alone might count all the stones on
earth, stars in the heavens, sand of the seashores, the salty
waves; but between the two seas, as far as hemmed-in Egypt
they will be established in the land of Canaan, your people, a
father's free-born, most excellent of nations."

* * *

XLVIIII
The nation was afraid, the flood-terror overcame their   447
gloomy spirits, the ocean threatened with death. The steep

Wæron beorh-hliðu   blode bestemed,
450 holm heolfre spaw,   hream wæs on yðum,
wæter wæpna ful,   wæl-mist astah.
Wæron Egypte   eft oncyrde,
flugon forhtigende,   fær ongeton,
woldon here-bleaðe   hamas findan,
455 gylp wearð gnornra.   Him ongen genap
atol yða gewealc,   ne ðær ænig becwom
herges to hame,   ac behindan beleac
wyrd mid wæge.   Þær ær wegas lagon,
mere modgode,   mægen wæs adrenced.
460   Streamas stodon,   storm up gewat
heah to heofonum,   here-wopa mæst.
Laðe cyrmdon   —lyft up geswearc—
fægum stæfnum,   flod blod gewod.
Rand-byrig wæron rofene,   rodor swipode
465 mere-deaða mæst,   modige swulton,
cyningas on corðre,   cyre swiðrode
sæs æt ende—   wig-bord scinon
heah ofer hæleðum,   holm-weall astah,
mere-stream modig.   Mægen wæs on cwealme
470 fæste gefeterod,   forð-ganges nep,
searwum æsæled.   Sand basnodon,
witodre fyrde,   hwonne waðema stream,
sin-calda sæ,   sealtum yðum
æf-lastum gewuna   ece staðulas,
475 nacud nyd-boda,   neosan come,
fah feðe-gast   se ðe feondum geneop.
    Wæs seo hæwene lyft   heolfre geblanden,
brim berstende   blod-egesan hweop,
sæ-manna sið,   oðþæt soð metod

cliffs were wet with blood, the sea spewed gore, a roar was in the waves, the water full of weapons, the slaughter-mist climbed up. The Egyptians were then routed, they fled terri- fied, realized the disaster, the battle-shy wanted to find their homes, their boasting became more lamentable. The terri- ble rolling of the waves darkened over them, none of that army came home, but fate enclosed them from behind with the wave. Where earlier paths had lain, the sea raged, the force was drowned.

The streams stood, the storm went up high to the heav- 460 ens, greatest of martial laments. The hateful ones screamed in fated voices—the sky above darkened—blood suffused the flood. The shield ramparts were riven, the greatest of sea-deaths scourged the sky, bold ones perished, kings in their splendor; the option grew weaker before the sea's van- guard—the shields shone high over the warriors, the seawall ascended, the brave sea-current. The force was firmly fet- tered in slaughter, the weak flow of the advance was hin- dered by armor. Sand awaited the doomed army, when the river of waves, the ever-cold sea, with salt surges came back from its diverted course to seek out its accustomed eter- nal foundations, the naked messenger of distress, the hostile wandering spirit who overtook the enemies.

The blue sky was mixed with gore, the bursting sea threat- 477 ened the sailors' journey with bloody terror, until the true

480 þurh Moyses hand   modge rymde,
wide wæðde,   wæl-fæðmum sweop.
Flod famgode,   fæge crungon,
lagu land gefeol,   lyft wæs onhrered,
wicon weall-fæsten,   wægas burston,
485 multon mere-torras,   þa se mihtiga sloh
mid halige hand,   heofon-rices weard,
þa wer-beamas   wlance ðeode.

Ne mihton forhabban   helpendra pað,
mere-streames mod,   ac he manegum gesceod
490 gyllende gryre.   Gar-secg wedde,
up ateah, on sleap.   Egesan stodon,
weollon wæl-benna.   Wit-rod gefeol
heah of heofonum   hand-weorc Godes —
famig-bosma,   flod-weard gesloh,
495 unhleowan wæg   alde mece
þæt ðy deað-drepe   drihte swæfon,
synfullra sweot.   Sawlum lunnon
fæste befarene,   flod-blac here,
siððan hie onbugon   brun yppinge,
500 mod-wæga mæst.

                    Mægen eall gedreas,
ða ðe gedrecte,   dugoð Egypta,
Faraon mid his folcum.   He onfond hraðe,
siððan grund gestah   Godes andsaca,
þæt wæs mihtigra   mere-flodes weard;
505 wolde heoru-fæðmum   hilde gesceadan,
yrre and egesfull.   Egyptum wearð
þæs dæg-weorces   deop lean gesceod,
forðam þæs heriges   ham eft ne com
ealles ungrundes   ænig to lafe,

creator swept away the brave by Moses's hand, widely it gushed, swept in with deadly embrace. The current foamed, the fated ones collapsed, the sea fell onto the land, the sky was stirred up, the ramparts gave way, the walls burst asunder, the sea-towers dissolved, when the mighty one, the guardian of the heavenly kingdom, struck with holy hand the dam's braces on the proud nation.

They could not hinder the path of those helpers, the intention of the sea-stream, but he destroyed the multitude with wailing terror. The sea raged, climbed up, slid on. Panic spread, mortal wounds gushed. The rod of punishment fell high from the heavens, the handiwork of God—the foamy-bosomed one, the guardian of the flood, struck the unsheltering wall with the ancient sword, so that the troops, the sinful band, perished by the death-blow. They lost their souls, firmly surrounded, the flood-pale army, when the dark towering mass, the greatest of willed-waves, turned them aside. 488

The force completely perished, those who had afflicted, the troop of Egyptians, Pharaoh with his nation. God's adversary quickly found out, when he reached the bottom, that the guardian of the sea-flood was mightier; he had wished to decide things in the press of combat in battle, angry and terrifying. The deep reward for the day's work became a punishment for the Egyptians, because none of all that capsized army came home afterward as a survivor, so 500

510 þætte sið heora   secgan moste,
bodigean æfter burgum   bealo-spella mæst,
hord-wearda hryre,   hæleða cwenum,
ac þa mægen-þreatas   mere-deað geswealh,
þa spel-bodan.   Se ðe sped ahte,
515 ageat gylp wera.   Hie wið God wunnon!
Þanon Israhelum   ece rædas
on mere-hwearfe   Moyses sægde,
heah-þungen wer,   halige spræce,
deop ærende.   Dæg-worc nemnað
520 swa gyt wer-ðeode,   on gewritum findað
doma gehwilcne,   þara ðe him Drihten bebead
on þam sið-fate   soðum wordum,
gif onlucan wile   lifes wealh-stod,
beorht in breostum,   ban-huses weard,
525 gin-fæsten god   gastes cægon.
Run bið gerecenod,   ræd forð gæð;
hafað wislicu   word on fæðme,
wile meagollice   modum tæcan
þæt we gesne ne syn   Godes þeodscipes,
530 metodes miltsa.   He us ma onlyhð—
nu us boceras   beteran secgað
lengran lyft-wynna.   Þis is læne dream,
wommum awyrged,   wreccum alyfed,
earmra anbid.   Eðellease
535 þysne gyst-sele   gihðum healdað,
murnað on mode,   man-hus witon
fæst under foldan   —þær bið fyr and wyrm,
open ece scræf   yfela gehwylces—

that the messengers must say of their journey, announce
across the cities the greatest death notice, to the men's
wives, the fall of the treasure-guardians, because the sea-
death had swallowed the force of attackers. He who owned
success emptied out the boast of men. They struggled
against God!

After that Moses, man of great virtue, announced eternal   516
counsels to the Israelites on the seashore, a holy speech, a
deep message. So the nations still relate that day's work, in
writings they find each one of those decrees, which the Lord
commended to them in true words during that journey, if
life's interpreter, the body's guardian, wishes to unlock the
abundant good, bright in the breast, with the keys of the
spirit.

The mystery is explained, counsel flows forth; he has wise   526
words in the bosom, should wish earnestly to teach minds,
so that we might not be lacking God's allegiance, the creator's mercy. He enlightens us more—now scholars explain
to us better concerning longer-lasting joys in heaven. This is
a transitory happiness, cursed with sorrows, granted to exiles, a tarrying for wretched ones. Deprived of the homeland
we keep this guesthouse with sorrows, mourn in mind, we
consider the home of wickedness secure under the earth—
where fire and worm are, the everlasting gaping pit of each

swa nu regn-þeofas   rice dælað,
540 yldo oððe ær-dead.

                        Eft-wyrd cymð,
mægen-þrymma mæst   ofer middan-geard,
dæg dædum fah.   Drihten sylfa
on þam meðel-stede   manegum demeð,
þonne he soðfæstra   sawla lædeð,
545 eadige gastas,   on up-rodor,
þær is leoht and lif,   eac þon lissa blæd;
dugoð on dreame   Drihten herigað,
weroda wuldor-cyning,   to widan feore.
Swa reordode   ræda gemyndig
550 manna mildost,   mihtum swiðed,
hludan stefne.   Here stille bad
witodes willan,   wundor ongeton,
modiges muð-hæl.   He to mænegum spræc:
      "Micel is þeos menigeo,   mægen-wisa trum,
555 fullesta mæst,   se ðas fare lædeð;
hafað us on Cananea   cyn gelyfed
burh and beagas,   brade rice;
wile nu gelæstan   þæt he lange gehet
mid að-sware,   engla Drihten,
560 in fyrn-dagum   fæderyn-cynne
  —gif ge gehealdað   halige lare—
þæt ge feonda gehwone   forð ofergangað,
gesittað sige-rice   be sæm tweonum,
beor-selas beorna.   Bið eower blæd micel!"
565   Æfter þam wordum   werod wæs on salum,
sungon sige-byman   (segnas stodon)
on fægerne sweg;   folc wæs on lande,
hæfde wuldres beam   werud gelæded,

and every evil—because now the arch-thieves, old age and early death, share dominion.

The last judgment will advance across the middle-earth, 540 the greatest of powers, a day colored by the accounts of deeds. The Lord himself will judge the multitudes at that meeting place, when he leads the souls of the righteous, the blessed spirits, into the firmament, where there is light and life, and also the glory of graciousness; in joy the company will praise the Lord, the glorious king of hosts, in life everlasting. So the mildest of men spoke, mindful of good counsels, mightily strengthened, in a loud voice. The army quietly awaited the wish of the chosen one, they understood the miracle, the healing words of the brave one. He spoke to the multitudes:

"Great is this company, the captain strong, greatest of 554 helpers, who leads this expedition; he has granted us in Canaan the people, city and rings, the broad kingdom; now the Lord of angels will fulfill what he long ago promised with sworn oaths, in ancient days to your paternal ancestors—if you keep the holy teaching—that henceforth you will overrun each enemy, occupy a victorious realm between the two seas, the beer-halls of men. Your glory will be great!"

After these words the company was joyful; the victory- 565 trumpets sang in beautiful music (the standards stood upright); the nation was on land, the glorious pillar had led

halige heapas,   on hild Godes.
570 Life gefegon   þa hie oðlæded hæfdon
feorh of feonda dome,   þeah ðe hie hit frecne geneðdon,
weras under wætera hrofas.   Gesawon hie þær weallas
standan,
ealle him brimu blodige þuhton,   þurh þa heora beado-
searo wægon.
Hreðdon hilde-spelle,   siððan hie þam herge wiðforon;
575 hofon here-þreatas   hlude stefne,
for þam dæd-weorce   Drihten heredon,
weras wuldres sang;   wif on oðrum,
folc-sweota mæst,   fyrd-leoð golan
aclum stefnum   eall-wundra fela.
580 Þa wæs eð-fynde   Afrisc meowle
on geofones staðe   golde geweorðod.
Handa hofon   hals-wurðunge,
bliðe wæron,   bote gesawon,
heddon here-reafes,   hæft wæs onsæled.
585 Ongunnon sæ-lafe   segnum dælan
on yð-lafe,   ealde madmas,
reaf and randas.   Heo on riht sceodon
gold and god-web,   Iosepes gestreon,
wera wuldor-gesteald.   Werigend lagon
590 on deað-stede,   driht-folca mæst.

the troop, the holy hordes, under God's protection. Those who had snatched life from the enemies' sentence rejoiced in life, though they had boldly risked it, the men under the roofs of water. They saw the walls stand up there, they appeared all bloodied to them, through which they carried their battle-gear. They celebrated with a battle-song after they had escaped from the army; the battalions, the men raised up a song of glory with loud voice, they praised God for the accomplished deed; the women in reply, greatest of hosts, with voices excited by awe sang a war-song about many a sheer miracle.

Then the African woman, adorned with gold, was easily 580 found on the ocean's shore. Hands lifted up neck ornaments, they were happy: they had seen the remedy, received the war-booty, and their captivity was undone. The sea-remnant began to share out among the cohorts the ancient treasures on the shore, clothing and shields. They rightly divided the gold and fine cloth, Joseph's treasure, the glorious possessions of men. The guards, the greatest of lordly nations, lay prostrate in the place of death.

DANIEL

L

    Gefrægn ic Hebreos   eadge lifgean
in Hierusalem,   gold-hord dælan,
cyningdom habban,   swa him gecynde wæs,
siððan þurh metodes mægen   on Moyses hand
5   wearð wig gifen,   wigena mænieo,
and hie of Egyptum   ut aforon,
mægene micle.   Þæt wæs modig cyn!
Þenden hie þy rice   rædan moston,
burgum weoldan,   wæs him beorht wela.
10   Þenden þæt folc mid him   hiera fæder wære
healdan woldon,   wæs him hyrde God,
heofon-rices weard,   halig Drihten,
wuldres waldend.
                  Se ðam werude geaf
mod and mihte,   metod alwihta,
15   þæt hie oft fela folca   feore gesceodon,
heriges helmum,   þara þe him hold ne wæs,
oðþæt hie wlenco anwod   æt win-þege
deofol-dædum,   druncne geðohtas.
Þa hie æ-cræftas   ane forleton,
20   metodes mægenscipe,   swa no man scyle
his gastes lufan   wið Gode dælan.
Þa geseah ic þa gedriht   in gedwolan hweorfan,
Israhela cyn   unriht don,
wommas wyrcean.   Þæt wæs weorc Gode!

248

I have heard tell of the Hebrews living blessedly in Jerusalem, sharing the gold-hoard, holding the kingdom, as was
natural for them, since through the creator's power an army
of many warriors was given into Moses's hand, and they journeyed out from Egypt by a great wonder. That was a brave
nation! While they were able to guide the kingdom, rule the
cities, their glory was bright. While that people intended to
keep their father's covenant with him, God was their protector, the guardian of heaven's kingdom, holy Lord, glory's
ruler.

He gave that company courage and strength, the maker
of all things, so that often, with helmed men of the army,
they harmed the life of many a nation that was not faithful
to him, until pride invaded them with devilish deeds at the
feast, drunken thoughts. Then at once they abandoned the
power of the Law, the creator's majesty, as no man should
cut off his spirit's love from God. Then I saw that company
turn to error, the nation of Israel did unrighteousness, com-
mitting sins. That was an affliction to God!

25   Oft he þam leodum   to lare sende,
        heofon-rices weard,   halige gastas,
        þa þam werude   wisdom budon.
        Hie þære snytro   soð gelyfdon
        lytle hwile,   oðþæt hie langung beswac,
30   eorðan dreamas,   eces rædes,
        þæt hie æt siðestan   sylfe forleton
        Drihtnes domas,   curon deofles cræft.
        Þa wearð reðe-mod   rices ðeoden,
        unhold þeodum   þam þe æhte geaf.
35   Wisde him æt frymðe,   ða ðe on fruman ær ðon
        wæron man-cynnes   metode dyrust,
        dugoða dyrust,   Drihtne leofost;
        here-poð tæhte   to þære hean byrig,
        eorlum el-ðeodigum,   on eðel-land
40   þær Salem stod   searwum afæstnod,
        weallum geweorðod.
                        To þæs witgan foron,
        Caldea cyn,   to ceastre forð,
        þær Israela   æhta wæron
        bewrigene mid weorcum;   to þam þæt werod gefor,
45   mægen-þreat mære,   man-bealwes georn.
        Awehte þone wæl-nið   wera aldor-frea,
        Babilones brego,   on his burh-stede,
        Nabochodonossor,   þurh nið-hete,
        þæt he secan ongan   sefan gehygdum
50   hu he Israelum   eaðost meahte
        þurh gromra gang   guman oðþringan.
        Gesamnode þa   suðan and norðan
        wæl-hreow werod,   and west foran
        herige hæðen-cyninga   to þære hean byrig.

Often the guardian of the heavenly kingdom sent holy 25
souls for the instruction of the people, who offered wisdom
to the troop. For a little while they believed in the truth of
that wisdom, until passion, the joys of the earth, deprived
them of eternal counsel, so that they themselves eventually
abandoned the Lord's decrees, chose the craft of the devil.
Then the prince of the kingdom grew belligerent, unfriendly
toward the people to whom he had given property. At the
start he had guided them, those who originally had been the
dearest of humankind to the creator, the dearest host, most
lovely to the Lord before that; he had showed them the line
of attack to the high city, to those foreign men, in the native land where Salem stood secured skillfully, honored with
walls.

To that place the magicians traveled, the nation of 41
Chaldeans, forward to the city, where the possessions of the
Israelites were protected with fortifications; against it the
troop advanced, the famous mighty band, eager for cruel
slaughter. The lord of men, Babylon's prince Nebuchadnezzar, had awoken the deadly malice through intense hatred in
his city, so that he began to search out in his mind's thoughts
how he could most easily enthrall men from among the Israelites through an advance of fierce ones. He summoned then
from south and from north a murderous band, and they
went west with an army of pagan kings to the high city.

55   Hæfdon Israela   eðel-weardas
        lufan, lif-welan,   þenden hie let Metod.
        Þa ic eðan gefrægn   eald-feonda cyn
        win-burh wera.   Þa wigan ne gelyfdon,
        bereafodon þa receda wuldor   readan golde,
60   since and seolfre,   Salomones templ.
        Gestrudan gestreona   under stan-hliðum,
        swilc eallswa þa eorlas   agan sceoldon,
        oðþæt hie burga gehwone   abrocen hæfdon,
        þara þe þam folce   to friðe stodon.
65   Gehlodon him to huðe   hord-wearda gestreon,
        feoh and freos,   swilc þær funden wæs,
        and þa mid þam æhtum   eft siðedon,
        and gelæddon eac   on langne sið
        Israela cyn,   on east-wegas
70   to Babilonia,   beorna unrim,
        under hand hæleð   hæðenum deman.
            Nabochodonossor   him on nyd dyde
        Israela bearn   ofer ealle lufen,
        wæpna lafe   to weorc-þeowum.
75   Onsende þa   sinra þegna
        worn þæs werudes   west toferan,
        þæt him þara leoda   land geheolde,
        eðne eðel,   æfter Ebreum.
        Het þa secan   sine gerefan
80   geond Israela   earme lafe,
        hwilc þære geogoðe   gleawost wære
        boca bebodes   þe þær brungen wæs.
        Wolde þæt þa cnihtas   cræft leornedon,
        þæt him snytro on sefan   secgan mihte,
85   nales ðy þe he þæt moste   oððe gemunan wolde

The guardians of the homeland of the Israelites had love 55
and life's joys while the ordaining Lord let them. I have
heard tell that the nation of ancient enemies then devas-
tated the people's festive city. Those warriors did not believe, they looted that glory of buildings, the temple of
Solomon, of red gold, treasure and silver. They plundered
treasure under the stone-cliffs, all that those men were
supposed to own, until they had broken each fortifica-
tion, those which had stood as security for the people. They
loaded up as booty the wealth of the treasurers, the money
and the nobles, such as was found there, and then with those
possessions traveled back, and also led the nation of Israel
on a long journey, on paths east to Babylon, an uncountable
number of men, to condemn the warriors in servitude to pagans.

Against all love, Nebuchadnezzar put them under servi- 72
tude, the children of Israel, the survivors of the weapons as
slaves. Then he sent a host of his own noblemen journeying
to the west, to hold for him the land of those people, the
wasted homeland, after the Hebrews. Then he commanded
his officials to seek throughout the wretched remnant of
the Israelites, for those of the youth that had been brought
there who were wisest in the books of the Law. He intended
that the young men should learn skill, so that he could tell
them the wisdom in his mind, not at all for the reason that

þæt he þara gifena   Gode þancode
þe him þær to duguðe   Drihten scyrede.
　Þa hie þær fundon   þry frea-gleawe
æðele cnihtas   and æfæste,
90　ginge and gode   in god-sæde;
an wæs Annanias,   oðer Azarias,
þridda Misael,   metode gecorene.
　Þa þry comon   to þeodne foran,
hearde and hige-þancle,   þær se hæðena sæt,
95　cyning corðres georn,   in Caldea byrig.
　Þa hie þam wlancan   wisdom sceoldon,
weras Ebrea,   wordum cyðan,
hige-cræft heane,   þurh halig mod.
　Þa se beorn bebead,   Babilone weard,
100　swið-mod cyning,   sinum þegnum,
þæt þa frum-garas   be feore dæde,
þæt þam gengum þrym   gad ne wære
wiste ne wæde   in woruld-life.

LI
　Þa wæs breme   Babilone weard,
105　mære and modig   ofer middan-geard,
egesful ylda bearnum.   No he æ fremede,
ac in ofer-hygde   æghwæs lifde.
　Þa þam folc-togan   on frum-slæpe,
siððan to reste gehwearf   rice þeoden,
110　com on sefan hwurfan   swefnes woma,
hu woruld wære   wundrum geteod,
ungelic yldum   oð edsceafte.
　Wearð him on slæpe   soð gecyðed,
þætte rices gehwæs   reðe sceolde gelimpan,
115　eorðan dreamas,   ende wurðan.

he could or would remember that he should thank God for the gifts which the Lord allotted him there for his benefit.

Then they discovered there three young men, nobly-wise, 88 princely and fixed on the law, young and good among the divine stock; one was Hananiah, the second Azariah, the third Mishael, chosen by the creator. These three came before the prince, steadfast and thoughtful, where the pagan sat, a king eager for pomp, in the city of the Chaldeans. Then the men of the Hebrews had to make known wisdom in words to the proud one, high intelligence though a holy mind. Then the warrior, the guardian of Babylon, the arrogant king, commanded his courtiers that the officials ensure, for the sake of their lives, that the three young ones should have no lack in this world's life of sustenance or clothing.

LI
The guardian of Babylon was then famous, mighty and 104 proud across middle-earth, terrifying to the children of men. He did not keep the Law, but in every way lived in great pride. Then in the first sleep, after the royal prince turned in to bed, the sound of a dream came to the tyrant, wandering into his mind, about how the world was wondrously transformed, unlike the ages before the new creation. In sleep the truth was made known to him that the cruel end of each empire must happen, must come about for earth's

Þa onwoc wulf-heort,   se ær win-gal swæf,
Babilone weard.   Næs him bliðe hige,
ac him sorh astah,   swefnes woma.
No he gemunde   þæt him meted wæs.
120   Het þa tosomne   sinra leoda
þa wiccungdom   widost bæron,
frægn þa ða mænigeo   hwæt hine gemætte,
þenden reord-berend   reste wunode.
Wearð he on þam egesan   acol worden,
125   þa he ne wisse   word ne angin
swefnes sines;   het him secgan þeah.
Þa him unbliðe   andswaredon
deofol-witgan   (næs him dom gearu
to asecganne   swefen cyninge):
130   "Hu magon we swa dygle,   drihten, ahicgan
on sefan þinne,   hu ðe swefnede,
oððe wyrda gesceaft   wisdom bude,
gif þu his ærest ne meaht   or areccan?"
Þa him unbliðe   andswarode
135   wulf-heort cyning,   witgum sinum:
"Næron ge swa eacne   ofer ealle men
mod-geþances   swa ge me sægdon,
and þæt gecwædon   þæt ge cuðon
mine aldorlege,   swa me æfter wearð,
140   oððe ic furðor   findan sceolde.
Nu ge mætinge   mine ne cunnon,
þa þe me for werode   wisdom berað.
Ge sweltað deaðe,   nymþe ic dom wite
soðan swefnes,   þæs min sefa myndgað."
145   Ne meahte þa seo mænigeo   on þam meðel-stede
þurh witigdom   wihte aþencean

joys. Then the wolf-hearted one awoke, Babylon's guardian, who previously had slept in a drunken stupor. He was not happy in mind, but sorrow mounted up in him, because of the dream's noise. He did not remember at all about what he had dreamt.

He commanded together those of his people who pa- 120 raded their witchcraft most widely, the gathering was to be asked what he had dreamt, while speech-bearers occupied a bed. He had been frightened in the terror, when he knew neither the words nor the origin of his dream; nevertheless he commanded them to speak. Then the devil's sorcerers answered him unhappily (the ability was not in them to explain the dream to the king): "Lord, how can we know things so hidden in your mind, how you dreamed, or what decrees of fate wisdom manifested, if you are not able first to explain its beginning?"

Then the wolf-hearted king answered his magicians an- 134 grily: "You are not as potent in intellect above all people as you told me, when you said that you understood my allotted life, what would happen to me afterward, or what I should encounter henceforth. Now you who present wisdom to me before the troop cannot interpret my dream. You shall suffer death, unless I know the judgment of the true dream, which my mind remembers."

Then that crowd in the assembly hall could not interpret 145 or understand anything at all by magic, when they were held

ne ahicgan,   þa hit forhæfed gewearð
þætte hie sædon   swefn cyninge,
wyrda gerynu—   oðþæt witga cwom,
150   Daniel to dome,   se wæs Drihtne gecoren,
snotor and soðfæst,   in þæt seld gangan.
Se wæs ord-fruma   earmre lafe
þære þe þam hæðenan   hyran sceolde.
Him God sealde   gife of heofnum
155   þurh hleoðor-cwyde   haliges gastes,
þæt him engel Godes   eall asægde
swa his man-drihten   gemæted wearð.
  Ða eode Daniel,   þa dæg lyhte,
swefen reccan   sinum frean,
160   sægde him wislice   wereda gesceafte,
þætte sona ongeat   swið-mod cyning
ord and ende   þæs þe him ywed wæs.
Ða hæfde Daniel   dom micelne,
blæd in Babilonia   mid bocerum,
165   siððan he gesæde   swefen cyninge,
þæt he ær for fyrenum   onfon ne meahte,
Babilonie weard,   in his breost-locan.
  No hwæðere þæt Daniel   gedon mihte
þæt he wolde metodes   mihte gelyfan,
170   ac he wyrcan ongan   weoh on felda
þam þe deor-mode   Diran heton,
se wæs on ðære ðeode   ðe swa hatte:
bresne Babilonige.   Þære burge weard
anne man-lican   ofer metodes est,
175   gyld of golde,   gumum arærde,
for þam þe gleaw ne wæs,   gum-rices weard,
reðe and rædleas,   riht . . .

back from explaining the dream, the mysteries of the fates, to the king—until the wise one came, Daniel to judgment, who was chosen by the Lord, wise and righteous, striding into the hall. He was the leader of the wretched remnant of those who had to serve the pagans. God gave him grace from the heavens through the utterances of a holy spirit, so that an angel of God explained everything to him, as his earthly lord had dreamt it.

Then Daniel went as the day lighted to explain the dream   158
to his lord, he told him wisely about the destiny of nations, so that the arrogant king immediately perceived the beginning and end of what had been revealed to him. Then Daniel had great esteem, glory in Babylon among the scholars, after he had explained the dream to the king, which for his sins the guardian of Babylon previously had not been able to grasp in his heart.

However, Daniel was unable to bring it about that he   168
would believe in the creator's power, but he began to build an idol on the plains that the brave ones called Dura, which was in the region that was called thus: Babylon the mighty. The guardian of the city raised up for men a human likeness, an idol of gold against the commandment of the creator, because the guardian of the empire was not wise, cruel and heedless, right . . .

* * *

Þa wearð hæleða hlyst   þa hleoðor cwom
byman stefne   ofer burh-ware.
180 Þa hie for þam cumble   on cneowum sæton,
onhnigon to þam herige   hæðne þeode,
wurðedon wih-gyld,   ne wiston wræstran ræd,
efndon unrihtdom,   swa hyra aldor dyde,
mane gemenged,   mode gefrecnod.
185 Fremde folc-mægen,   swa hyra frea ærest,
unræd efnde   (him þæs æfter becwom
yfel ende-lean),   unriht dyde.
    Þær þry wæron   on þæs þeodnes byrig,
eorlas Israela,   þæt hie a noldon
190 hyra þeodnes dom   þafigan onginnan,
þæt hie to þam beacne   gebedu rærde,
ðeah ðe ðær on herige   byman sungon.
Ða wæron æðelum   Abrahames bearn,
wæron wærfæste,   wiston Drihten
195 ecne uppe,   ælmihtigne.
Cnihtas cynegode   cuð gedydon,
þæt hie him þæt gold   to gode noldon
habban ne healdan,   ac þone hean cyning,
gasta hyrde,   ðe him gife sealde.
200 Oft hie to bote   balde gecwædon
þæt hie þæs wiges   wihte ne rohton,
ne hie to þam gebede   mihte gebædon
hæðen heriges wisa,   þæt hie þider hweorfan wolden,
guman to þam gyldnan gylde,   þe he him to gode geteode.
205 Þegnas þeodne sægdon   þæt hie þære geþeahte wæron
    —hæftas hearan   in þisse hean byrig—
"þa þis hegan ne willað   ne þysne wig wurðigean,
    þe ðu þe to wuldre   wundrum teodest."

* * *

Then came about the obedience of the heroes when the 178
summons, the voice of the trumpet, went out over the citizens. When they went down on their knees before that image, the heathen nation bowed to that idol, worshipped the
pagan god, they did not know a nobler counsel, performed
an unrighteousness act, just as their lord did, sullied by sin,
made arrogant in mind. The populace did as their lord did
first, acted without heed, did an unrighteous thing (an evil
reward later came to them for that).

There were three in that prince's city, men of the Israel- 188
ites, who would in no way begin to accept the prince's edict,
that they should lift up prayers to that token, even though
the trumpets sounded there at the idol. These were by noble
descent sons of Abraham, they were faithful to the covenant,
they knew the Lord, eternally on high, the Almighty. The
royal youths made it known that they would neither have
nor hold that gold as their god, but rather the high king, the
shepherd of souls, who gave them grace. In addition, they
often boldly said that they did not care at all for that idol,
nor could that pagan people's guide command them to pray,
that they should turn there, the men toward the golden idol,
which he had set up as a god for them.

The courtiers told the prince that they were of that 205
mind—the more noble captives in this high city—"who do
not wish to do this, nor honor this idol, which you have
wondrously set up to your glory." Then enraged, the guard-

Ða him bolgen-mod   Babilone weard
210 yrre andswarode,   eorlum onmælde
grimme þam gingum,   and geocre oncwæð,
þæt hie gegnunga   gyldan sceolde
oððe þrowigean   þrea-nied micel,
frecne fyres wylm,   nymðe hie friðes wolde
215 wilnian to þam wyrrestan,   weras Ebrea,
guman to þam golde,   þe he him to gode teode.
Noldon þeah þa hyssas   hyran larum
in hige hæðnum.   Hogedon georne
þæt æ Godes   ealle gelæste,
220 and ne awacodon   wereda Drihtne,
ne þan mæ gehwurfe   in hæðendom,
ne hie to facne   freoðo wilnedan,
þeah þe him se bitera deað   geboden wære.

LII
    Þa wearð yrre an-mod cyning,   het he ofn onhætan
225 to cwale cnihta feorum   forðam þe hie his cræftas
                                                           onsocon.
Þa he wæs gegleded   swa he grimmost mihte,
frecne fyres lige,   þa he þyder folc samnode,
and gebindan het,   Babilone weard,
grim and gealh-mod,   Godes spel-bodan.
230 Het þa his scealcas   scufan þa hyssas
in bæl-blyse,   beornas geonge.
Gearo wæs se him geoce gefremede;   þeah þe hie swa
                                                           grome nydde
in fæðm fyres lige,   hwæðere heora feorh generede
mihtig metodes weard,   swa þæt mænige gefrunon.
235 Halige him þær help geteode,   sende him of hean rodore
    God, gumena weard,   gast þone halgan.

ian of Babylon answered them angrily, grimly advised the young men, and harshly said that they immediately should worship, or suffer great oppression, the terrible surge of fire, unless they would pray to that most terrible thing for protection, the men of the Hebrews, the men to the gold, which he had set up as a god for them. However, those youths in their counsel would not listen to the pagan teaching. They eagerly intended that they would completely fulfill God's Law, and not deprecate the Lord of hosts, nor convert to paganism at all, nor desire peace from that evil thing, even though the bitter death was offered to them.

LII
224
Then the obstinate king became angry, he commanded the oven be heated for the extinction of the young men's lives because they had denied his powers. When it was heated as it most cruelly could be with the terrible flame of fire, then he summoned the people there, and the guardian of Babylon, grim and bloody-minded, commanded God's messengers to be bound. Then he commanded his servants to shove the youths, the young men, into the baleful blaze. He was ready who made their rescue. Although he had forced them so cruelly into the embrace of the fire's flame, nevertheless the mighty sentinel of the creator saved their life there, just as many have heard tell. He established holy help for them there, God, the guardian of people, sent them that holy spirit from high heaven.

Engel in þone ofn   innan becwom

237a   þær hie þæt aglac drugon,

freo-bearn fæðmum beþeahte   under þam fyrenan hrofe.

Ne mihte þeah heora wlite   gewemman owiht

240   wylm þæs wæfran liges,   þa hie se waldend nerede.

Hreoh-mod wæs se hæðena þeoden,   het hie hraðe

bærnan.

Æled wæs ungescead micel.   Þa wæs se ofen onhæted,

isen eall ðurhgleded.   Hine ðær esnas mænige

wurpon wudu on innan,   swa him wæs on wordum

gedemed;

245   bæron brandas on bryne   blacan fyres

(wolde wulf-heort cyning   wall onsteallan,

iserne ymb æfæste),   oðþæt up gewat

lig ofer leofum   and þurh lust gesloh

micle mare   þonne gemet wære.

250   Ða se lig gewand   on laðe men,

hæðne of halgum.   Hyssas wæron

bliðe-mode,   burnon scealcas

ymb ofn utan,   alet gehwearf

teonfullum on teso;   ðær to geseah

255   Babilone brego.   Bliðe wæron

eorlas Ebrea,   ofestum heredon

Drihten on dreame,   dydon swa hie cuðon

ofne on innan,   aldre generede.

Guman glæd-mode   God wurðedon,

260   under þæs fæðme   þe geflymed wearð

frecne fyres hæto.   Freo-bearn wurdon

alæten liges gange,   ne hie him þær lað gedydon.

Næs him se sweg to sorge   ðon ma þe sunnan scima,

ne se bryne beot mæcgum   þe in þam beote wæron,

The angel went there, inside the furnace where they en-   237
dured that terror, wrapped the noble youths in his embrace
under the fiery roof. Indeed, the surge of the licking flame
could not mar their beauty at all, when the ruler saved them.
The pagan prince was furious, commanded them to be incinerated immediately. The pyre was unreasonably large.
Then the oven was intensely hot, the iron utterly incandes-
cent. Many servants threw wood inside it there, as had been
commanded them by orders; they bore brands into the blaze
of the gleaming fire (the wolf-hearted king wished to found
an iron wall around those who kept the Law), until a flame
went up over the dear ones, and through over-excitement
slew many more than was fitting.

Then the flame turned on the hateful men, to the hea-   250
then from the holy ones. The youths were blissful, the servants around were incinerated outside the oven, the fire
turned in hurt to the harmful ones; the prince of Babylon
looked on there. Happy were the men of the Hebrews,
speedily they praised the Lord with delight, did as they
knew how inside the furnace, when their lives were saved.
Glad in heart the men worshipped God, within the embrace
that had put to flight the terrible heat of the fire. The noble
youths had been freed from the advance of flame — the Bab-
ylonians did them no harm there.

The roar was no more painful to them than the sun's radi-   263
ance, nor did the burning injure those men who were under

265 ac þæt fyr fyr scynde   to ðam þe ða scylde worhton,
hwearf on þa hæðenan hæftas   fram þam halgan cnihton,
werigra wlite minsode,   þa ðe ðy worce gefægon.
Geseah ða swið-mod cynig,   ða he his sefan ontreowde,
wundor on wite agangen;   him þæt wræclic þuhte.
270 Hyssas hale hwurfon   in þam hatan ofne,
ealle æfæste ðry;   him eac þær wæs
   an on gesyhðe,   engel ælmihtiges.
   Him þær on ofne   owiht ne derede,
   ac wæs þær inne   ealles gelicost
275 efne þonne on sumera   sunne scineð,
and deaw-drias   on dæge weorðeð
winde geondsawen.   Þæt wæs wuldres God
þe hie generede   wið þam nið-hete.
Ða Azarias   in-geþancum
280 hleoðrade halig   þurh hatne lig,
dreag dæda georn,   Drihten herede,
wer womma leas   and þa word acwæð:
   "Metod alwihta, hwæt!   Þu eart mihtum swið
niðas to nergenne.   Is þin nama mære,
285 wlitig and wuldorfæst   ofer wer-ðeode.
Siendon þine domas   in daga gehwam
soðe and geswiðde   and gesigefæste,
swa þu eac sylfa eart.
Syndon þine willan   on woruld-spedum
290 rihte and gerume,   rodora waldend.
Geoca user georne nu,   gasta scyppend,
and þurh hyldo help,   halig Drihten,
nu we þec for þreaum   and for ðeo-nydum
and for eað-medum   arna biddað,
295 lige belegde.   We ðæs lifgende

that threat, but the fire rushed fire against those who committed the crime, turned toward the pagan slaves from the holy youths, diminished the beauty of those wretches, those who rejoiced in the work. Then the obstinate king saw, when he trusted in his mind, a miracle going on in the torture; that seemed alien to him. The youths roamed safely in the hot oven, all three who kept the Law; there was another one visible there with them, the angel of the almighty.

Nothing harmed them at all there in the furnace, but inside there it was most of all just like when the sun shines in summer, and dewdrops are scattered by the wind when it becomes day. That was the God of glory who saved them from the cruel hatred. Then holy Azariah spoke from his inner thoughts through the hot flame, eager for deeds he persisted, the man without crimes praised the Lord and spoke these words: 273

"Maker of all things, listen! You are potent in might to save men. Great is your name, beautiful and glorious over the nations. Each day your judgments are true and made mighty and triumphant, as you yourself are also. Your wishes are right and bountiful in worldly goods, ruler of the skies. Assist us eagerly now, creator of spirits, and help us through grace, holy Lord, now that we for our afflictions and constraints and humiliation beg for mercies, surrounded by flame. Living in the world we brought this about, and our el- 283

worhton on worulde,   eac ðon wom dyde
user yldran;   for ofer-hygdum
bræcon bebodo   burh-sittende,
had oferhogedon   halgan lifes.

300 "Siendon we towrecene   geond widne grund,
heapum tohworfene,   hyldelease;
is user lif   geond landa fela
fracoð and gefræge   folca manegum,
þa usic bewræcon   to þæs wyrrestan

305 eorð-cyninga   æhta gewealde,
on hæft heoru-grimra,   and we nu hæðenra
þeow-ned þoliað.   Þæs þe þanc sie,
wereda wuldor-cyning,   þæt þu us þas wrace teodest.
Ne forlet þu usic ana,   ece Drihten,

310 for ðam miltsum   ðe ðec men hligað,
and for ðam treowum   þe þu, tirum fæst,
niða nergend,   genumen hæfdest
to Abrahame   and to Isaace
and to Iacobe,   gasta scyppend.

315 "Þu him þæt gehete   þurh hleoðor-cwyde,
þæt þu hyra frum-cyn   in fyrn-dagum
ican wolde,   þætte æfter him
on cneorissum   cenned wurde,
and seo mænigeo   mære wære,

320 had to hebbanne   swa heofon-steorran
bebugað bradne hwyrft,   oððe brim-faroþæs,
sæ-faroða sand,   geond sealtne wæg
in eare gryndeð,   þæt his unrim a
in wintra worn   wurðan sceolde.

325 Fyl nu frum-spræce,   ðeah heora fea lifigen!
Wlitiga þinne word-cwyde   and þin wuldor on us!

ders also committed crimes; in arrogance the citizens broke commandments, despised the calling of holy life.

"We are exiled across the wide earth, dispersed in crowds, 300 without protection; throughout many lands our life is despised and a byword among many peoples, who have banished us as chattels to the rule of the worst of earth's kings, into the captivity of warlike men, and we now suffer servitude to the pagans. To you be thanks for this, wondrous king of hosts, that you have made this punishment for us. Do not abandon us, eternal Lord, because of the mercies that people attribute to you, and for the covenants which you, firm in glory, savior of men, have taken up with Abraham and Isaac and Jacob, creator of souls.

"You promised them by utterances that in distant days 315 you would increase their offspring, which would be born in generations after them, and the multitude should be famous, promised to raise the kindred, as the stars of heaven encircle their broad orbit, or as the sand of the ocean shore, of the seashore, throughout the salt wave, forms the bottom of the sea, promised that for many years an uncountable number of them should continue forever. Fulfill now that oath, though few of them be alive! Embellish your promise and your glory in us! Make known the power and might that

Gecyð cræft and miht   þæt þa Caldeas
and folca fela   gefrigen habbað,
ða þe under heofenum   hæðene lifigeað,
330 and þæt þu ana eart   ece Drihten,
weroda waldend,   woruld-gesceafta,
sigora settend,   soðfæst metod!"
　　Swa se halga wer   hergende wæs
metodes miltse   and his mihta sped
335 rehte þurh reorde.   Ða of roderum wæs
engel ælbeorht   ufan onsended,
wlite-scyne wer   on his wuldor-haman,
se him cwom to frofre   and to feorhnere
mid lufan and mid lisse.   Se ðone lig tosceaf,
340 halig and heofon-beorht,   hatan fyres,
tosweop hine and toswende   þurh þa swiðan miht,
ligges leoman,   þæt hyra lice ne wæs
owiht geegled,   ac he on andan sloh
fyr on feondas   for fyren-dædum.
345 　　Þa wæs on þam ofne,   þær se engel becwom,
windig and wynsum,   wedere gelicost
þonne hit on sumeres tid   sended weorðeð
dropena drearung   on dæges hwile,
wearmlic wolcna scur.   Swylc bið wedera cyst,
350 swylc wæs on þam fyre   Frean mihtum
halgum to helpe.   Wearð se hata lig
todrifen and todwæsced   þær þa dæd-hwatan
geond þone ofen eodon,   and se engel mid,
feorh nerigende   —se ðær feorða wæs—
355 Annanias   and Azarias
and Misael.   Þær þa mod-hwatan
þry on geðancum   ðeoden heredon,

the Chaldeans and many nations have heard about, those who live as pagans under the heavens, and that you alone are the eternal Lord, ruler of hosts, of worldly creatures, giver of victories, creator firm in truth!"

So the holy man was praising the creator's mercy and told 333 with his voice the abundance of his might. Then a radiant angel was sent from the skies above, a beautiful man in his glorious robe, who came as a comfort and as a lifesaver to them with love and with kindness. He, holy and heaven-bright, forced back the flame, the heat of the fire, swept away and scattered the radiance of the flame by great force, so that their body was not at all harmed, but in enmity he struck fire on the enemies for their wickedness.

Then in that oven, when the angel arrived, it was breezy 345 and pleasant, the weather most like when it happens in summertime that a sprinkling of drops is sent at the time of day, a warm shower from the clouds. Just as the best of climates is, so it was in that fire by the Lord's might as a help to the saints. The hot flame was driven back and extinguished where the deed-bold ones, Hananiah, Azariah and Mishael, went throughout the furnace, and the angel with them, saving life—he was the fourth there. There the stouthearted

bædon bletsian   bearn Israela
eall land-gesceaft   ecne Drihten,
360 ðeoda waldend.   Swa hie þry cwædon,
modum horsce,   ʾþurh gemæne word:

"Ðe gebletsige,   bylywit Fæder,
woruld-cræfta wlite   and weorca gehwilc.
Heofonas and englas,   and hluttor wæter,
365 þa ðe ofer roderum   on rihtne gesceaft
wuniað in wuldre,   ða þec wurðiað.
And þec, ælmihtig,   ealle gesceafte,
rodor-beorhtan tunglu,   þa þe ryne healdað,
sunna and mona,   sundor anra gehwilc
370 herige in hade.   And heofon-steorran,
deaw and deor scur,   ða ðec domige.
And þec, mihtig God,   gastas lofige.
Byrnende fyr   and beorht sumor
nergend hergað.   Niht somod and dæg,
375 and þec landa gehwilc,   leoht and þeostro,
herige on hade,   somod hat and ceald.

"And þec, Frea mihtig,   forstas and snawas,
winter-biter weder   and wolcen-faru,
lofige on lyfte.   And þec ligetu,
380 blace, berhtm-hwate,   þa þec bletsige.
Eall eorðan grund,   ece Drihten,
hyllas and hrusan   and hea beorgas,
sealte sæ-wægas,   soðfæst metod,
ea-stream yða   and up-cyme,
385 wæter-sprync wylla,   ða ðec wurðiað.
Hwalas ðec herigað,   and hefon-fugolas,
lyft-lacende,   þa ðe lago-streamas,

three praised the prince in their thoughts, the children of Israel commanded all land-creatures to bless the eternal Lord,
the ruler of nations. So those three, clever in mind, said in
unison:

"Gracious Father, let the beauty of the world's virtues and
works bless you. The heavens and the angels, and clear waters, those which over the skies continue in glory in correct
order, these worship you. And you, almighty, all creatures,
the sky-bright stars, those which you hold on course, the
sun and moon, let each of these praise you individually in
its place. And the stars of heaven, dew and fierce shower, let
these honor you. And let the spirits praise you, mighty God.
Burning fire and bright summer praise the savior. Night together with day, and each land, light and darkness, hot and
cold, let them praise you in their place.

"And, mighty Lord, let the frosts and snows, winter-bitter
weather, and the bank of clouds, praise you on high. And
lightning, bright and sudden as a blink, let these bless you.
The entire surface of the earth, eternal Lord, hills and plains
and high mountains, salt sea-waves, righteous creator, the
torrent of the waves and the rising and water-spring of wells,
these honor you. Whales praise you, which move in the
ocean currents and bodies of water, and the birds of the

LIII
362

377

wæterscipe wecgað.   And wildu deor
and neata gehwilc   naman bletsie.
390 "And manna bearn   modum lufiað,
and þec Israela,   æhta scyppend,
herigað in hade,   herran þinne.
And þec haligra   heortan cræftas,
soðfæstra gehwæs   sawle and gastas,
395 lofiað Lif-Frean,   lean sellende
eallum ead-modum,   ece Drihten.
Annanias ðec   and Adzarias
and Misael   metod domige
breost-geðancum.   We þec bletsiað,
400 Frea folca gehwæs,   Fæder ælmihtig,
soð Sunu metodes,   sawla nergend,
hæleða helpend,   and þec, Halig Gast,
wurðiað in wuldre,   witig Drihten.
We ðec herigað,   halig Drihten,
405 and gebedum bremað.   Þu gebletsad eart,
gewurðad wide-ferhð   ofer worulde hrof,
heah-cyning heofones,   halgum mihtum,
lifes leoht-fruma,   ofer landa gehwilc."
    Ða þæt ehtode   ealdor þeode,
410 Nabochodonossor,   wið þam nehstum
folc-gesiðum: "Þæt eower fela geseah,
þeode mine,   þæt we þry sendon,
geboden to bæle   in byrnende
fyres leoman.   Nu ic þær feower men
415 geseo to soðe   —nales me selfa leogeð."
Ða cwæð se ðe wæs   cyninges ræswa,
wis and word-gleaw: "Þæt is wundra sum
þæt we ðær eagum   on lociað.

heavens flitting in the sky. And let the wild beasts and all cattle bless your name.

"And the children of men love you in their hearts, and the 390 Israelites your servants, praise you in their place, creator of possessions. And the virtues of the holy of heart, the souls and spirits of each of the righteous, praise you, the Lord of life, eternal Lord, giving reward to all the humble of heart. Let Hananiah and Azariah and Mishael honor the creator in their inner thoughts. We bless you, Lord of all nations, Father almighty, true Son of the creator, savior of souls, help of heroes, and you, Holy Spirit, we worship you in your glory, wise Lord. We praise you holy Lord, and extol you in our prayers. You are blessed, worshipped forever above the roof of the world, high-king of heaven, in your holy majesty, radiant source of life, across every land."

Then Nebuchadnezzar, the nation's leader, considered it 409 with his closest advisors: "Many of you saw, my people, that we sent three into the burning fire's flames, commanded to the pyre. Now I truly see four people there—I do not deceive myself at all." Then one who was a wise counselor of the king, shrewd of speech, said: "It is a certain miracle that we are gazing on there with our eyes. Consider, my prince,

Geðenc, ðeoden min,   þine gerysna.

420   Ongyt georne   hwa þa gyfe sealde
gingum gædelingum.   Hie God herigað,
anne ecne,   and ealles him
be naman gehwam   on neod sprecað,
þanciað þrymmes   þristum wordum,

425   cweðað he sie ana   ælmihtig God,
witig wuldor-cyning,   worlde and heofona.
Aban þu þa beornas,   brego Caldea,
ut of ofne.   Nis hit owihtes god
þæt hie sien on þam laðe   leng þonne þu þurfe."

430   Het þa se cyning to him   cnihtas gangan.
Hyssas hearde   hyrdon lare,
cyrdon cynegode   swa hie gecyðde wæron,
hwurfon hæleð geonge   to þam hæðenan foran.
Wæron þa bende forburnene   þe him on banum lagon,

435   lað-searo leoda cyninges,   and hyra lice geborgen.
Næs hyra wlite gewemmed,   ne nænig wroht on hrægle,
ne feax fyre beswæled,   ac hie on friðe Drihtnes
of ðam grimman gryre   glade treddedon,
gleaw-mode guman,   on gastes hyld.

440   Ða gewat se engel up   secan him ece dreamas
on heanne hrof   heofona rices,
heh-þegn and hold   halgum metode.
Hæfde on þam wundre gewurðod   ðe þa gewyrhto
                                                            ahton.

Hyssas heredon Drihten   for þam hæðenan folce,

445   septon hie soð-cwidum   and him sædon fela
soðra tacna,   oðþæt he sylfa gelyfde
þæt se wære mihta waldend   se ðe hie of ðam mirce
                                                            generede.

your proper duty. Understand clearly who has granted that grace to these young companions. They are praising God, the one everlasting, and call on him by each and every name in necessity, they thank him for victory with bold words, they say that he is alone almighty God, wise king of glory, of the world and heavens. Summon the men, prince of the Chaldeans, out of the furnace. It is not at all good that they should be in pain longer than you need."

Then the king ordered the young men to come to him. 430 The bold youths obeyed the order, the noblemen turned as they were instructed, the young heroes went before the pagan. The bonds they had tied on their limbs, the hateful knots of the king's people, were incinerated, and their bodies protected. Their looks were not harmed, nor was any damage done to their clothes, nor hair scorched by fire, but they gladly stepped out of that grim terror in the Lord's surety, wise-minded men, in the spirit's protection. Then the angel, a chief minister and one loyal to the holy creator, ascended into the firmament to seek the eternal joys of the kingdom of heaven. In that miracle he had honored those who had merit.

The youths praised the Lord before the pagan nation, 444 they taught them in true words and gave them many true explanations, until the king himself believed that he who had saved them from the smoke is the wielder of powers.

Gebead þa se bræsna   Babilone weard
swið-mod sinum leodum,   þæt se wære his aldre scyldig,
450 se ðæs onsoce   þætte soð wære mære
mihta waldend,   se hie of þam morðre alysde.
Agæf him þa his leoda lafe   þe þær gelædde wæron
on æht eald-feondum,   þæt hie are hæfdon.
Wæs heora blæd in Babilone,   siððan hie þone bryne
                                                                    fandedon,
455 dom wearð æfter duguðe gecyðed,   siððan hie Drihtne
                                                                    gehyrdon.
Wæron hyra rædas rice,   siððan hie rodera waldend,
halig heofon-rices weard,   wið þone hearm gescylde.
     Þa ic secan gefrægn   soðum wordum,
siððan he wundor onget,
460 Babilone weard,   þurh fyres bryne—
hu þa hyssas þry   hatan ofnes,
fær-gryre fyres,   oferfaren hæfdon.
Wylm þurhwodon,   swa him wiht ne sceod
grim gleda nið,   Godes spel-bodan,
465 frecnan fyres,   ac him frið Drihtnes
wið þæs egesan gryre   aldor gescylde.
Ða se ðeoden ongan   geðinges wyrcan;
het þa tosomne   sine leode,
and þa on þam meðle   ofer menigo bebead
470 wyrd gewordene   and wundor Godes,
þætte on þam cnihtum   gecyðed wæs:
     "Onhicgað nu   halige mihte,
wise wundor Godes!   We gesawon
þæt he wið cwealme gebearh   cnihtum on ofne,
475 lacende lig,   þam þe his lof bæron;
forþam he is ana   ece Drihten,
dema ælmihtig,   se ðe him dom forgeaf,

278

Then the brazen guardian of Babylon commanded his people: that the life would be forfeit of anyone who denied that he who had rescued them from that slaughter is the true wielder of powers. Then he returned the heirlooms of the people to them, which had been brought there in the possession of those ancient enemies, so that they had honor. Glory was theirs in Babylon, after they passed the test in the fire, their honor was made known among the seasoned troop, after they had obeyed the Lord. Their counsels were potent, after the ruler of the skies, the holy guardian of the heavenly kingdom, shielded them against that harm.

Then I discovered by true words, the moment when   458
he, the protector of Babylon, understood the miracle—how the three youths had passed through the sudden terror of the fire, of the oven's heat. They had walked through the surge, as the grim hatred of the flames, the fire's hostility, did not harm them at all, God's preachers, but the surety of the Lord shielded their lives against the awful terror. Then the prince began to summon an assembly; he ordered his people together, and then in the gathering he announced across the multitude the accomplished feat and God's miracle, which was made known in the young men:

"Consider now the holy might, the wise miracle of God!   472
We saw that he sheltered the youths against death in the oven, in the jumping flame, those who lifted up his praise; therefore he alone is the eternal Lord, the almighty judge, he who gave them honor, thriving success, those who carry

spowende sped,　þam þe his spel berað.

Forðon witigað　þurh wundor monig
480　halgum gastum　þe his hyld curon.

Cuð is þæt me Daniel　dyglan swefnes
soðe gesæde,　þæt ær swiðe oðstod
manegum on mode　minra leoda,
forþam ælmihtig　eacenne gast
485　in sefan sende,　snyttro cræftas."

　　Swa wordum spræc　werodes ræswa,
Babilone weard,　siððan he beacen onget,
swutol tacen Godes.　No þy sel dyde,
ac þam æðelinge　ofer-hygd gesceod,
490　wearð him hyrra hyge　and on heortan geðanc
mara on mod-sefan　þonne gemet wære,
oðþæt hine mid nyde　nyðor asette
metod ælmihtig,　swa he manegum deð
þara þe þurh ofer-hyd　up astigeð.

LIV

495　　Þa him wearð on slæpe　swefen ætywed,
Nabochodonossor;　him þæt neh gewearð.
Þuhte him þæt on foldan　fægre stode
wudu-beam wlitig,　se wæs wyrtum fæst,
beorht on blædum.　Næs he bearwe gelic,
500　ac he hlifode　to heofon-tunglum,
swilce he oferfæðmde　foldan sceatas,
ealne middan-geard,　oð mere-streamas,
twigum and telgum.　Ðær he to geseah,
þuhte him þæt se wudu-beam　wilddeor scylde,
505　ane æte　eallum heolde,
swylce fuglas eac　heora feorhnere
on þæs beames　bledum name.

his message. Therefore he prophesies by many a wonder through holy souls who choose his protection. It is known to me that Daniel spoke truly about my secret dream, which earlier had perplexed many of my people in their mind, because the almighty sent a potent spirit, wise skills, into his mind."

Thus spoke in words the prince of the troop, the guardian of Babylon, after he understood the sign, the clear proof of God. He did no better, but arrogance damaged the prince, a haughtier mind developed in him, and in his heart's pondering came grander thoughts than was fitting, until the almighty creator necessarily cast him down, as he does to many of those who through arrogance climb upward. 486

Then it happened that in sleep a dream was revealed to Nebuchadnezzar; it turned out to be about him. It seemed to him that a beautiful tree stood pleasantly on the earth, which was sound in its roots, bright in its fruits. It was not like a forest tree, but it towered to the stars of heaven, and also it reached over the plains of the earth, all middle-earth, as far as ocean streams, with twigs and with branches. While he looked on, it seemed to him that the tree shielded wild animals, it alone held food for them all, so also birds took their nourishment from the tree's fruit. LIV 495

Ðuhte him þæt engel   ufan of roderum
stigan cwome   and stefne abead,
510   torhtan reorde.   Het þæt treow ceorfan
and þa wildeor   on weg fleon,
swylce eac þa fugolas,   þonne his fyll come.
Het þonne besnædan   seolfes blædum,
twigum and telgum—   and þeh tacen wesan,
515   wunian wyrt-ruman   þæs wudu-beames
eorðan fæstne,   oðþæt eft cyme
grene bleda,   þonne God sylle.
Het eac gebindan   beam þone miclan
ærenum clammum   and isernum,
520   and gesæledne   in susl don,
þæt his mod wite   þæt migtigra
wite wealdeð   þonne he him wið mæge.
    Þa of slæpe onwoc   —swefn wæs æt ende—
eorðlic æðeling.   Him þæs egesa stod,
525   gryre fram ðam gaste   ðe þyder God sende.
Het þa tosomne   sine leode,
folc-togan feran,   frægn ofer ealle
swið-mod cyning   hwæt þæt swefen bude,
nalles þy he wende   þæt hie hit wiston,
530   ac he cunnode   hu hie cweðan woldon.
Ða wæs to ðam dome   Daniel haten,
Godes spel-boda.   Him wæs gæst geseald,
halig of heofonum,   se his hyge trymede.
On þam drihten-weard   deopne wisse
535   sefan sidne geþanc   and snytro cræft,
wisne word-cwide.   Eft he wundor manig
metodes mihta   for men ætbær.
    Þa he secgan ongan   swefnes woman,

DANIEL

It seemed to him that an angel descended from the skies 508
above and gave orders in a clear voice. He commanded the
tree to be cut down, and the wild animals and also the birds
to flee, when its fall should come. He commanded the tree
itself to be shorn of its fruit, twigs and branches—but nevertheless there should be a token, a stump to remain of the
tree firm in the earth, until green shoots should come again,
when God should grant it. He also commanded the great
tree to be bound with brass and iron chains, and when
bound, given to be tortured, so that his mind should know
that a mightier one controls the punishment than he is able
to resist.

Then the earthly prince awoke from sleep—the dream 523
was at an end. The fright remained with him, the terror from
the spirit that God had sent there. Then he commanded his
people together, the national leaders to come, the arrogant
king asked them all what the dream meant, not at all because he thought they knew it, but he tested how they would
speak. Then Daniel was summoned to that judgment, God's
messenger. The spirit was given to him, holy from the heavens, which strengthened his mind. In that mind the lord
protector knew there to be a deep and wide intelligence,
wise skill and sagacious speech. Afterward he presented before the people many a wonder of the creator's might.

Then the guide of the army, arrogant and pagan, began to 538

283

heah-heort and hæðen   heriges wisa,
540   ealne þone egesan   þe him eowed wæs.
Bæd hine areccan   hwæt seo run bude,
hofe haligu word   and in hige funde
to gesecganne   soðum wordum
hwæt se beam bude   þe he blican geseah,
545   and him witgode   wyrda geþingu.
He ða swigode,   hwæðere soð ongeat,
Daniel æt þam dome,   þæt his drihten wæs,
gumena aldor,   wið God scyldig.
Wandode se wisa;   hwæðre he worde cwæð,
550   æ-cræftig ar,   to þam æðelinge:
      "Þæt is, weredes weard,   wundor unlytel,
þæt þu gesawe   þurh swefen cuman,
heofon-heane beam   and þa halgan word,
yrre and egeslicu,   þa se engel cwæð,
555   þæt þæt treow sceolde,   telgum besnæded,
foran afeallan,   þæt ær fæste stod,
and þonne mid deorum   dreamleas beon,
westen wunian,   and his wyrt-ruman
foldan befolen,   fyrst-mearc wesan
560   stille on staðole,   swa seo stefn gecwæð,
ymb seofon tida   sæde eft onfon.
      "Swa þin blæd lið.   Swa se beam geweox,
heah to heofonum,   swa þu hæleðum eart
ana eallum   eorð-buendum
565   weard and wisa.   Nis þe wiðer-breca,
man on moldan,   nymðe metod ana.
Se ðec aceorfeð   of cyningdome,
and ðec wineleasne   on wræc sendeð,
and þonne onhweorfeð   heortan þine,

talk about the dream's noise, all the terror that was revealed to him. He ordered him to say what the mystery signified, that he should rouse himself and find in his mind holy words to explain in true sentences what the tree signified, which he had seen shining, and prophesy matters of destiny for him. He then went silent. However, Daniel at that judgment understood the truth, that his lord, the leader of men, was guilty before God. The wise one hesitated; however, the messenger skilled in the Law spoke in a word to the prince:

"Guardian of the troop, that is no small wonder that you   551 saw advancing in your dream, the heaven-high tree and the holy words, angry and terrifying, that the angel spoke, saying that the tree, trimmed of its branches, beforehand must be felled, that which formerly stood fast, and then must be joyless among the wild beasts, must remain in the desert, and its stump buried in the earth, be still for a set time in its foundation, just as the voice said, and after seven seasons it will regenerate.

"So your glory lies. As the tree grew, high to the heavens,   562 so are you the guardian and guide for men, alone among all dwellers of the earth. There is no rival for you, a man on the earth, except the creator alone. He will cut you off from your kingdom, and send you friendless into exile, and then he will transform your heart, so that you do not remember

570 þæt þu ne gemyndgast   æfter man-dreame,
ne gewittes wast   butan wildeora þeaw,
ac þu lifgende   lange þrage
heorta hlypum   geond holt wunast.

"Ne bið þec mæl-mete   nymþe mores græs,
575 ne rest witod,   ac þec regna scur
weceð and wreceð   swa wildu deor,
oðþæt þu ymb seofon winter   soð gelyfest,
þæt sie an metod   eallum mannum,
reccend and rice,   se on roderum is.

580 Is me swa þeah willa   þæt se wyrt-ruma
stille wæs on staðole,   swa seo stefn gecwæð,
and ymbe seofan tide   sæde onfenge.
Swa þin rice   restende bið,
anwalh for eorlum,   oðþæt þu eft cymst.

585 Gehyge þu, frea min,   fæstlicne ræd.
Syle ælmyssan,   wes earmra hleo,
þinga for ðeodne   ær ðam seo þrah cyme
þæt he þec aworpe   of woruld-rice.
Oft metod alæt   monige ðeode

590 wyrcan bote,   þonne hie woldon sylfe,
fyrene fæstan,   ær him fær Godes
þurh egesan gryre   aldre gesceode."

No þæs fela Daniel   to his drihtne gespræc
soðra worda   þurh snytro cræft,

595 þæt þæs a se rica   reccan wolde,
middan-geardes weard,   ac his mod astah,
heah fram heortan;   he þæs hearde ongeald.
Ongan ða gyddigan   þurh gylp micel
Caldea cyning   þa he ceastre weold;

600 Babilone burh   on his blæde geseah,

human happiness, nor be aware of any intellect except the
way of wild animals, but you will continue living for a long
time on the courses of the deer across the forest.

"There will be no food for you except the grass of the   574
moor, nor resting place fixed for you, but the shower of
rain will waken and pursue you like a wild animal, until after
seven years you believe the truth, that there is one creator
for all people, a ruler and a power, who is in the heavens.
Nevertheless, it appears to me his will is that the stump be
fixed on its foundation, as the voice said, and should regenerate after seven seasons. So your kingdom will abide, undiminished before men, until you again return. Consider, my
lord, reliable advice. Give alms, be the protector of the weak,
place a petition before the prince, before that time should
come when he cast you out of the empire. Often the creator
allows many a nation fixed in sin to make remedy, when they
themselves wish to, before God's sudden attack deprives
them of life with frightening terror."

Daniel could not speak enough true words through wise   593
skill about this to his lord that would make the potentate,
middle-earth's guardian, take account of it, but his mind
climbed up, high from the heart; he paid hard for that. The
king of the Chaldeans began to brag in a great boast when
he ruled the city; in his glory he saw the city of Babylon tow-

Sennera feld   sidne bewindan,
heah hlifigan.   Þæt se here-tyma
werede geworhte   þurh wundor micel,
wearð ða an-hydig   ofer ealle men,
605   swið-mod in sefan,   for ðære sundor-gife
þe him God sealde,   gumena rice,
world to gewealde   in wera life:
   "Ðu eart seo micle   and min seo mære burh
þe ic geworhte   to wurðmyndum,
610   rume rice.   Ic reste on þe,
eard and eðel   agan wille."
Ða for ðam gylpe   gumena drihten
forfangen wearð   and on fleam gewat,
ana on ofer-hyd   ofer ealle men.
615   Swa wod wera   on gewin-dagum
geocrostne sið   in Godes wite,
ðara þe eft lifigende   leode begete,
Nabochodonossor,   siððan him nið Godes,
hreð of heofonum,   hete gesceode.
620   Seofon winter samod   susl þrowode,
wildeora westen,   win-burge cyning.
   Ða se earfoð-mæcg   up locode,
wilddeora gewita,   þurh wolcna gang.
Gemunde þa on mode   þæt metod wære,
625   heofona heah-cyning,   hæleða bearnum
ana ece gast.   Þa he eft onhwearf
wodan gewittes,   þær þe he ær wide bær
here-wosan hige,   heortan getenge.
Þa his gast ahwearf   in Godes gemynd,
630   mod to mannum,   siððan he metod onget.
Gewat þa earm-sceapen   eft siðian,

ering high, encompassing the broad field of Shinar. The general had built that great marvel for the troop, and grew stubborn over all people, arrogant in mind, because of the unique grace God had given him, the empire of men, the world to rule in mortal life:

"You are mine, the great and famous city that I built to 608 my honor, a broad empire. I repose in you, city and homeland I will possess." Then for that boast the lord of men became seized with madness and departed in flight, alone in his pride over all people. So he departed from men in days of toil, on the most difficult journey in God's punishment, of those who surviving afterward might return to their people, after God's enmity, swift from the heavens, in hostility had cut off Nebuchadnezzar. The king of the wine-city suffered punishment in the wilderness of wild beasts for seven years altogether.

Then the wretch looked up, the savage-minded one, 622 through the drift of clouds. He remembered then in his heart that the creator should be high-king of the heavens, the one eternal spirit for the children of men. Then after that he returned from his mad mind, where formerly he widely bore a belligerent mind close to his heart. Then his spirit turned to the memory of God, his heart to the people, after he understood the creator. Then the humiliated one

nacod nyd-genga,   nið geðafian,
wundorlic wræcca   and wæda leas,
mætra on mod-geðanc,   to man-cynne,
635 ðonne gumena weard   in gylpe wæs.
    Stod middan-geard   æfter man-drihtne,
eard and eðel   æfter þam æðelinge,
seofon winter samod,   swa no swiðrode
rice under roderum   oðþæt se ræswa com.
640 Þa wæs eft geseted   in aldordom
Babilone weard,   hæfde beteran ðeaw,
leohtran geleafan   in lif-fruman,
þætte God sealde   gumena gehwilcum
welan swa wite,   swa he wolde sylf.
645 Ne lengde þa   leoda aldor
witegena word-cwyde,   ac he wide bead
metodes mihte   þær he meld ahte,
sið-fæt sægde   sinum leodum,
wide waðe   þe he mid wilddeorum ateah,
650 oðþæt him Frean Godes   in gast becwom
rædfæst sefa,   ða he to roderum beseah.
    Wyrd wæs geworden,   wundor gecyðed,
swefn geseðed,   susl awunnen,
dom gedemed,   swa ær Daniel cwæð,
655 þæt se folc-toga   findan sceolde
earfoð-siðas   for his ofermedlan.
Swa he ofstlice   god-spellode
metodes mihtum   for man-cynne,
siððan in Babilone   burh-sittendum
660 lange hwile   lare sægde,
Daniel domas.   Siððan deora gesið,
wildra wær-genga,   of waðe cwom,

went journeying back to mankind, the beggar naked and
without clothes, accepting the chastisement, a miraculous
exile, more measured in intellect than that protector of men
had been in his boasting.

The middle-earth still stood afterward for the sovereign,   636
land and native soil afterward for the prince, seven years
altogether, so that his empire under the heavens had not
diminished until its prince returned. When the guardian of
Babylon was again established in lordship, he had a better
manner, a more enlightened belief in the source of life, that
God gave to each man prosperity or punishment, as he himself desired. The lord of the people did not hesitate then
over the discourses of the prophets, but he widely announced the creator's might where he had proclamations
made, told of the journey to his people, widely of the wandering that he had made with the wild beasts, until a reliable mind came into his spirit from the Lord God, when he
looked to the heavens.

Destiny was fulfilled, a miracle manifested, the dream   652
proved true, the punishment beaten, the judgment carried
out, just as Daniel earlier had said, that the sovereign must
discover the way of hardship because of his great pride. So
he urgently preached concerning the creator's power before
mankind, when Daniel for a long while announced his doctrine and judgments to the citizens in Babylon. After Nebuchadnezzar returned from the wandering, from the journey

Nabochodonossor   of nið-wracum,
siððan weardode   wide rice,
665 heold hæleða gestreon   and þa hean burh,
frod, fore-mihtig   folca ræswa,
Caldea cyning,   oðþæt him cwelm gesceod,
swa him ofer eorðan   andsaca ne wæs
gumena ænig   oðþæt him God wolde
670 þurh hryre hreddan   hea rice.
Siððan þær his aferan   ead bryttedon,
welan, wunden gold,   in þære widan byrig,
ealh-stede eorla,   unwaclice,
heah hord-mægen,   þa hyra hlaford læg.

LV
675 Ða in ðære ðeode awoc   his þæt þridde cneow.
Wæs Baldazar   burga aldor,
weold wera rices,   oðþæt him wlenco gesceod,
ofer-hyd egle.   Ða wæs ende-dæg
ðæs ðe Caldeas   cyningdom ahton.
680 Ða metod onlah   Medum and Persum
aldordomes   ymb lytel fæc,
let Babilone   blæd swiðrian,
þone þa hæleð   healdan sceoldon.
Wiste he ealdor-men   in unrihtum,
685 ða ðe ðy rice   rædan sceoldon.
Ða þæt gehogode   ham-sittende,
Meda aldor   —þæt ær man ne ongan—
þæt he Babilone   abrecan wolde,
alh-stede eorla,   þær æðelingas
690 under wealla hleo   welan brytnedon.
    Þæt wæs þara fæstna   folcum cuðost,
mæst and mærost   þara þe men bun,

of wild animals, of unruly refugees, back from his banishment, then he guarded his wide empire, looked after the treasures of the heroes and the high city, a wise, pre-eminent guide of the nations, the king of the Chaldeans, until death harmed him, so that no man was a rival to him across the earth, until God wished to deprive him of the high kingdom through his demise. Afterward there his heirs shared undiminished the prosperity, wealth, twisted gold, the great mass of treasure, when their lord lay dead.

Then into that nation was born the third generation after him. Belshazzar was lord of the cities and wielded human empire, until pride destroyed him, despicable presumptuousness. It was then the final day in which the Chaldeans held sovereignty. Then, within a short while, the ordaining Lord granted dominion to the Medes and Persians and let the glory of Babylon, which those men should have guarded, dwindle away. He knew that the elders, those who should have guided the empire, were involved in wrongful deeds. Then the lord of the Medes, waiting at home, decided that he would destroy Babylon—no-one had undertaken that before—the city of men, where princes enjoyed prosperity under the protection of the walls.

That was the fortress best known to the nations, greatest and most famous of those which men inhabit, Babylon

LV
675

691

Babilon burga,   oðþæt Baldazar
þurh gylp grome   Godes frasade.
695 Sæton him æt wine   wealle belocene,
ne onegdon na   orlegra nið,
þeah ðe feonda   folc feran cwome
herega gerædum   to þære heah-byrig
þæt hie Babilone   abrecan mihton.
700 Gesæt þa to symble   siðestan dæge
Caldea cyning   mid cneo-magum,
þær medu-gal wearð   mægenes wisa.
    Het þam æðelum beran   Israela gestreon,
husl-fatu halegu,   on hand werum,
705 þa ær Caldeas   mid cyne-ðrymme,
cempan in ceastre,   clæne genamon,
gold in Gerusalem,   ða hie Iudea
blæd forbræcon   billa ecgum,
and þurh hleoðor-cyme,   herige genamon
710 beorhte frætwe.   Ða hie tempel strudon,
Salomanes seld,   swiðe gulpon.
Ða wearð bliðe-mod   burga aldor,
gealp gramlice   Gode on andan,
cwæð þæt his hergas   hyrran wæron
715 and mihtigran   mannum to friðe
þonne Israela   ece Drihten.
    Him þæt tacen wearð   þær he to starude,
egeslic for eorlum   innan healle,
þæt he for leodum   lige-word gecwæð,
720 þa þær in egesan   engel Drihtnes
let his hand cuman   in þæt hea seld,
wrat þa in wage   worda gerynu,
baswe boc-stafas,   burhsittendum.

of the cities, until Belshazzar by his hostile boasting tested
God. They sat at their wine enclosed by the wall, not at all
fearing the hatred of enemies, even though a nation of foes
came advancing equipped as an army to the high city, so that
they might destroy Babylon. The king of the Chaldeans then
sat at feasting on the ultimate day with his relatives, when
that guide of that army became drunk.

He commanded the princes to carry in the treasures   703
of the Israelites, the sacred liturgical vessels, in the hands of
men, which the Chaldeans formerly had cleanly taken away
with royal triumph, the warriors in the city, gold in Jerusalem, when they had destroyed the glory of the Judeans with
the edges of swords, and in the cry of warfare had seized the
bright treasure in battle. When they plundered the temple,
Solomon's hall, they boasted greatly. Then the leader of the
cities was happy-minded, boasted tauntingly in hostility to
God, said that his armies were more high and mighty as a
surety to people than the eternal Lord of the Israelites.

To him the proof was sent where he gazed, terrifying be-   717
fore men within the hall, that he spoke lying words before
the people, when frighteningly an angel of the Lord allowed
his hand to come into the high hall, then wrote enigmatic
words on the wall, purple letters, for the citizens. Then the

Ða wearð folc-toga   forht on mode,
acul for þam egesan.   Geseah he engles hand
in sele writan   Sennera wite.
Þæt gyddedon   gumena mænigeo,
hæleð in healle,   hwæt seo hand write
to þam beacne   burh-sittendum.
Werede comon   on þæt wundor seon.
     Sohton þa swiðe   in sefan gehydum,
hwæt seo hand write   haliges gastes.
Ne mihton arædan   run-cræftige men
engles ærend-bec,   æðelinga cyn,
oðþæt Daniel com,   Drihtne gecoren,
snotor and soðfæst,   in þæt seld gangan.
Ðam wæs on gaste   Godes cræft micel,
to þam ic georne gefrægn   gyfum ceapian
burhge weardas   þæt he him boc-stafas
arædde and arehte,   hwæt seo run bude.
Him æ-cræftig   andswarode,
Godes spel-boda,   gleaw geðances:
     "No ic wið feoh-sceattum   ofer folc bere
Drihtnes domas,   ne ðe dugeðe can,
ac þe unceapunga   orlæg secge,
worda gerynu   þa þu wendan ne miht.
Þu for anmedlan   in æht bere
husl-fatu halegu,   on hand werum.
On þam ge deoflu   drincan ongunnon,
ða ær Israela   in æ hæfdon
æt Godes earce,   oðþæt hie gylp beswac,
win-druncen gewit,   swa þe wurðan sceal.
No þæt þin aldor   æfre wolde
Godes gold-fatu   in gylp beran,

sovereign became scared in his mind, fearful before the terror. He saw the angel's hand write in the hall the punishment of the people of Shinar. Many men discussed that, men in the hall, what the hand might have written as a sign to the citizens. Crowds came to look at that wonder.

They sought earnestly in their minds' thoughts concerning what the hand of the holy spirit had written. The men skilled in mysteries, the race of princes, were not able to read the angel's missive, until Daniel came into the hall, chosen by the Lord, wise and righteous. God's great power was in his spirit, so that, I have readily heard, the city's guards bargained with bribes so that he would read and interpret the letters, what the enigma signified. The one skilled in the Law answered them, God's messenger, wise of thought: 731

"I do not present the Lord's judgments to the nation for coins, nor can I do it for your benefit, but I will tell you your fate without haggling, the riddle of words that you cannot translate. For pride you would parade in captivity the sacred liturgical vessels in the hands of men. You have taken to drinking to devils with them, which the Israelites formerly used lawfully at the ark of God, until boasting seduced them, their intelligence intoxicated, as shall happen to you. Not at all would your father ever vauntingly parade God's golden vessels, nor the more quickly boast, even though he 743

755 ne ðy hraðor hremde,   ðeah ðe here brohte
Israela gestreon   in his æhte geweald,
ac þæt oftor gecwæð   aldor ðeoda
soðum wordum   ofer sin mægen,
siððan him wuldres weard   wundor gecyðde,
760 þæt he wære ana   ealra gesceafta
Drihten and waldend;   se him dom forgeaf,
unscyndne blæd   eorðan rices —
and þu lignest nu   þæt sie lifgende,
se ofer deoflum   dugeþum wealdeð."

brought the treasures of the Israelites with his army as possessions under his rule, but the leader of nations more often
announced to his forces in true words, after the guardian of
glory had made known a miracle to him, that he alone is
Lord and ruler of all created things; he gave him honor, the
unsullied glory of earth's empire—and now you deny that he
is living, who rules in majesty over the devils."

AZARIAS

Him þa Azarias   in-geþoncum
hleoþrede halig   þurh hatne lig,
dreag dædum georn,   Dryhten herede,
wis in weorcum,   ond þas word acwæð:
5 "Meotud all-wihta,   þu eart meahtum swið
niþas to nerganne.   Is þin noma mære,
wlitig ond wuldorfæst   ofer wer-þeode.

    "Sindon þine domas   on dæda gehwam
soðe geswiðde   ond gesigefæste,
10 eac þinne willan   in woruld-spedum
ryhte mid ræde.   Rodera waldend,
geoca us georne,   gæsta scyppend,
ond þurh hyldo help,   halig Dryhten,
nu we þec for þearfum   ond for þrea-nydum
15 ond fore eað-medum   arena biddaþ,
lege bilegde.   We þæs lifgende
worhton in worulde,   eac þon wom dydon
yldran usse,   in ofer-hygdum
þin bibodu bræcon   burg-sittende,
20 had oferhogedon   halgan lifes.

    "Wurdon we towrecene   geond widne grund,
heapum tohworfne,   hylda lease;
wæs ure lif   geond londa fela
fracuð ond gefræge   fold-buendum.
25 Nu þu usic bewræce   in þas wyrrestan

302

Then holy Azariah spoke from his inner thoughts through the hot flame, eager for deeds he persisted, wise in works he praised the Lord and spoke these words: "Maker of all things, you are ready in might to save men. Great is your name, beautiful and glorious over the nation.

"In each deed your judgments truly are made mighty and triumphant, and also your will has guided with good counsel to worldly prosperity. Ruler of the skies, assist us eagerly, creator of spirits, and help us by your favor, holy Lord, now that we in our needs and tortures and humiliation beg for grace, surrounded by flame. Living in the world we brought this about, and our elders also committed crimes; in arrogance the citizens broke your commandments, despised the calling of holy life.

"We were exiled across the wide earth, dispersed in crowds, without protection; throughout many lands our life is despised and a byword among earth-dwellers. Now you have banished us to the rule of the worst of earth's kings as

eorð-cyninges   æht-gewealda,
in hæft heoro-grimmes,   sceolon we þær hæþenra
þrea-nyd . . .

* * *

“. . . hæfdes

30 to Abrahame   ond to Isace
ond Iacobe,   gæsta scyppend.
  “Þu him gehete   þurh hleoþor-cwidas
þæt þu hyra from-cynn   on fyrn-dagum
ycan wolde,   þæt hit æfter him
35 on cyne-ryce   cenned wurde,
yced on eorþan,   þæt swa unrime,
had to hebban,   swa heofon-steorran
bugað bradne hwearft   oð brim-flodas,
swa waroþa sond   ymb sealt wæter,
40 yþe geond ear-grund,   þæt swa unrime
ymb wintra hwearft   weorðan sceolde.
Fyl nu þa frum-spræce,   þeah þe user fea lifgen,
wlitega þine word-cwidas   ond ðin wuldor us!
Gecyð cræft ond meaht,   nu þec Caldeas
45 ond eac fela folca   gefregen habban
þæt þu ana eart   ece Dryhten,
sige-rof settend   ond soð meotod,
wuldres waldend   ond woruld-sceafta!”
  Swa se halga wer   hergende wæs
50 meotudes miltse,   ond his mod-sefan
rehte þurh reorde.   Ða of roderum wearð
engel ælbeorhta   ufon onsended,
wlite-scyne wer   in his wuldor-homan,
cwom him þa to are   ond to ealdornere
55 þurh lufan ond þurh lisse.   Se þone lig tosceaf,

AZARIAS

possessions, into the captivity of warlike men, and where we
must suffer servitude to the pagans . . .

* * *

". . . you have to Abraham and Isaac and Jacob, maker of
spirits.

"You promised them in discourses that in distant days 32
you would increase their offspring, which would be born in
generations after them, increased on earth so that the kindred should become so innumerable, be exalted as the stars
of heaven revolving in their broad orbit, even to the ocean
streams, and as the sand of the shores about the salt water,
by the wave across the sea's expanse, should become so innumerable, across the circuit of the years. Fulfill now that
oath, though few of them should be alive, embellish your
promises and your glory in us! Make known your power and
might, now the Chaldeans and many nations have heard
about you, that you alone are the eternal Lord, triumphant
founder and true creator, ruler of glory, and of worldly creatures!"

So the holy man was praising the creator's mercy and 49
spoke his mind aloud. Then from the skies above a radiant angel was sent, a beautiful man in his glorious robe, who
came as a favor and as a lifesaver to them in love and in kindness. He, holy and heaven-bright, forced back the flame,

305

halig ond heofon-beorht,   hatan fyres,
þæt se bittra bryne   beorgan sceolde
for þæs engles ege   æfæstum þrim.
Tosweop ond toswengde   þurh swiðes meaht
60   liges leoman,   swa hyra lice ne scod,
ac wæs in þam ofne,   þa se engel cwom,
windig ond wynsum,   wedere onlicust
þonne on sumeres tid   sended weorþeð
dropena dreorung   mid dæges hwile.
65   Se wæs in þam fire   for Frean meahtum
halgum to helpe.   Wearð se hata lig
todrifen ond todwæsced,   þær þa dæd-hwatan
þry mid geþoncum   þeoden heredon,
bædon bletsian   bearn in worulde
70   ealle gesceafte   ecne Dryhten,
þeoda waldend.   Swa hi þry cwædon,
modum horsce,   þurh gemæne word:
    "Bletsige þec,   bilwit Fæder,
woruld-sceafta wuldor   ond weorca gehwylc,
75   heofonas ond englas   ond hluttor wæter,
ond eal mægen   eorþan gesceafta.
Bletsige þec, soðfæst cyning,   sunne ond mona,
leohte leoman,   lifgende God,
hædre ond hlutre   ond heofon-dreame
80   wæstem weorðian.   Ful oft þu, wuldor-cyning,
þurh lyft lætest   leodum to freme
mildne morgen-ren;   monig sceal siþþan
wyrt onwæcnan,   eac þon wudu-bearwas
tanum tydrað;   trymmað eorð-welan,
85   hleoð ond hluttrað.   Næfre hlisan ah
meotud þan maran   þonne he wið monna bearn

the heat of the fire, so that the bitter blaze should preserve those three observant in the law by the angel's terror. He swept away and scattered the radiance of the flame by great force, so that their body was not harmed, but when the angel arrived it was breezy and pleasant in that oven, the weather most similar to when in summertime it happens that a sprinkling of drops is sent at daytime.

He was in that fire by the Lord's might, as a help to 65 the saints. The hot flame was driven back and extinguished where the valiant ones, the three, praised the prince in their thoughts, the men commanded all land-creatures in the cosmos to bless the eternal Lord, the ruler of nations. So those three, clever in mind, said in unison:

"Gracious Father, let the glory of the world's creatures 73 and works bless you, the heavens and the angels, and clear waters, and all forces of the earthly creatures. Righteous king, let the sun and moon bless you, the beams of light, living God, brightly and clearly with heavenly bliss honor you in their fullness. Very often, king of glory, you send mild morning rain through the sky as a comfort to people; many plants must be roused afterward, the forest groves also bring forth branches; it makes strong the richness of the earth, protects and purifies. The creator never has the more fame than when he does benevolent deeds for the children of

wyrceð wel-dædum.   Wis bið se þe con
ongytan þone geocend,   þe us eall good syleð
þe we habbað   þenden we her beoð,

90   ond us milde meotod   mare gehateð,
gif we geearniað,   elne willað,
ðonne feran sceal   þurh Frean hæse
sundor anra gehwæs   sawl of lice.

"Ond þec, God Dryhten,   gæstas hergen,

95   byrnende fyr   ond beorht sumor,
wearme weder-dagas,   waldend manna,
Frean on ferðe.   Fremest eorð-welan
þurh monigne had,   milde Dryhten,
ond þec dæg ond niht,   domfæst cyning,

100   lofigen ond lufigen,   lux et tenebre,
þe þas wer-þeoda   weardum healdað.
Deop Dryhtnes bibod   drugon hi þæt longe.

"Ond þec, Crist cyning,   ceolas weorðian,
Fæder, forst ond snaw,   folca waldend,

105   winter-bitera weder   ond wolcna genipu,
ond þec liexende   ligetta hergen,
blace, breahtum-hwate,   bryten-rices weard,
dyrne Dryhten.   A þin dom sy
god ond genge—   þu þæs geornlice

110   wyrcest, wuldor-cyning.   Wæstmum herge,
bletsien bledum,   ond þin blæd wese
a forð ece,   ælmihtig God.
Wesað ond weaxað   ealle wer-þeode,
lifgað bi þam lissum   þe us se leofa cyning,

115   ece Dryhten,   ær gesette
sinum bearnum to brice,   bremen Dryhten.

"Ond þec, halga God,   hea duna

308

men. Wise is he who is able to perceive in you the sustainer, who gives us all the good that we have while we are here, and the mild creator promises us more, if we merit it, desire it zealously, when we must travel at the Lord's behest, each soul be separated from the body.

"And Lord God, let spirits praise you, burning fire and 94
bright summer, warm weather days, ruler of men, Lord in spirit. You bring about earthly goods in many a degree, mild Lord, and let day and night praise and love you, glorious king, light and darkness, those which the nations carefully observe. They have performed that for a long time, the deep command of the Lord.

"And let frosts honor you, king Christ, Father, rime and 103
snow, ruler of peoples, winter-bitter weather and the bank of clouds, let the shining lightning praise you, bright and sudden as a flash, dear Lord, guardian of the spacious kingdom. May your judgment always be good and sure—you readily bring that about, king of glory. May you be praised by fertile things, let them bless you in their foliage, and let your glory be ever eternal, almighty God. The entire nation continues and grows, we live by the grace that the dear king, the eternal Lord, earlier established for us, the glorious Lord for his children to enjoy.

"And, holy God, high hills across middle-earth should 117

geond middan-geard   miltsum hergen,
fæger folde   ond Fæder rice,
120 forðon waldend scop   wudige moras,
lofe leanige   leohtes hyrde.
Bletsige þec, soðfæst cyning,   sæs ond wætra,
hea holmas,   haligne Dryhten,
domlice deop wæter;   ond Dryhtnes bibod
125 geofon-floda gehwylc   georne bihealdeð,
þonne mere-streamas   meotudes ræswum
wæter onwealcað.   Witon eald-gecynd
þæt ær gescop   ece Dryhten
lagu-floda bigong,   leohtes hyrde,
130 on þam wuniað   wid-ferende
siðe on sunde   seldlicra fela.

    "Bletsien þec þa ealle,   ece Dryhten,
þurh þinne willan,   wuldorfæst cyning,
ond þec ealle æ-sprynge,   ece Dryhten,
135 heanne hergen.   Ful oft þu hluttor lætest
wæter wynlico   to woruld-hyhte
of clife clænum.   Þæt us se cyning gescop
monnum to miltse   ond to mægen-eacan.
Bletsien þec,   bilwit Fæder,
140 fiscas ond fuglas,   fela-meahtigne,
ealle þa þe onhreorað   hreo wægas
on þam bradan brime,   bremen Dryhten,
hergen haligne,   ond heofon-fuglas,
þa þe lacende   geond lyft farað.
145 Bletsien þec, Dryhten,   deor ond nyten.
    "Meotud monna bearn   miltsum hergen
ond ecne God,   Israhela cynn.
Bletsien þe þine sacerdas,   soðfæst cyning,
milde mæsseras   mærne Dryhten,

praise you for your mercies, the pleasant earth and Father's empire, because the ruler created the wooded slopes, with praise they should repay the shepherd of light. Righteous king, may the seas and waters bless you, high seas, holy Lord, gloriously deep water; and by the Lord's decree each ocean stream eagerly keeps its way, when by the creator's counsels the sea currents surge around the waters. They know their ancient nature which the eternal Lord had created, the expanse of seas, the shepherd of light, in which dwell many strange creatures traveling far and wide in the deep.

"Let them all bless you, eternal Lord, according to your   132
wishes, and all fountains, glorious king, eternal Lord, should praise you on high. Very often you let clear water fall cleanly off the cliff, joyfully in worldly delight. The king created that for us, for men in mercy and for fertility. Merciful Father, let fishes and birds bless you, omnipotent one, all those that stir up fierce waves on the wide sea, glorious Lord, and let birds of the air, who travel flitting through the air, praise the holy one. May wild beasts and cattle bless you Lord.

"Let the nation of Israel, children of men, praise the cre-   146
ator, the eternal God for his mercies. May your priests and mild mass-priests bless you, righteous king, glorious Lord,

150 ond þine þeowas,   ðeoda hyrde,
swylce haligra   hluttre saule,
ond, ece God,   eað-mod-heorte.
Nu þec Ananias   ond Azarias
ond Misahel, meotud,   miltsum hergað.
155 Nu we geonge þry   God bletsiað,
fela-meahtigne   Fæder in heofonum,
þone soðan Sunu   ond þone sigefæstan Gæst.
Forþon us onsende   sigora waldend
engel to are,   se þe us bearg
160 fyr ond feondas,   ond mid fiþrum bewreah
wið bryne-brogan."
                        Breahtmum hwurfun
ymb þæt hate hus   hæðne leode,
ða þæt ongeaton   Godes ondsacan
þæt hi ne meahtan   —ne meotod wolde—
165 acwellan cnyhta æ,   ac hy Crist scilde.
Hwearf þa to healle,   swa he hraþost meahte,
eorl acol-mod,   þæt he ofer his ealdre gestod.
Abead þa for þære duguðe   deop ærende,
haligra gehyld   (hlyst wæs þær inne),
170 grom-hydig guma: "Þæt ic geare wiste,
þæt we III hæfdon,   þeoda wisa,
geonge cniehtas,   for gæst-lufan
gebunden to bæle   in byrnendes
fyres leoman.   Na ic þær IIII men
175 sende to siðe: nales me sylfa gerad.
Hweorfað nu æfter heorðe,   nængum hat sceþeð,
ofnes æled,   ac him is engel mid,
hafað beorhtne blæd;   ne mæg him bryne sceþþan
wlitigne wuldor-homan."

and your servants, shepherd of the nations, likewise those pure in soul and humble of heart, eternal God. Now, creator, Hananiah and Azariah and Mishael praise you for your mercies. Now we three young ones bless God, omnipotent Father in the heavens, the true Son and the victorious Spirit. Therefore ruler of victories, you have sent us an angel as a favor, who has blocked fire and enemies for us, and with wings covered us against the terrifying blaze."

With shouts the pagan people moved around that hot 161 house, when they understood that they could not kill God's messengers, the law of the youths—the creator did not wish it—but Christ sheltered them. A terrified nobleman moved then to the hall as quickly as he could, so that he stood before his lord. The fierce-minded man then announced the profound message before the troop, the protection of the saints (there was attention in there): "I readily knew, guide of the nations, that for spiritual love we had bound for burning three young lads in the blazing beams of fire. I did not send four people there to their fate: that was not at all my own arrangement. Now they move about across the hearth, the heat does not harm any of them, the flame of the furnace, but an angel is with them, they have a bright radiance; the blaze cannot harm his beautiful glory-raiment."

Ða þam wordum swealg

180 brego Caldea, gewat þa to þam bryne gongan
an-hydig eorl, þæt he ofer þam ade gestod.
Het þa of þam lige lifgende bearn
Nabocodonossor near ætgongan.
Ne forhogodon þæt þa halgan, siþþan hi hwæt-mode

185 woruld-cyninges weorn gehyrdon,
ac eodon of þam fyre feorh unwemme
wuldre gewlitegad, swa hyra wædum ne scod
gifre gleda nið, ac hi mid gæst-lufan
synne geswencton ond gesigefæston,

190 modum gleawe, in mon-þeawum,
þurh fore-þoncas fyr gedygdon.

When the prince of the Chaldeans swallowed those 179
words, he went to the blaze, the arrogant man, so that he
stood in front of the pyre. He then commanded the living
men to come out of the flame and go before Nebuchadnezzar. The saints did not despise that, when they courageously
obeyed the admonition of the earthly king, but they went
from the fire, life unharmed, the miracle glorified, so that
even their clothes were not damaged by the greedy hostility
of the flames, but with spiritual love they crushed sin, and
became victorious, wise in their minds, in their customs,
and with prudence escaped the fire.

Appendix

Three lines of verse appear as captions to illustrations in Junius XI. They have been edited by A. J. Bliss, "Some Unnoticed Lines of Old English Verse," *Notes and Queries* 216 (1971): 404.

p. 3
Hu se engyl ongon   ofer-mod wesan
How the angel began to be insolent

p. 3
Her se hælend gesce(op)   helle heom to wite
Here the savior created hell as a punishment for them

p. 7
Her be todælde   dæg wið nihte
Here day and night are separated

A fourth shows metrical rhythm but lacks alliteration:

p. 6
(Her h)e gesyndrode   wæter and eorðan
Here he divided the water and the earth

Note on the Texts

This edition of the poems in this volume has necessarily not included discussion of many of the complex problems faced by editors of Old English verse. It is my own, though I consulted a number of editions when establishing the text. These are listed in the Bibliography. In the edition and the translation of the poems from Junius XI I have included a system of fitt numbering that corresponds to the sometimes sporadic (and in *Genesis* confused) numbering of sectional divisions in the manuscript. I have not noted scribal corrections to the text where these have produced acceptable readings. Modern punctuation has been added. Abbreviations in the manuscripts have been expanded without comment, with the Tironian symbol 7 expanded as *and* unless otherwise stated. I have maintained this convention despite some evidence in the text of *Genesis A* for a preferred spelling of *ond*.

Notes to the Texts

9 swið-feorm: swið ferom   23 dwæl: dæl   52 bryttigan: brytti-
gin   63 yrre: yr   65 Sceof: Sceop   82 buað: buan   100 geseted:
gesetet   116 gyta: gyt   131 gesceaft: gescaft   135 timber: tiber
150 flod: fold   155 gyta: gyt   184 freolice: freo licu   186 Eue: *not in*
MS   221 Þæra: þære anne: *not in MS*   222 se: sæ   255 wæstm:
wæwtm   317 geswinc: gewrinc   344 cwæð se: *abbreviation for* þæt *in-*
serted between   346 winnan: widnan *with* d *marked for deletion*   357 ham:
not in MS   382 ymbe:ymb   459 metod:metot   476 he:heo   506 hearran: hearan   625 ond: ond *written out*   626 gieng: gien   644 laðe:
lað   656 bliðe: blið   696 hell-geþwing: hell ge þwin *with letter following*
erased   702 him: hire   752 heofon-rice: heofon rices   826 þinum:
þinu   857 þam:þa   875 ne: *not in MS*   906 werig: werg   907 bradre:
brade   917 hu:nu   954 hie:he   959 gehwilcre:gehilcre   980 asteah:
hyge wælmos teah   1011 wærfæstne: wærfæsne   1022 ædre: *not in*
MS   1040 þe: *not in MS*   1056 fæsten: *Not in MS*   1088 æres:
ærest   1093 sumne: sune   1098 ic: *not in MS*   1118 eðel-stæfe: edulf
stæfe   1120 and: *runic* wyn *for Tironian abbrev. of* et.   1128 leod:
leof   1131 he: heo   1133 Sethes: sedes   1148 þurh: þur   1155 Cainan:
Cain *with two following letters erased*   1160 Cainanes: caines   1162 feowertig: feowertigum   1191 eaforan: eafora   1195 and: ond *written*
out   1211 feran:frean   1219 þissa:þisse   1232 and:*not in MS*   1234 eaforan: eafora   1307 þæt: þær   1308 and: *not in MS*   1314 fremede:
freme   1335 ond: ond written out   1338 oðerra: oðe ra *with erasure af-*
ter e   1401 heof: heo   1405 ed-modne: ed monne   flod: *not in*

321

MS 1416 torhtne: torht 1428 þæra: þære 1469 gesittan: gesette 1491 liðe: hliðe 1492 geþeahtne: geþeahte 1508 þæt: þa 1515 and: *not in MS* heofon-fuglas: heofon fugla 1522 þæra: þære 1525 sece: seðe 1539 and: *not in MS* 1549 metode: metod 1567 inne: innne 1617 Chanan: cham 1628 Nebroðes: nebreðer 1630 swa: wwa 1638 wid-folce: wid folc 1642 frod: forð 1664 bearm: bearn 1676 stænenne: stænnene 1693 tohlocon: tohlodon 1711 freond: freod 1718 driht-folca bearn: drihta bearnum 1783 Sicem: siem 1795 landa: lande 1809 hneawlice: hnea lice 1829 onegan: on agen 1879 on: Tironian *sign for* and 1912 teon of: teon wit of 1924 neorxna-wange: neoxnawange oðþæt: on þæt 1929 ealle lædde: *not in MS* 1938 Loth: leoht 1953 hleow-lora: hleor lora 1957 mode: mod 1986 þryðge: þrydge 2032 ahreded: ahred 2038 feollan: feallan 2042 þeoden-holdra: þeonden holdra 2046 folc-getrume: folce getrume 2049 wæron: waron 2055 hie: he 2058 eaðe: eað 2080 wæron: *Not in MS* 2096 folce: folc 2097 wegen: wegan 2107 Wæs: wær 2141 and: *not in MS* 2149 rices: rice selfa: *not in MS* 2159 ac ne-fuglas: eacne fuglas 2160 blodige: blodig 2161 wæle: wæl 2191 and: *not in MS* 2195 mæg-burge: mæg burh 2210 swa: twa 2211 Wendelsæ: wendeð sæ 2225 se: seo 2251 drehte: drehta gehwam: geham 2255 ece: *not in MS* 2267 Sarrai: sarran 2290 and: *not in MS* 2293 frum-garan: frum garum awæcniað: apæc-niað 2368 gelæstan: gelætan 2372 wegan: wesan 2396 word-gehat: worn gehat 2402 Lothes: leohtes 2416 fyr: *not in MS* 2419 wite-laces: wite loccas 2439 sunnan: sunne 2482 wine-þearfende: þine þearfende 2528 sprycest: spryst 2559 leg: *not in MS* geador: eador 2577 he eft: heft 2604 genearwod: genearwot 2615 folces: folc 2629 hie: *not in MS* 2631 Abrahames: abrames 2645 beheowan: be-heopan þæne: þære 2658 wið god: *not in MS* 2662 ærendu: ærenda 2668 gesprecan: sprecan 2676 geworhte: orht *on an erasure* 2697 alædde: alæded 2721 weorc-þeos: weorc feos spræc: written twice 2728 Sarrai: sarran 2730 flett-paðas: flett waðas 2748 ecan: agan 2751 arna: arra 2758 weard: wearð 2768 mid: *not in MS* 2784 siðian: siððan 2814 on: *not in MS* 2838 þæt: þær 2839 lond: lono 2861 frean: frea 2894 gedæde: gedæd 2900 stowe: *not in MS* 2935 ær and sið: sið and ær

DANIEL

Exodus

8 weroda: werode   15 andsacan: andsaca   17 mago-ræswan: mago
ræs wum   22 feonda: feonda feonda   40 ðrysmyde: dryrmyde
45 feond: freond   55 mago-ræswa: mago ræwa   63 Heht: EHT *with
space for capital*   tir-fæste: tir fæstne   81 segle: swegle   105 segl: swegl
113 sceado: sceaðo   118 hæð-broga: hæð   119 on fer-clamme: ofer
clamme getwæfde: getwæf   128 leod-mægne: leo mægne   145 antwigða: an twig. ða   151 hie: he   157 eofer-holt: ofer holt   162 hreopon: hwreopon *with second* o *altered from* a   167 fyl: ful   169 genæged:
gehæged   176 wæl-hlencan: hwæl hlencan   178 fyrdgetrum: syrd get-
rum   onsegon: onsigon   181 heoru-wulfas: heora wulfas   186 ealde:
eade   216 bemum: benum   226 mode-rofra: mode rofa   233 wace:
wac   243 on: *not in MS*   248 gerad: rad   249 bidon: buton   253 beadu-hata: beo hata   277 þeoden: þeod   283 on: *Tironian
sign for* and   288 tid: *not in MS*   290 brim: bring   291 spaw: span
313 on onette: an on orette   321 leon: leor   326 Þracu: þraca
334 manna: man   340 forð: *not in MS*   345 gar-secge: gar secges
364 drence-floda: dren floda   368 gefræge: fr fræge   371 gehwæs: ge-
hæs   373 missenlicra: mismicelra   392 alh: alhn   399 fægenra: fæg ra
411 Abraham þa: *not in MS*   414 metod: god   432 He: ne   442 sand:
sund   444 in-geðeode: incaðeode   471 basnodon: barenodon   487
þa: *not in MS*   494 flod-weard gesloh: flodwearde sloh   499 onbugon:
on bogum   500 mod-wæga: modewæga   502 onfond: on feond
503 grund: *not in MS*   505 heoru-fæðmum: huru fæðmum   510 heora:
heoro   514 þa: *not in MS*   517 Moyses: moyse   535 healdað: healdeð
538 gehwylces: gehylces   546 is: *not in MS*   556 us on: ufon   570 gefegon: gefeon   574 herge: *not in MS*   578 golan: galan   587 sceodon:
sceo   590 mæst: mæ

Daniel

9 weoldan: weoldon   22 þa: þe   25 to: *not in MS*   29 hie: me
34 þeodum: þeoden   35 wisde: wisðe   38 tæhte: *not in MS*   53 foran:
faran   55 Hæfdon: *not in MS*   57 ic: eac   66 feoh: fea   73 ofer: otor
76 west: wes   77 leoda: leode   88 þry: to   97 cyðan: cyðdon

119 meted: metod   138 gecwædon: gcwædon   141 Nu: Ne   142 berað: bereð   152 wæs: þæs   170 weoh: woh   195 ælmihtigne: ælmihtne
208 wuldre: *not in MS*   221 gehwurfe: gen hwyrfe   226 gegleded:
gelæded   239 owiht: *not in MS*   246 onsteallan: onstealle   255 Bliðe:
biliðe   264 þe: þen   265 scynde: scyde   þe: we   273 on ofne: *not in*
MS   281 dreag: *not in MS*   292 hyldo: *not in MS*   298 burh-sittende:
burhsittendum   304 usic: us ec   320 had: hat   321 oððe: oð *followed*
by abbreviation for þæt   brim-faroþæs: brimfaro. þæs   323 in eare: me
are   327 þa: *abbreviation for* þæt   342 leoman: leoma   hyra: hyre
365 ofer: of   392 heran: herran   396 ead-modum: *not in MS*
403 wurðiað: wurðað   406 wide-ferhð: ferhð   409 ealdor: ealde
410 nehstum: nehstam   412 þeode: þeoden sendon: syndon
421 gædelingum: gædelinge   434 bende: benne   444 heredon: heredo
445 septon: stepton   453 on æht: 7 nahte   464 godes: ac godes
477 dema: *not in MS*   491 mara on: maran   500 hlifode: hlfode
515 wyrt-ruman: wyrtrumam   527 feran: *not in MS*   550 æ-cræftig: ar
cræftig   570 gemyndgast: gemydgast   584 anwalh: anwloh   590
bote: *not in MS*   615 wod: woð   681 ymb: ym   694 frasade: frea
sæde   703 æðelum: *not in MS*

Azarias

61 ofne: hofne *with* h *marked for deletion*   69 bletsian: bletsunge   77 mona: monan   100 lufigen: lifigen   et: *Tironian abbrev. for*
and   133 wuldorfæst: woldor fæst   143 heofon-fuglas: heofon fugulas
with last u marked for deletion   148 sacerdas: sacerdos   soðfæst: saðfæst
150 þeowas: þas   171 wisa: wisan   174 na: nu   188 nið: *not in MS*

Notes to the Translations

1–3   The phrasing suggests a debt to and evocation of the preface to the Canon of the Mass; see Michel. There are also echoes of *Cædmon's Hymn:* see Doane (1978), 225.

110–16   The poet here combines elements of the openings of John's Gospel (1:1 *uerbum;* l. 109 *word*) and Gen. 1:1 to mark a transition to the creation account; see Frank, 73.

168–69   The missing text corresponds to Gen. 1:10–2:17. Note that even in the damaged text it is apparent that the poet had reworked the two Genesis accounts of creation into one narrative, shown in his transposition of the account of Eden's rivers (Gen. 2:10–14) to after the creation of Eve.

234–35   Text is obviously missing, but it is difficult to say how much. The narrative flow is not greatly disturbed, especially as the reader has not yet been informed of the injunction against the forbidden fruit. *Genesis B* begins at l. 235 — albeit in a damaged sentence — with this important detail.

441–42   Two leaves have been lost at this point. The enemy (*andsaca*) referred to at l. 442 is not Satan, but a subordinate.

588–99   The casual antifeminism of the passage appears, in the wider context, to be designed to mitigate Eve's culpability; Adam, as the more intelligent, should have been better equipped to resist the devil's complex reasoning.

816–26   The poet's invocation of the medieval antifeminist tradition is complex. Eve's repentance stands in contrast to Adam's desire to blame her; he repents only that he asked God for a compan-

325

ion. Eve's attitude would appear to be more exemplary for the sinner.

852 *Genesis A* resumes.

987–1001 The image of the branches of sin is used by the poet to link Cain's sin, the first murder, to Eve's sin in the garden (though the *Genesis A* account of the fall has been lost); see Introduction, p. x; Wright.

1111–12 The lines *Me ece sealde sunu selfa* present a metrical irregularity, and many editors rearrange to *sunu sealde*.

1268 *gigant-mæcgas* (giant-kinsmen). This understanding of Gen. 6:4 was standard in the Middle Ages, based on the Vulgate Latin, *gigantes;* in the poem, under the influence of apocryphal traditions, they are now a family, or race, at war with God. See *Beowulf* 111–14, 1688–93.

1400–1401 The passage is very difficult and almost certainly corrupt. I have followed the emendation of Krapp, *Junius Manuscript.* I have read *Þam* (among them) as referring to those outside the ark, of whom *nan* (no one) remains; *to gedale* is anomalous, but I have read it as "to be killed." MS *heo* becomes *heof* (grief, lament), as suggested by Eduard Sievers, noted by Cosijn, 448.

1545–48 The apocryphal names of the wives of Noah and his sons are extrametrical and are probably included as the result of a marginal note in an earlier copy of the poem subsequently making its way into the body of the text.

1610 *Geomor.* This spelling appears to make the biblical name Gomer conform to West Saxon dialect (with palatalization), either by scribal habit or by error, producing a word meaning "sad."

1710 The poet does not include the text of Genesis describing Abraham's new name (Gen. 17:5) and simply calls him Abraham throughout. *Abrames* at l. 2631 is a scribal error.

1723 There is some confusion in the poem about how to spell and inflect Sarah's name, introduced here as *Sarra.* As with Abraham, the poet omits reference to her changed name (Gen. 17:15). See ll. 2745, 2267, 2728.

1951 *full-wona bearn.* The poet numbers himself and his audience among Abraham's descendents who sing his praises, as the "children of baptism." See Gal. 3:6–7.

1982   *francan.* The OE literally means "Frankish spears," a striking anachronism.

2319–25 The poet does not describe the physical act of circumcision, but offers a spiritual reading that draws on Gen. 17:11, which describes it as a sign of the covenant (*in signum foederis*). In his homily on the circumcision of the Lord, Ælfric of Eynsham does describe it and warns his listeners not to think circumcision is foolish, though he provides an allegorical reading of it as prefiguring baptism; see *Ælfric's Catholic Homilies,* 224–31.

2381–82 A leaf has been cut out of the manuscript. The missing text corresponds to Gen. 18:1–12.

2418–19 A leaf has been cut out of the manuscript. The poet's modification of the text, apparent in his treatment of Gen. 18:17–22, makes it difficult to appreciate what has been lost, though the missing text presumably corresponded to Gen. 18:23–33.

2512–13 A leaf has been cut out of the manuscript, presumably containing text corresponding to Gen. 19:14–17.

2599–600 A leaf has been cut out of the manuscript, which must have contained the text corresponding to Gen. 19:31–32.

2806–7   A leaf has been cut out of the manuscript, which would have contained the text corresponding to Gen. 21:15–21.

2906–8   *sencan.* The passage presents difficulties, focused on the word *sencan* (to sink, submerge). I have read this in the sense "plunge," though this leaves the inflection of *dreore* as an anomaly.

2935   The reordering of *sið and ær,* suggested by Holthausen, restores alliteration.

Exodus

34   *gedrenced.* Some editors emend to *gedrecced* (afflicted), though the MS reading can stand with a metaphoric sense of "drowned," especially if this is read as an anticipation of the fate awaiting the Egyptians.

39   *bana.* Compare Exod. 12:29; the "destroyer" is either the angel of death or God himself.

47–48   In an example of his technique of combining the literal and figurative interpretations of events, the poet points out that Pass-

over was an event famous across the world, while the universal
significance of the event for Christians (rather than for the Jew-
ish people) is also suggested.

75–92   The maritime imagery is striking, and deliberately incongruous
when describing people moving through the desert. The description anticipates the sea crossing (for which no ship will be
required) but also evokes the Church, an assembly associated
with a ship in medieval commonplace.

116–24   The anthropomorphism creates a giant monster of the night
out of the pillar of fire.

141–42   Text is clearly missing, though as the poet's source is not obvious, it is difficult to know how much has been lost. The lost text
presumably explained the story of Joseph.

157   *eofer-holt.* Emended following Sedgefield and Lucas.

161   The text is confused here, and probably about half a line of verse
has been lost.

224–45   The poet's close interest in the arrangement of the army and the
selection of fighters does not suggest a typological reading. The
passage is important in the presentation of the Israelites as heroic warriors, as they must at least appear eager to fight, even
though they do not join battle. The poet is careful not to present a cowardly rout.

253   *beadu-hata.* MS *beo-hata* makes little sense, and I agree with Lucas that the word is parallel, and similar in meaning, to *hilde-calla*
(messenger, courier, herald).

353   *an fæder.* Probably a reference to Abraham, who received the
promise of land, though Israel may be intended as one who begot a generation of kinsmen (l. 356).

358   *onriht Godes.* An etymological wordplay on the name of Israel
(*rectus Domini*), as pointed out by Robinson, 25–26.

373   *missenlicra.* MS *mis micelra* renders little sense.

386   The poet moves the sacrifice to Mount Zion.

413   I have retained MS *eagum,* where many editors emend to *ecgum.*
The poet is often interested in emotional responses to dramatic
situations, and here Abraham's "red eyes" reveal his emotion in
conflict with his obedience. It is also hard to see how the sword's
blades could be called "red" before the sacrifice of the ram.

414   MS *god* has been emended to *metod* for alliteration, with little change in meaning.

432–46   These descendents of Abraham are now those crossing the sands of the seafloor; the Christian nations of the world become his offspring by faith. The poet maintains a balance between the literal and the typological.

446–47   Between these two lines we find two blank pages in the manuscript and an obvious lacuna in the text. The numbering of the fitts shows that at least a whole numbered section (XLVIII) is missing.

467   *sæs* has been retained, despite the problem with alliteration, because other proposed emendations disrupt the sense.

470   *nep.* Taken here as meaning "neap-(tide)," the tide with the smallest difference between high and low water, and so the weakest in its current. I have translated as "weak flow," here applied to the Egyptians; see Lucas, *Exodus,* 134.

487   *wer-beamas.* A notorious crux, emended to *werge beornas* (cursed men) by Holthausen. OE *wer* (m.) can mean "dam" or "weir," a sense which seems appropriate here; the word also appears in compounds: *wer-bære* (fish-pond), *wer-bold* (weir-building), *wer-stede* (weir-place). I have taken the MS *wer-beamas* to mean something like the wooden supports or braces of the wall of a weir or dam, which here have given way and fallen on the Egyptians. The result is not ideal metrically but preserves the MS reading, which clearly has a meaningful context.

501   *ða ðe gedrecte.* An onomastic pun on "Egyptians" (those who afflicted); see Robinson, 28.

516–53   These lines appear to be a homiletic comment by the poet, drawing out the Christian meaning of the Exodus, before Moses begins his speech.

Daniel

1–71   The poet draws on a number of biblical books to provide a historical context for the action of the poem, especially 2 Chronicles and 2 Kings; see http://fontes.english.ox.ac.uk.

91–92   The names of the youths follow the Vulgate text.

150   *Daniel to dome.* The poet is clearly aware of the etymology of Daniel's name (*judicium*) and is developing an onomastic pun; see Farrell, 56. See also ll. 531, 547.

177–78 A page has been cut out of the manuscript, with loss of the text corresponding to Dan. 3:2–6.

205–208 The passage shows strained meter and disrupted syntax in the transition from narration to direct speech. The general sense, however, seems clear.

237a   The text here follows Farrell, whose lineation from this point departs from Krapp's edition. However, by numbering the single half-line 237a, this edition keeps with Krapp's subsequent lineation to the end of the poem.

276   *deaw-drias.* I follow Farrell and earlier editors in retaining the word, which appears to mean "dew-fall." Emendations based on the poet's presumed understanding (or lack of it) of atmospheric phenomena are not sufficiently convincing.

281   *dreag,* found in *Azarias* 3, is added to restore sense and meter.

401–3   The anachronistic Trinitarian doxology is probably a reflex of the liturgical use of the canticle.

409–29 No such character is found in the source, nor in *Azarias* (compare *Azarias* ll. 166–81). The unidentified *ræswa* is unlikely to be the prophet Daniel, who (although he has the role of interpreting divine communications to the king) could hardly be watching the three youths cast in the furnace.

435   *lað-searo.* The meaning of this unique compound (literally, "hateful-device") is suggested by the fact that it is parallel to *bende,* and with these bonds the *lað-searo* are incinerated. This would suggest the *lað-searo* are either locked chains (which would be expected to melt rather than burn) or elaborately skillful knots.

608–35 The poet's choice not to include any description of the king's physical transformation (compare Dan. 4:32–33) shifts the focus of the episode, and the poem more generally, to the king's psychological state and the process of inner conversion.

752   The poem ends on the last line of a page and gathering of leaves; it is uncertain whether this was the original ending or if some lines have been lost. The latter seems more likely.

Azarias

31–32   The missing text parallels *Daniel,* ll. 307–12

77–144   The elaborations on the biblical source suggest that the *Azarias* poet was more interested in the dynamic processes of nature than the *Daniel* poet was.

166–81   These lines correspond to *Daniel,* ll. 409–29, where events are presented differently. Both poems introduce a nonbiblical character.

174–75   There are some difficulties here. Using the text of *Daniel* as a guide is problematic, as the two poems' narratives clearly diverge at this point. The speaker here is not the king (as in *Daniel*), but his "fierce-minded" officer; in the *Azarias* account Nebuchadnezzar seems to have no clear sight of the furnace. The messenger is obliged to report to the king that his royal wish has not been carried out, and therefore explains that he did not (MS *nu* becomes *na*) disobey the king and send four people into the furnace and that what has happened was not his own "arrangement" (from *geradian,* "to arrange"; OE *gerad* has a range of meanings, including "account," "manner," "condition").

Bibliography

Ælfric's Catholic Homilies: The First Series: Text. Ed. Peter Clemoes, EETS ss 17. Oxford, 1997.

Anderson, Earl R. "Style and Theme in the Old English *Daniel.*" In Liuzza, *The Poems of MS Junius 11,* 229–60, 245–53. New York, 2002.

Anlezark, Daniel. "Old English Biblical and Devotional Poetry." In *Blackwell's Companion to Medieval Poetry.* Edited by Corinne Saunders, 101–24. Oxford, 2010.

Auerbach, Erich. *"Figura."* In *Scenes from the Drama of European Literature,* 11–76. New York, 1959.

Bede's Ecclesiastical History of the English People. Edited by Bertram Colgrave and R. A. B. Mynors. Oxford, 1969.

Blackburn, Francis A., ed. *Exodus and Daniel.* Boston, 1907.

Bliss, A. J. "Some Unnoticed Lines of Old English Verse." *Notes and Queries* 216 (1971): 404.

Chambers, R. W., Max Förster, and Robin Flowers, eds. *The Exeter Book of Old English Poetry.* London, 1933.

Cosijn, P. J., "Anglosaxonica." *Beiträge* 19 (1894): 441–61.

Doane, A. N., ed. *Genesis A: A New Edition.* Madison, Wis., 1978.

——. *The Saxon Genesis: An Edition of the West Saxon Genesis B and the Old Saxon Vatican Genesis.* Madison, Wis., 1991.

Farrell, R. T., ed. *Daniel and Azarias.* London, 1974.

Frank, Roberta. "Some Uses of Paronomasia in Old English Scriptural Verse." In Liuzza, *The Poems of MS Junius 11,* 69–98.

Fulk, R. D. *A History of Old English Meter.* Philadelphia, 1992.

——, ed. and trans. *The Beowulf Manuscript: Complete Texts and The Fight at Finnsburg.* DOML 3. Cambridge, Mass., 2010.

Godden, M. R. "The Trouble with Sodom: Literary Responses to Biblical Sexuality." *Bulletin of the John Rylands University Library* 77 (1995): 97–119.

Gollancz, Israel, ed. *The Cædmon Manuscript of Anglo-Saxon Biblical Poetry: Junius XI in the Bodleian Library.* London, 1927.

Hauer, Stanley R. "The Patriarchal Digression in the Old English *Exodus,* Lines 362–446." In Liuzza, *The Poems of MS Junius 11,* 173–87.

Holthausen, F., ed. *Die Ältere Genesis.* Heidelberg, 1914.

Irving, Edward B., Jr. "Exodus Retraced." In *Old English Studies in Honour of John C. Pope.* Edited by Robert B. Burlin and Edward B. Irving, Jr., 203–23. Toronto, 1974.

———, ed. *The Old English Exodus.* New Haven, Conn., 1953.

Jones, A. "*Daniel* and *Azarias* as Evidence for the Oral Formulaic Character of Old English Poetry." *Medium Ævum* 35 (1966): 95–102.

Junius, Franciscus, ed. *Caedmonis monachi paraphrasis poetica: Genesios ac praecipuarum sacrae paginae historiarum.* Amsterdam, 1655. Reprint with introduction by Peter J. Lucas, ed., Amsterdam, 2000.

Krapp, George Philip, ed. *The Junius Manuscript.* Anglo-Saxon Poetic Records I. New York, 1931.

Krapp, George Philip, and Elliott van Kirk Dobbie, eds. *The Exeter Book.* Anglo-Saxon Poetic Records III. New York, 1936.

Liuzza, R. M., ed. *The Poems of MS Junius 11: Basic Readings.* New York, 2002.

Lucas, Peter J., ed. *Exodus.* London, 1977. Rev. ed. Exeter, 1994.

Marsden, Richard. "Wrestling with the Bible: Textual Problems for the Scholar and Student." In *The Christian Tradition in Anglo-Saxon England: Approaches to Current Scholarship and Teaching.* Edited by Paul Cavill, 69–90. Cambridge, 2004.

Michel, L. "*Genesis A* and the Praefatio." *Modern Language Notes* 62 (1947): 545–50.

Muir, Bernard J., ed. *A Digital Facsimile of Oxford, Bodleian Library, MS. Junius XI.* Ed. Oxford, 2004.

———. *The Exeter Anthology of Old English Poetry.* Exeter, 2006.

———. *The Exeter Anthology of Old English Poetry: An Edition of Exeter Dean and Chapter MS 3501.* 2 vols. Exeter, 1996.

Remley, Paul G. "*Daniel,* the *Three Youths* Fragment and the Transmission of Old English Verse." *Anglo-Saxon England* 31 (2002): 81–140.

———. *Old English Biblical Verse: Studies in Genesis, Exodus and Daniel.* Cambridge Studies in Anglo-Saxon England 16. Cambridge, 1996.

Renoir, Alain. "Eve's I.Q. Rating: Two Sexist Views of *Genesis B.*" In *New Readings on Women in Old English Literature.* Edited by Helen Damico and Alexandra Hennessey Olsen, 262–72. Bloomington, Ind., 1990.

Robinson, Fred C. "The Significance of Names in Old English Literature." *Anglia* 86 (1968): 14–58.

Sedgefield, W. J., ed. *An Anglo-Saxon Verse Book.* Manchester, 1922.

Thorpe, Benjamin, ed. *Cædmon's Metrical Paraphrase of Parts of the Holy Scriptures in Anglo-Saxon.* London, 1832.

Timmer, B. J., ed. *The Later Genesis.* Rev. ed. Oxford, 1954.

Turville-Petre, Joan, ed. *The Old English Exodus: Text, Translation, and Commentary by J. R. R. Tolkien.* Oxford, 1981.

Wright, Charles D. "The Blood of Abel and the Branches of Sin: *Genesis A, Maxims I* and Aldhelm's *Carmen de Virginitate.*" *Anglo-Saxon England* 25 (1996): 7–19.

Index